The Decline of the Sacred
in Industrial Society

S. S. ACQUAVIVA

The Decline of
the Sacred
in Industrial Society

Translated by Patricia Lipscomb

HARPER & ROW PUBLISHERS
NEW YORK, EVANSTON, SAN FRANCISCO

Standard Book Number 0-06-136180-1
Library of Congress Catalog Card Number 78·59910

This edition is a translation of *L'eclissi del Sacro Nella Civiltá Industriale*, second edition, published by Edizioni di Communita, Milan, 1966.

To my wife Eugenia

Contents

Introduction
by Gabriel Le Bras

In the space of only five years, Sabino Samele Acquaviva has given us two books and fifteen articles on sociology which show him to be as gifted in philosophy as in mathematics, in traditional methodology as in modern techniques. All of these talents have been brought to bear in this new book in which we find, between a chapter on the concept of the sacred and on its destiny, a synthesis of world religious practice and a theory of the general movement of 'desacralization'.

Using surveys conducted throughout the world on seasonal as well as on regular religious practice, Acquaviva reveals the almost universal decline of practice. No other work offers such complete statistics on the public acts of the Catholic faith.

Such purely external adherence, manifested through measurable acts, generally implies a favourable attitude toward the orders of the hierarchy, morality, and even a political policy favourable to the churches. On it can be based certain conjectures about the power of the ecclesiastical institution, and certain comparisons between the statistics of practice and demographic coefficients or the results of elections. But beyond this elementary sociography, which we have always held to be necessary if not sufficient, sociology proper attempts to determine the strictly religious value of attitudes and the causes of variations. With these considerations Sabino Samele Acquaviva is deeply concerned.

This leads him to a thorough examination of the notion of the sacred, the significance of myth and ritual, the psychological problems of 'motivation' and of the person, all with a view toward explaining the phenomena of the world's conversion to the profane. Acquaviva conducts with vigour this philosophical analysis which displays the whole breadth of the religious phenomenon. He utilizes and discusses not only the works of distinguished scholars, but also, to our advantage, introduces us to less widely known pamphlets and articles.[1]

From proto-history to the irreligion of the future, Acquaviva seeks out the phases in the decline of the sacred in order to discover the relationship between social structures and the religious life. Among the modern revolutions, the technological and the environmental furnish him with the essential keys. As he observes the current disaffection toward the sacred, he sees us floundering through a long night during which perhaps the light glows faintly in the unconscious. But he rejects and refutes the linear conception of history. He knows that the Middle Ages were not totally dedicated to piety and that even today under the bushel the light of religion shines.

Like Acquaviva, we too reject the dogma of the linear, of the irreversible. The tortuous curves of history, its internal contradictions, its illusory appearances strike us with ever greater force. From Remus to Cicero, from Cicero to Lucretius, from Lucretius to Augustine: how many turns in the curve! And who can say that the Catholicism of the eighteenth (or of the fourteenth) century was stronger than that of our own day?

Professor Acquaviva's principal merit is that of breaking down the barriers between disciplines which can and must join together to give us a deeper understanding of religious societies. Such an enterprise could not produce perfectly harmonious results on its first attempt: between proto-history and psychoanalysis, statistics and philosophy, the connections are difficult to establish, and how can one introduce the methods of sociology into all of these sciences at one stroke?

Great progress has been made in the sociology of religion. As we have always hoped it would, it is going beyond the techniques of 'numbers and paper' and allying itself more solidly with psychology and history. By utilizing all of the human sciences, by taking advantage of all favourable currents, it is raising itself in the hierarchy of sciences.

Acknowledgements

I should like to thank those who have helped me during and after the drafting of the manuscript, both with particular themes and with general arguments.

First, Prof. Albino Uggé, who with his moderate counsel has often prevented me from taking extreme positions; Prof. Marcello Boldrini, Prof. Camillo Pellizzi, Prof. Michele Marotta, and Prof. Giorgio Braga, who has given me useful systematic advice, especially in relation to the central nucleus of the work; also Prof. Mario Manzini, Prof. Cleto Corrain, the late Prof. Luigi Caiani, Prof. Gabriel Le Bras whose thought has inspired much of my work, Prof. Mircea Eliade of the University of Chicago to whom I owe much in the discussion of the concept of the experience of the sacred, Prof. Jean Chelini of Aix-en-Provence, Prof. Abbé Houtart of the Centres des Recherches Socio-religiueses of Brussels. Prof. Conor K. Ward of the University of Dublin has furnished me with valuable data on Great Britain. I should also like to thank Prof. Geck of the Sociology Institute of the University of Bonn; the Centro de Estudios de Sociologia Aplicada di Madrid; Prof. Vinas y May of the University of Madrid; Prof. Edvard Vogt of the University of Oslo; Prof. Gottfried Eisermann of the University of Bonn; Prof. Norman Birnbaum of Nuffield College Oxford; Prof. Dietrich Goldschmidt of the University of Berlin; Prof. Luciano Gallino of the University of Turin; Dr. Bryan Wilson of All Souls College Oxford, Prof. Giulio Girardi of the Gregorian University of Rome; Prof. Luigi Gaudenzio to whom I am indebted for stylistic improvements; and many others, both Italian and foreign, whose expert advice has influenced my orientation both on particular problems and in general.

Special thanks are due to my wife who has read the manuscript and the proofs of the Italian edition and who has given me much valuable advice in both stylistic and systematic matters.

The Theme

The scale of the subject with which this book is concerned is such that perhaps not even a generation of researchers could do it adequate justice. Even if they did, the subject itself would by then have taken on new forms, thus superseding both their research and its conclusions. Yet, we cannot, because of this, merely leave discussion of these issues to pamphleteers. The development of the human spirit, and its relation to changes in customs and ideas is of far wider interest. What an individual makes of the contemporary religious crisis necessarily affects his attitude to the modern world at large. We must all come to terms with industrial society, and thus we must, implicitly or explicitly, take a position vis à vis the religious crisis that accompanies the process of industrialization. Yet few people do this on the basis of knowledge of all the elements that ought to be considered. The choice they make often appears to be strictly ideological, and it is a rare individual who takes into account the way and the extent to which this choice is an expression of his own 'human condition', of the time and circumstances of his own life, and of the influences inevitably exercised on him by the attitudes adopted by earlier generations.

Man is continuously conditioned by his environment — in his desire for self-preservation, in his productive activities, and in a complex net of innumerable concerns both past and present, since

> no product of his culture is so detached from the larger groundwork of existence that he can impute to his individual powers what alone has been made possible by countless generations of men and by the underlying co-operation of the entire system of nature. [1]

This influence is exercised in a variety of ways, but primarily in and through work. Work alone permits man to master his circumstances and to achieve that balance between internal and external demands necessary for his continued existence, and for his inevitably transitory struggle against death.

The development of the individual and his integration into the group takes place through language, that is through that set of symbols and meaningful signs, represented by images, sounds, words, and objects, which enable thought and action to be transmitted across space and time. The dynamics of the symbol are the dynamics of life, since art, literature, religion, philosophy, and so on, are possible only by the development of symbols. Through myths and history

> man . . . lives in a time-world that transcends the limitations of his local environment: the world of the past, the present, and the possible; or, if you will, the real, the realizing and the realizable. Once he loses hold on any of these dimensions of his experience, he cuts himself off from a part of reality. [2]

To understand the great contemporary crisis in religion it is necessary to take the past, the present, and the possible into account as well as the more or less symbolic expressions of those factors — from the biological and psychological to the more widely spiritual — which in their interaction give new momentum to the crisis. But to attain this understanding, it is also necessary to be aware of the values and the features of religion itself, and an understanding of religion will be attained only with the assistance of the social sciences. The crisis of religion is the drama of our times, but it has its roots in the origins of humanity itself, and it arises particularly with the consciousness of the existence of death. In his struggle against death, man has made of it

> the center of his most valued efforts, cutting temples out of the rock, heaping pyramids high above the desert, transposing the mockeries of human power into visions of godlike omnipotence, translating human beauty into everlasting stone, human experience into printed words and time itself, arrested in art, into a simulacrum of eternity.
>
> Death happens to all living things; but man alone has created out of the constant threat of death a will-to-endure, and out of the desire for continuity and immortality in all their many conceivable forms, a more meaningful kind of life, in which Man redeems the littleness of individual man. [3]

The consciousness of death has left its imprint on all civilizations. As industrial society advances and, as the sacred is progressively made profane, the consciousness of death increasingly projects that bleak image which makes the present both fascinating and profoundly saddening.

1

The Sacred

1. THE LIMITATIONS AND THE SIGNIFICANCE OF
THE STUDY OF THE SACRED

How many of those who assert that religion is in a state of crisis are in
fact referring to the same phenomenon? To what extent do we
consider this crisis to be the expression of those psychological, social,
cultural, and biological factors which together make up the complexity of the human personality, and to what extent a manifestation
of other aspects of reality? Is an adequate analysis of the religious
crisis of modern society possible solely on the basis of data furnished
by the empirical sciences such as sociology, psychology, the history of
religion, and so forth, and what are the ultimate limitations of such
an analysis?

These are significant questions. Religion has always exerted a
profound influence on many aspects of human life and personality.
In itself, religion is so complex that it virtually defies description.
Thus one might expect that any discussion of the religious crisis
should begin with a definition of the religious phenomenon itself
before proceeding to an analysis of the nature and extent of the
crisis. But religion virtually defies description, and is rarely taken as
a departure point.

Many identify religious experience exclusively with their own
personal experience of religion, and are content to let matters rest
there. In speaking of the religious crisis, they identify it with their
own personal crisis, or they fail to distinguish the personal aspects of
the problem from the wider issues that are of concern to mankind at
large.

The majority of those who have tried to define the object of socio-
religious enquiry have contented themselves either with specifying
the external relations between socio-religious phenomena and other
aspects of social life, or with producing definitions that commit them,

more or less openly, to particular ideological positions. The ease with which such normative elements become involved arises because the interpretation of the data of a sociographic study of religion pre-supposes not only a quantitative comparative analysis of these data, but a more refined qualitative interpretation of religious phenomena.[1] Thus it becomes essential, in pursuing the enquiry at hand, to deal at the outset with some problems of definition, to solve which involves using various scientific techniques.

We must first clarify, within the limits of concern of this study, the concept of religion. Just what we take to be the religious crisis of our times, must depend on what we conceive to be religion, indeed on this definition depends whether we perceive a crisis at all.

In one of his writings, Camillo Pellizzi argues as follows:

> Unlike ancient science, and much more clearly than magic, modern science received its initial impulse from a specific religious motive, that is from the desire for 'revelation' (i.e. the giving of a ritual and sacred representation) of the intrinsic value of experienced reality and of the world as God's creature, and thus our own sister. If there is any truth in this idea . . . then em-pirical science appears as a 'religious fact' animated by a living, and thus always mutable, system of ritual and myth which is specified to it.[2]

Were we to accept this thesis, we could no longer speak of the religious crisis of industrial society, but would have to believe that the modern world had been conquered by a new religious impulse — that of science. We might even be led to regard modern society, more than any previous society, as one dominated by religion.

On the other hand, others narrowly restrict the application of the term 'religious' to those cases where there is an awareness of the existence of a personal God. Were we to accept this definition, not only could we demonstrate the existence of a crisis, but we might also maintain that a large portion of humanity is not, and never has been, religious: we need think only of the Buddhists.

The definition we need is one which avoids any personal *Weltanschauung*. Although it may be only an operational definition, it must take into account the problems of our society and its culture. It must certainly employ essential logical categories, but it must be sufficiently malleable and elastic to be applicable to a variety of societies, and above all to a variety of cultures.[3] The significance of the problem has been widely recognized.[4]

To determine the empirical characteristics of the central nucleus of religion is, however, not enough. We must also determine the religious significance of other and more specifically social aspects of religious phenomenology. We must concern ourselves with such matters as the limits and significance of ritual and myth, and the extent to which there is a coincidence between what we might term *secularization* and *desacralization*.

There are difficulties in the attempt to formulate a useful non-ontological definition of religion (ontological definitions being the province of the philosophy of religion). On the one hand, in the search for an objective and universally valid definition we come dangerously close to ontology; on the other, while we remain on the empirical level, we find it very difficult to shed the psychological, logical, and cultural baggage of the civilization of which we are a part. To free ourselves from these folk categories of European societies, as Bohannan calls them, is sometimes so difficult that it becomes almost impossible for us to assess the religious phenomenologies connected with other cultures. The European definitions of religious phenomena reveal the influence of the cognitive and cultural perspectives available to those who have formulated them. These influences stem not simply from the cultural setting as such, but from the specific circumstances of the time, and from those aspects of the culture to which the student is particularly committed, and which constitute fundamental pre-suppositions in the construction of his specific theory. Nineteenth-century definitions exemplify this type of influence. As scientific research made available new knowledge about human religion in its various forms in space and time, various students each produced a new theory which differed from earlier ones exactly in that it sought to take into account the new findings of science.[5]

In this framework, one can readily understand the theory of Tylor, which viewed the cult of the dead and animism as the central facts of the development of religion. What he did was nothing more than to construct an empirical definition based on the data which the science of his time and his culture made available. In the same way, later research led Marrett to question the traditional distinctions between magic and religion, and religion and science, and to introduce rigorous concepts of ritual, the sacred, the non-logical, the magical, and the religious. From there it was but a short step to Durkheim's distinction between sacred and profane, and his contention that all populations recognize the existence of a radical dichotomy between these two realms. [6]

One may challenge Durkheim's assertion, and one may ask whether the distinction is sufficient and fruitful. Others have asserted the value of subsuming all supernatural forces under one category, but if we do this, shall we not have more difficulty in distinguishing the sphere of the sacred from that of the profane, or the natural, and the non-spiritual? The distinction between sacred and profane adopted by Durkheim appears at first sight to be fairly acceptable, even in its wider implications, and all the more so in that it leads to a view of religion as the set of beliefs and practices pertaining to the sacred. Durkheim appealed to Robertson Smith in maintaining the contrast between religion and magic, the former being based in society, and the latter in individuality. [7]

Although there are gaps and difficulties in its progress, the enormous category of the sacred was elaborated by Marrett, taken up again by Durkheim and Radcliffe-Brown, and established in con-temporary thought through Pareto and Parsons. Yet various weaknesses in the concept have not been eliminated. The sociological distinction, made by Durkheim, between magical and religious values appears to be untenable. Warner has maintained, perhaps rightly, that magic has its own church, and even though it may be true that this association is different in kind, the differences are often a matter of nuance. Durkheim, however, appears to be guilty of confusing two different types of association with the simple absence of association. This purely external distinction, based on the type of associative bond that characterizes the group under study is not sufficient to determine the boundaries of religion vis-à-vis magic. Like many others, Durkheim has constructed a category of the sacred that proves to be inapplicable to a number of cultures and to a number of aspects of man's psychological life. Thus, he is eventually compelled to fall back on the social manifestations of religion (and of the phenomena from which he wishes to distinguish it) in order to specify the boundaries of religion itself. He resorts to this device, because he is aware of the difficulties involved in a conceptual distinction between magic and religion, and this obliges him to appeal to external categories.

The same objections are incurred by Malinowski when he asserts that ritual magic and lay ceremony are distinguishable from religious ritual by virtue of their practical goals. But do not many religious rituals have practical goals?

The distinction between sacred and profane, even in its most rigorous formulation, which is valid for some cultures, is not valid for others, so that in some circumstances it is impossible to employ it. The distinction which these authors make is based on a rational distinction between the two spheres which does not form a part of the logical and psychological equipment of many peoples, and particularly not of primitive peoples. The confusion is particularly evident with respect to magic, but even in Roman Catholicism there are magical elements — the cult of saints, for example, which are not distinguished from religious practice.

In some cases it appears easy to transfer magic into the realm of the phenomenology of the sacred, and then to distinguish it from the more properly religious phenomenology on the basis of the different kinds of associational structures to which they respectively give rise. This is what Durkheim does. Frazer, on the other hand, tells us that magic is a kind of bastardized science, and thus it is at the same time both logical and non-logical to speak of the distinction between the 'magical' and the 'profane'. Yet Parsons holds that

> Side by side with this system of rational knowledge and technique, however, and specifically not confused with it, was a system of magical beliefs and practices. These beliefs concerned the possible intervention in the situation of forces and entities which are 'supernatural' in the sense that they are not from our point of view objects of empirical observation and experience, but rather what Pareto would call 'imaginary' entities with a specifically sacred character.[8]

Thus magic is held to have a sacred value, and when we speak of the sacred must we therefore include also magic? Or has it no place in the discourse? At least, we can be sure that among the experts there is considerable confusion.[9]

The same situation exists with respect to religion in the narrower sense of the term. Parsons distinguishes between the sphere of the supernatural, on the one hand, and the sphere of the rational and utilitarian, on the other. But Evans-Pritchard tells us that the Azande, for example, make no distinction corresponding to that made by Europeans[10] between the supernatural and the natural-utilitarian, and that in general this distinction is not universally accepted among primitive peoples. And into what category do we then put magic, which (at least according to Frazer's critics) is utilitarian but not rational?

Whether they include or exclude magic from the realm of the sacred, or whether they place the sacred in the realm of the irrational or the rational, the various definitions are unsatisfactory, in that they either fail to include among religious phenomena more or less extensive areas which we should maintain are undoubtedly religious, or they account for these areas inadequately. These difficulties appear to arise because even though the sacred-profane dichotomy is basically valid, in its various manifestations over space and time, it assumes very different aspects. In order to grasp both the differences and the basic unity of this sacred-profane dichotomy in its variety of manifestations, we must seek by deeper analysis to introduce some order into this complicated subject.

Confusion in definition arises from three sources: from the use of certain more or less uniform logical categories; from the fact that these definitions are derived from the European philosophical tradition; and from the character of the particular documents which they have selected for their analysis. Recent developments in the social sciences have made it apparent that definitions based on external and incomplete information can themselves only be external and inadequate.[11] This is particularly true with respect to the deeper phenomena of human psychology such as religion.

The themes that concern us have usually been discussed within the perspective of one particular discipline rather than through an integrated inter-disciplinary approach. The approaches of 'pure' sociologists, historians of religion, paleo-ethnologists, ethnologists or others, characteristic of scholars at the turn of the century, and also of some more contemporary writers, have been one-sided even when they have been brilliant.[12] Clearly, discussion of the resulting deficiencies would involve going into the complex issue of the inadequacies of general methodology, from which the deficiencies in this particular field arise.[13] The incongruities and contradictions between the theories on the one hand, and the data of experience and research on the other, have their origin in these methodological inadequacies.

In re-opening discussion, we shall examine again the categories of the sacred and the profane, but this time at different levels, employing a different type of approach, to culture as well as to history, and above all centring everything on the human individual. In this way we can interpret variations in religious phenomena over time and space, and perhaps arrive at a malleable and elastic definition which will permit us to pursue a coherent argument.[14]

2. SACRED AND SECULAR AT THE GROUP AND INDIVIDUAL LEVEL

The relations that link one man with another in the religious sphere cannot be understood without some conception of the structure of personality, of what constitutes *homo religiosus*, and the nature of the religious experience.[15] We need, then, some conception of group relations, as well as an analysis of personality structure, with special reference to those aspects of personality of importance for religion, and an adequate religious phenomenology.[16, 17]

Others, particularly Howard Becker, have approached the sociology of religion by employing a distinction between the sacred and the profane, whilst being aware of the difficulties that would be encountered were this distinction made too rigid. According to Becker, the terms *sacred* and *secular* imply a value-judgment.[18] This judgment generally arises from the recognition of the needs that relate object to subject. Man has both material and immaterial needs, private and public needs, and to meet these needs relations are established: the needs give rise to values. There is, then, a general relationship between value and need. Becker related individual value judgments to certain general value judgments which, even though individual judgments vary from person to person, are strongly affected by the range of social experiences typical of the society at large. Becker rejects the idea that concepts of the sacred and the secular are to be regarded as individual psychological attitudes, and he connects the sacred with reluctance to initiate change, and the secular to the readiness for change. On the basis of readiness or reluctance to change, he constructs a scale of sacredness and secularity.

Becker regards holiness as the greatest sacred value, followed by loyalism (understood as loyalty to one's race, class, faction, or party, or as patriotism), sacred intimacy, moral sacredness, and a type of sacredness that I should designate 'formal', which has to do with decency, profanity, etc. Ceremonial sacredness, an auxiliary element, functions at each of the various levels of intensity of the sacred from holiness to custom.

Basically, Becker is facing an old problem — first of locating, and then of measuring, the data of intimate, individual, and irrepeatable experience. He seeks to solve it by externalizing the datum. Rather than trying to force the particular experience into a set of logical classifications, he deals with its external manifestations. Thus, he does not consider the sacred and the secular as individual experiences, but he looks at them in some of their social and phenomenological manifestations as reluctance or readiness to accept social change.

He provides a new construction for the categories of the sacred and the secular (or profane), and his procedure is perhaps, at least partially, adequate. And yet, even though his logical constructions may be used to classify the external expressions of the sacred and the secular, his scale appears to be quite arbitrary. It is also difficult to see how these external expressions correspond to that intimate individual sacredness of which each external manifestation of readiness or reluctance vis-à-vis social change, is supposed to be an expression.

For example, we can admit that a series of determinate expressions of custom are, from the standpoint of reluctance to accept change, less sacred than, say, loyalism, as defined above — but what of individual experience? Might it not be the case that individuals attach a greater sacredness to their customs than to their loyalties? And is it not possible that the utilization of these categories might dispose us to regard as religious, social phenomena that have, outside this frame of reference, little claim to be so regarded? Whilst it is true that religious groups and individuals have a tendency to conserve existing social structures, customs, and traditions, it is a long step from saying this to the point where we might think of conservative groups as necessarily religious (much less define them as such), or go on to use the concept of conservatism as part of the definition of religion. In such fashion one would soon reach the paradoxical position of declaring as sacred or religious some social fact or act that is not so perceived by those who experience it. When we ask these individuals if they have had an experience of the sacred, will they answer with reference to the same object?

Becker's logical-psychological solutions do not, then, appear to be adequate. Although the phenomenon is to be approached from the perspective of a broad range of disciplines, it must also be studied in its own proper frame of reference, that is to say on a religious plane. To approach the subject through philosophy, philology, psychology, economics, linguistics, is all very well, but we must never overlook the irrepeatable *quid* that it claims a sacred character. We agree with Eliade

> we do not deny the usefulness of approaching the religious phenomena from alternative points of view, but first of all it should be considered in itself, in what it possesses that is irreducible and original.

If, instead, we remain within the framework of more or less equivocal and external definitions, we may orient our work toward substantially negative solutions such as that of Caillois, who gives up the search for a concrete definition of the sacred and limits himself to determining its contrast with the profane, as does Becker. He observes that 'No formula, however elementary it may be, is applicable to the labyrinthine complexity of facts,'[19] and holds that the sacred fact, when it is removed from its cultural context, from the set of beliefs to which it refers, is nothing more than a mere abstraction. In religious matters more than in any other sphere, every generalized conclusion is valid for an 'average' which in no case corresponds to the reality. In spite of this, Caillois stresses the necessity for a series of 'utilitarian' generalizations, which are regarded as working tools rather than as interpretations of the sacred fact in itself. Along these lines, and drawing on the analyses of Durkheim, Hubert, Hertz, and Mauss, he formulates his theory.

With Caillois we agree only partially. We accept as working tools some generalized interpretations. But we need a more precise characterization of the sacred[20] and one sufficiently clear to allow us, when necessary, unequivocally to decide whether we are, or are not, dealing with a sacred fact. In stating this desideratum, we do not assert the necessity of a philosophical definition of the sacred: our intention is more limited.

In our definition we need to have regard to what might be called the constants of human psychology, and here we turn to the work of Otto, Clark, Allport, and Pratt, among others; and also to the variables that arise from culture, environment, and history which affect the experience of the sacred. Here we shall draw upon Le Bras, Eliade, Pellizzi, Cassirer, and de Martino. In discussing the sacred and the profane, we shall not be concerned with the opposition of two abstractions, but essentially with human psychology.[21] In the light of these considerations, the conclusions of Caillois seem unacceptable. In proposing the simple contrast, sacred-profane, as a basis of comparison and standard of judgment, Caillois observes that:

> Sooner or later, through logical considerations or direct observation, everyone must admit that the religious man is above all the one for whom there exist two complementary spheres: one in which he can act without distress or fear but, within it, his activity engages only superficially his personality; the other one in which a feeling of intimate dependence restrains, represses, guides each one of his impulses and within which he feels engaged without reserve. These two spheres, the sacred and the profane, are strictly defined the one through the other.[22]

But this is not a definition. One reality is not contrasted with another, and there is insufficient account of the historical, cultural, and psychological context. One cannot define either term merely by declaring it different from the other, there must be some reference to the structure of components.

Nor are some of Caillois' other considerations of much help. He observes that

> The profane sphere reveals itself as being the house of evidence, of gestures which need no precaution and develop in the space — often narrow — left to men for their own non-constricted activities. The sacred sphere, on the contrary, appears as the house of danger and prohibition: no individual can approach it without setting ungovernable forces in motion before which his weakness is absolutely disarmed. Nevertheless, without their aid, no ambition can escape failure; they are the location of each success, of each power, of each fortune. However, by stirring up these forces we must fear to be their first victim.[23]

Even this attempt to consider the psychological aspects of the distinction between sacred and profane is still external and descriptive. It moves towards a morphology of the sacred, but it does not bring its inner significance into focus. Even Caillois appears to have failed to grasp the full significance of the sacred in the realm of the individual psyche.

Although Becker's approach has weaknesses at other levels, it is, from the psychological point of view, more promising. Becker observes that although human judgment is unique and unrepeatable, it is easier to find elements of definition at the personal level. In spite of their diversity, it is possible to identify a common element at this level in those individual experiences of the religious. This common element is necessary for a definition of our area of concern.

In practice, it has been shown that a purely psychological approach is not in itself sufficient, however. Used in isolation, it does no more than locate sets of psychological relations that are constant within one personality, but which vary from one man to another: we are thus led to the conclusion that there is no one single form of religious feeling.

This is the conclusion reached by Allport,[24] who maintains, with Dunlap, that not only is there no single religious feeling, but that neither is there a single fundamental religious concept. The explanation offered for this, is that religion responds to certain requirements of the personality, and that these requirements vary from individual to individual. However, Allport says:

> in nearly all instances, however, we find that in the course of development the religion of the individual has been refracted by: (1) his bodily needs; (2) his temperament and mental capacity; (3) his psychogenic interests and values; (4) his pursuit of rational explanation; and (5) his response to the surrounding culture.[25]

Although these factors enter into the religious phenomenon in different ways and to different degrees, and are partly rational and partly irrational, in the mind of the religious man they are a unity in which emotion and logical thought are fused, in which the vital demands of existence and the need to understand and explain the meaning of life and of the world become one.

If this exhausted the possibilities of understanding the meaning of religious experience, we should have to conclude with Allport that:

the roots of religion are so numerous, the weight of their influence in individual lives so varied, and the forms of rational interpretation so endless, that uniformity is impossible.[26]

If we accept Allport's thesis, at least in its more radical interpretation, then we must also accept Camillo Pellizzi's broad interpretation of religion. He maintains that it is only by virtue of the similarity of particular psychological reactions to certain facts that we classify certain determinate phenomena as religious. It is because of this that we may speak of the religiosity of the human response to a science, a response that may often be analogous to the religious response.[27]

However, Allport's conclusions are acceptable only in a rather restricted form. One may recognize that in every religious phenomenon there are a variety of characteristics that express psychological, cultural, historical, and other elements. This in itself does not, however, indicate the absence of a common characteristic on which, for example, the sacred-profane distinction might be based, even though the concrete experiences of the sacred vary with cultural, historical, and other influences.

To stress the psychological features of religion does not provide an adequate definition of it, of course, but, given the psychological consequences of the industrial revolution, emphasis on the psychological brings into sharper focus the transformations in religious phenomenology during that period.

In these considerations, we have not completely overcome the logical contradictions which Becker also encountered, between individual experience and group phenomena, and between the demand for a unitary interpretation and definition of the religious phenomenon, and psychologism's tendency toward fragmentation.

Religious awareness and experience are difficult to explain purely on the basis of general psychology. One might acknowledge the existence of some psychological 'facts' that differ from others by, for example, their reference to a divinity: at the same time, psychology cannot accept the concept of divinity as a standard for its own judgment.

To delimit the field of the sociology of religion and of religion as an individual phenomenon presupposes an *at least partial* understanding of the significance of internal experience. The understanding is to be achieved through the interpretation of the objective expression of that experience. However, since this interpretation in turn requires the analysis of the internal experience itself, we seem to be caught in a vicious circle. On the one hand, psychology requires an external standard of judgment which allows it to classify as religious a certain set of psychological facts. On the other hand, it must reject an externally imposed typology, even though, as an empirical and classificatory science, it encounters difficulty in creating its own category of the sacred and religious. Furthermore, since the forms which such experiences take are so varied and so internally differentiated, it becomes difficult to locate the object of the religious experience. Each experience becomes mixed with other experiences and phenomena that are not of a religious nature.

If we take the nucleus of individual religiosity to be an experience, then at least in certain respects, religiosity may be regarded as a particular modality of general psychic activity. If we analyse the components of religious experience in greater detail, we see that there exists, first and foremost, a belief in certain not yet logically crystallized ideas which in turn become translated into cult practices. At the same time, an awareness exists of the superiority of certain beings and/or values. This belief in certain truths and superior entities is one of the first elements in the differentiation of the psycho-religious fact from other psychic facts. *Thought*, *will*, and *feeling* are all involved in this belief in superior entities.

These considerations may partially differentiate religiosity from other psychic states, but they do not show its markedly sacred character. Our broad interpretation of religion is still tenable, but it yields no more than a clear distinction between religious states and facts and other states and facts that are certainly not religious. Up to this point, we have not shown that the psycho-religious fact, and the social act or fact that follows from it, is specifically religious with respect to its internal structure, however.[28]

At the psychological level, numerous proposals have been advanced. Some, for example, suggest that within the variety of religious phenomena, the object of religiosity is a sort of experience of God, who can be characterized 'locally', in the sense of the logic of the situation. That is to say, man may experience God in different forms according to the times, the peoples, and the cultures con-

cerned. But given the forms taken by religious experience, this
solution appears too restrictive.

Another method for delimiting the field of religiosity, and thus
indirectly of the sociology of religion, might be to define as religious
every experience which is said to be religious by those who have
experienced it. But this suffers the objection that in confining
religion to the facts and acts said to be religious by individuals, we
might ignore social structures and social acts which transcend individual religious experience.

Some psychologists, such as Allport, have rejected the possibility of
constructing a definition of religion grounded on logical extra-
psychological elements, and they have encountered the difficulties
already indicated. Other psychologists have put forward a conceptualization derived from external sources. Among these is Clark,
who defines religion as follows:

> religion can be most characteristically described as the inner
> experience of the individual when he senses a Beyond, especially
> as evidenced by the effect of this experience on his behaviour
> when he actively attempts to harmonize his life with the Beyond. [29]

This definition allows us — at least at the phenomenological level —
to locate the field of religion, its psychology and its sociology. But
Clark, too, must face the usual criticism. His concept is an expression
of a particular cultural context and his data are limited to particular
historical periods and to particular geographical areas. He himself
recognizes that his definition refers only to 'the more characteristic
types of religious experience'. If we are obliged to accept an external
definition, then we must invoke other disciplines, such as the history
of religion, ethnology, and cultural anthropology, which provide
more generalized definitional categories.

The relationship between the sacred and the profane and the
concept of the experience of the sacred are among the most general
concepts. They are therefore capable, at least potentially, of
providing a logical structure for discussion which develops on so
many, and at such diverse, levels. In spite of the criticisms we have
made, the concepts of sacredness and of the experience of the sacred
seem to be among the most fertile. One of the reasons for the difficulties encountered in using these concepts is that they have been
regarded as rational values to be applied as standards of judgment to

various religions and civilizations. They have been proposed, that is, as rigid concepts, and thus when confronted with the variety of manifestations of the religious phenomenon, they appeared to be incapable of coming to terms with different historical situations and with the multiform manifestations of human psychology and culture. The contrast between sacred and profane, put forward by Becker, Durkheim, and others, should be preserved, but it should be employed at different levels and on different planes, and not only in conjunction with an abstract and logico-rational definition which at best has only historical validity. Furthermore, the idea of the sacred takes on its form and significance within the psychology of the individual who entertains it. It is, as we have said, to a great extent an expression of his own experiences. Thus it follows that we can take our point of departure from the psychological experience of the sacred, no matter how encrusted it may be with elements from a particular cultural and historical context. Let us by all means discuss the problems posed by Durkheim and Becker, but at the same time we must take into account all those factors which make up their concrete configuration. It must be recognized from the outset, that to provide a definition of religious experience is difficult. Once this has been grasped we may look for the objective and rational aspects of the experience of the sacred. Then, on the basis of the individual's rational awareness of his own experience, we may study the cultural, historical, and other aspects of the religious experience, to arrive finally at the widest, most elastic, and open-ended definition possible.

What we seek, in short, is a definition which utilizes Durkheim's and Becker's dichotomy, but on the subjective-objective level rather than at the purely objective level. The definition must also take account of those nuances and other factors that we have mentioned, and especially of the historical dimension of the problem.

The experience of the sacred is initially an individual psychological fact. Only subsequently is it recognized as a specifically religious experience which becomes the pivot for all religiously relevant social acts and facts.

But even if we ignore the requirements of rigidity and comprehensiveness for our definition, it is still difficult to define the exact limits of the sacred, and not only because of the psychological and social-psychological problems. There is an infinite variety and multiplicity of facts which are, or at first glance appear to be, sacred. Closer attention reveals that all of them have certain common characteristics which might make the construction of general categories possible.

To begin with, the experience of the sacred is founded on one or more hierophanies, or manifestations of the sacred. This fact further complicates the problem; not only because there is such a multiplicity of hierophanies, but also because each of them is experienced and interpreted differently by different individuals and groups, for example by the populace as opposed to the religious elites. Furthermore, the hierophany itself has certain characteristics which make its interpretation difficult. For example, although it is easy to interpret 'manifest' hierophanies, such as a sacred space, a sacred stone, a sacred river, and so on which exhibit 'the modality of the sacred', it is much more difficult to interpret 'cryptic' hierophanies, which are highly symbolic and sometimes almost completely conceal the sacred. Such a cryptic hierophany would be certain sorts of moral behaviour impelled originally by religious sanctions. This variety does, however, allow us to widen our horizons and seek a broader understanding of the concept of sacredness. An analysis of hierophanies shows us that everything that has ever existed, that man has touched, or loved, has been, actually or potentially, a manifestation of the sacred. These range from the most abstract, such as the sacredness of the perfect forms — a common category of the divine in Olympic Greece, to the most concrete, such as the sacredness of a stone, of mystical eroticism, etc. They range also from the most ancient, such as the Great God of the primitives, to the most recent. Nor should we ignore contemporary facts, since no analysis of the sacred can be entirely based on the experience of others, on myths, hierophanies, and expressions of the experiences of preceding generations. On the contrary, it is our own experience and creation of myths, sacred and profane, which allows us to understand and to live hierophanies which would otherwise be dead or incomprehensible. These considerations have brought us to the centre of the problem.

3. EXPERIENCE AND PHENOMENOLOGY OF THE SACRED

It is useless to avail ourselves of the various specialized disciplines of modern science, if we are to ignore the particular way in which the sacred finds expression in social life. [30]

Both the sociology and the psychology of religion are essential for the understanding of the forms which religion takes on, and for comprehension of its intrinsic character. But it is also true that, by exhibiting the specific cultural and historical forms of the experience of the sacred, the history of religion will help us in the construction of the broad categories which we require. However, in the absence of a psychological and socio-psychological clarification of these categories, the history of religion itself must utilize procedures that are borrowed from philosophy and logic, and the rigidity of which makes them inadequate for our purposes.

To distinguish the various aspects of the sacred we may, following Becker, set the sacred and profane over against one another. But even using these categories it is very difficult to isolate the area to which the concept of the sacred applies, or to observe its characteristics in a 'pure state', that is to say as purely psychological phenomena which have not yet acquired particular cultural and social expression. On the other hand, it is difficult to 'isolate' *any* phenomenon of social significance.

But we may certainly approach a solution to the problem by focussing our attention on a sufficient number of sacred facts and attempting a comparative analysis. Unfortunately there are far too many for any student to be able to know and catalogue them all. But there are certain qualities of the sacred which we may regard as fundamental. It is necessary to examine these characteristics one at a time to discover by comparison the elements that are common beneath the specific local cultural overlay. As Eliade tells us, an approach of this type makes possible the study of each individual element of the sacred, and reveals (1) one expression of the sacred, (2) the psychological, social and cultural attitude of men with respect to that expression, and (3) the historical circumstances of the experience of the sacred.

Undoubtedly the ways in which the sacred may be expressed are infinite, are differently perceived by the different men who live them, and are found in all cultures and all periods of history. There are hundreds of thousands of documents pertaining to the sacred which could be examined. There is also a vast qualitative difference, from the exotic brilliance of many primitive sacred hierophanies, to the manifold expression of the popular religiosity of the Aryan peoples, to the great religions of the East and the West. Each of these religious traditions, in turn, contains innumerable and diverse manifestations of the sacred, each of which must be individually interpreted.[31]

To these difficulties, as Eliade points out, must be added those encountered in the analysis of documents which are as heterogeneous in their structure (ranging, for example, from vegetal myths to myths connected with animal and human sacrifice) as they are in their history.[32]

The sacred in its multiform manifestations, 'bloweth where it listeth', changing its mythical and ritual symbolism with changes in spiritual life. Man's religious psychological experience leaves its imprint on every cultural context and on every period of history.

Within the larger framework of general history, the history of religion tells us where to find the sacred and allows us to grasp the states of mind, the psychological, psycho-social, and cultural realities within which the sacred patterns themselves are expressed. In a word, it throws into relief the bonds between personality structure and the experience of the sacred. From this psychological aspect we may again approach a definition. Naturally, the more fluid and relative the historical and psychological background and the more rapid the changes in human consciousness with respect to experience of the sacred, the more fluid and relative must be our definition. And the more firmly it is grounded on the empirical sciences, the greater will be its independence of philosophical and theological considerations.

But although our analysis is based on the history of religion, we will leave its further development to the specialists. The reader will find implicit in the psychological and social considerations which follow those elements of the history of religion which are necessary for an understanding of our discussion.

Thus, from certain standpoints, the psychological experience of the sacred may be considered to be an irrepeatable and ineffable *unicum*. But from other points of view this concept is open to discussion, and it is for this reason that we are able to continue our argument. In any form of knowledge, man always compares the quality and the object he is considering with something else, a *quid aliud*. Thought is never directed to this or that thing, this or that property or quality, alone, but always involves a process of comparison.[33] An absolute religious experience is unknowable in its immediacy and its totality *except for the man who lives it and in the moment in which he lives it*. Even becoming aware of it already involves some elements of comparison which reveal the internal and external relations of the experience itself. Psychologically speaking, the immediacy of experience is possible, and not only possible, but in the most complete forms of mystical experience the whole personality is pervaded by it. Although these phenomena are of no use for our argument, we may still have to reflect on the experience and, in so doing, decompose it into the elements of which it is formed.

Rudolph Otto tries to characterize the experience of the sacred, or as he calls it, the *numinous*, in his book, *The Idea of the Holy*.[34] The value of Otto's work lies not so much in his attempt to arrive at philosophical definitions or to conceptualize the experience of the sacred, but rather in his construction of categories which prove to have an unexpected validity from the viewpoint of psychology and the history of religion.[35]

It is significant then that the first attribute Otto discovers in the numinous is psychological, creature-consciousness, a sentiment of gratitude, of humble submission, of devotion and dependence. But is this element intrinsic or extrinsic to the experience of the sacred? That is, does the experience express itself in the feeling of dependency, or does this feeling develop to the extent that one has had prior experience of the sacred? The *ad extra* and *ad intra* relations between the sacred as experience and this creature-consciousness are so close as to make a precise answer very difficult. There are many cases in which the sentiment is clearly mostly *a posterius* with respect to the experience, but an equal number of cases in which it *seems* to be part of the experience itself.

It is difficult to say whether this feeling is internal or external to the experience, but even if it is internal, it does not represent the central nucleus of that experience. It is always caused, contemporaneously or nearly so, by another state of consciousness. The creature-consciousness presupposes the 'awareness of something numinous and sacred of which one feels himself to be the creature.'

The sacred, of which the creature-consciousness is an expression, is always something which must be won, and which once attained is again lost and must again be won. It is difficult to maintain that the genuine experience of the sacred is or can be in us *a priori*, even though the final result of the experience may well be the identification of the ego with the sacred.

Although on the ontological plane they postulate *a priori* the existence of an absolute self, even the Indian philosophers and mystics think of it as a goal to be reached. Although the spirit is 'eternally pure, impassible, autonomous, irreducible', it can be 'accompanied' by psychic experience.

According to Otto, the second element of the sacred experience is *mysterium tremendum*. In general, the argument developed above applies also here.

During ceremonies, in the echoes which ritual and cult awake in us,

> the feeling of it (*mysterium tremendum*) may at times come . . . sweeping like a gentle tide, pervading the mind with a tranquil mood of deepest worship[36]

in the same way that it is possible to 'sink to an almost grisly horror and shuddering.'[37] But it is also true that the experience of the sacred cannot be resolved into this feeling of the hidden and tremendous. The *tremendum* is merely a partial expression of it.

The numinous horror may refer to the world of ghosts, to the phantasms of medieval castles, as well as to the more formidable rites of the Indian deities, or the mystic ecstasies of Meister Eckhart. It occurs in both sacred and non-sacred manifestations, and thus it is neither an exclusive and immediate expression of the sacred nor the central nucleus of it. What is involved here is a 'fear' of things that are different from the usual, not only quantitatively but also qualitatively.

Fear is not the essence of the experience of the sacred, although in the anger of God 'there is always present something which gives a sense of unease which normal anger cannot arouse'. But this difference may be due to the fact that the anger of others does not give us a sense of our own total incapacity to intervene and resist such as we feel when faced with divine wrath.

From this sense of helplessness we move to the other characteristic of the experience of the sacred, the feeling of being overwhelmed. Here, too, Otto's argument is controversial. In the subject who lives the experience being overwhelmed amounts to

> the feeling of one's own abasement, of being but 'dust and ashes' and nothingness. And this forms the numinous raw material for the feeling of religious humility. [38]

The characteristics of the religious experience which we have so far discussed may be attributed to all the modalities of the sacred. But here (at least in Otto's example of being overwhelmed) we are dealing with a feeling which applies only to some categories of religion. (And this point holds, if to a lesser extent, also for the concept of the *mysterium tremendum*.) It is not at all certain, for example, that the feeling of being overwhelmed characterizes the modalities of the sacred in some Oriental religions. It is known, in fact, that in these religions this concept becomes that of being overwhelmed in oneself. This quality does not derive from something outside, but, *in nuce*, stems from the ego itself.

These aspects of the sacred experience in turn give rise to a fourth, that of energy and the enthusiastic vitality connected with the numinous, which affects the person who lives the sacred experience and who is overcome by a feeling of emotional fullness, of 'will, force, movement, excitement, activity, impetus' to use Otto's words. It goes without saying that also this is a retrospective interpretation of the experience.

The experience is fascinating and extremely attractive. It grips the personality, sometimes totally paralysing it, first by attraction and then by repulsion. Sometimes this fascination produces the divine demoniac so common in some manifestations of medieval religiosity; the demoniac is more characteristic of archaic than of advanced manifestations of religiosity. This phenomenon disappears with the passage of time and as mankind develops. The demoniac, this fascinating *tremendum*, seems to be connected with the rites aimed at mastering mysterious reality, and thus also with magic, witchcraft, etc. This is true of manifestations of supernatural power, typical among them taboo, where the sacred and the unclean become confounded. Taboo occurs with respect to objects, actions, or persons which *because of a break in the natural ontological level* acquire a 'more or less uncertain force of nature'. [39]

Around these expressions, *the tremendous*, *the mysterious*, *the portentous*, *fascination*, and *energy*, Otto constructs the concept of the experience of the sacred. He compares these feelings (and concepts) of the sacred (clarifying the qualitative difference) with profane feelings which, although analogous, are different to the extent that they have no sacred reference. What is typical of the experience of the sacred, and thus different from analogous profane feelings, he refers to as the non-rational, 'a hidden depth inaccessible to our conceptual thought, which we . . . call the "non-rational" '.[40]

Our spirit finds within itself the *tremendum*, the portentous, the fascinating, etc., but it does not find their source within itself. The experience of the sacred remains of purely 'emotive' value, for which no conceptualization is adequate. From this it is but a short step to the affirmation that the sacred is an *a priori* category.

In short, according to Otto, the experience of the sacred comes from

> a hidden 'predisposition' of the human spirit, which awakens when aroused by diverse excitations.
>
> That there are 'predispositions' of this sort in individuals no one who has given serious study to the history of religion can deny. They are seen as propensities 'predestining' the individual to religion, and they may grow spontaneously to quasi-instinctive presentiments, uneasy seeking and groping, yearning and longing, and become a religious *impulsion* that only finds peace when it has become clear to itself and attained its goal.[41]

But to what extent can one really maintain that the sacred is an *a priori* category? It is difficult to do so on the basis of the psychology, the history, and the sociology of religion. The categories we have mentioned so far are of an essentially empirical nature. At bottom we have done no more than enumerate the attributes of the sacred: in doing so we did not intend to maintain that the sacred can be known only through and in these attributes. But if what is knowable about the sacred is only indirectly and marginally knowable, is it then possible to give an adequate description of it? If it should turn out that the sacred is an *a priori* category, then any interpretation we might give of it will of necessity be uncertain.

Even the indices proposed by Otto (and by others) can easily mislead us, all the more so in that all the 'feelings' referred to by this author have analogous 'profane' feelings with which they may be confused. Thus when confronted with an alleged hierophany we may experience the sense of the tremendous or the fascinating, even though the phenomenon itself is not sacred. The truth is that religion—being, as Bergson observes, coextensive with our existence, with our species—must be and is involved in our psychic structure and in our total personality. For this reason, when they are resolved into their psychological components and viewed, so to speak, from outside experiences of the sacred are often confused with other experience. But even in this confusion and uncertainty we realize that there is something which will help us to characterize the sacredness of an experience.

Since man is capable of reflection, he is, even to himself a focal point, a centre, in the immensity of the universe. Reflection allows the individual to become aware of his own psychic states, and to grasp as an intimate psychical unity facts which may otherwise appear as random and incidental. The various biological and psychic aspects of human nature come together into a psychic unity centred on the consciousness of self. The affective psychic components that we have been discussing are those which elicit the experience of the sacred. Affectivity surrounds it, takes part in it, and orientates the will towards this experience. The experience itself is a complex dynamic fact, the measure and the meaning of which is the individual's self-consciousness of the experience. The mind knows by means of comparisons, contrasts, and relations. Thus, at the time when the sacred experience arises in the ego, the mind forges the instruments for grasping its sacredness, for perceiving the way in which the sacred differs from the profane. The ego, in living the experience perceives it in its psychic unity. Thus, the ego grasps, both as a fact of self-consciousness and as a rational logical fact, the *wholly other*—that is to say, other than the profane life, other than normal experience, and other than the dimensions of human nature. For the person who lives the experience, it is something incommensurable with our own being. Although Otto has recognized the existence of this difference and of the ego's consciousness of it, he did not make it a basic standard of judgment. He preferred his own understanding of the sacred as an *a priori* category, and thus overlooked the fact that the gap between the rational ego and the sacred is logically bridged by means of the *wholly other* when viewed in the context of the relational theory of knowing.[42] When we cease to think of this bridge as a philosophical category and instead consider it as a psychological category, then its explanatory value becomes apparent.

Although this was not Otto's intention, his thesis represents a true bridge between psychic and historical-religious reality. It allows us to understand that alongside the psychological element involved in religious and sacred experiences, there is a common element the existence of which is witnessed by the history of religion. The history of religion documents the existence of a *wholly other* which manifests itself as a *psychological* trait common to different experiences of the sacred, and these can be connected — almost demand to be connected with the set of experiences analysed by Otto.

This new approach leading to the analysis of the *wholly other* is itself full of difficulties, however. We might ask, for example, whether this *wholly other*, in which the hierophanic experience becomes concrete, is not only, so to speak, defined as something different from the profane. Otto defines the sacred as that which is different from the profane, but how does this difference express itself in actual cases? Is it possible to find logical connections between the various forms of the *wholly other* as it manifests itself historically and locally, or does the immediate, individual, irrepeatable and essentially incommunicable character of these sacred experiences make it impossible to subsume them under a single logical category?

Yet, in this variety of experiences there is a common element: everything that is worshipped as hierophanic is venerated to the extent that it is no longer what it was. Thus an object or an act is sacred to the extent to which it embodies (or reveals, as Eliade would say) something which is different from itself. The object becomes a hierophany at that moment at which it ceases to be what it was and acquires a new character.[43] The history of religion is the history of the sacred as it finds a diverse and changing cultural variety of expressions throughout history, among different peoples, in different settings and conditions of life, in different religious systems — but always as something which is qualitatively different from the profane.[44]

At the beginning, Mircea Eliade remarks, all of human life was felt as a single sacrament, and sacred life and social life were practically identical. Subsequently the sacred became less pronounced in increasingly wider areas of human life. Primitive man projected himself by means of ritual beyond time into eternity and thought of most of his sacralized acts as repetitions of a primeval gesture made at the beginning of time by a divinity or a mythical being. Progressive 'desacralization' has occurred, and has led modern man to be keenly aware of precariousness and of irreparable caducity.

Undoubtedly the best way of defining the sacred is by means of a concept based on an interpretation of the sacred by those who actually experience it: but not in an immediate and direct way such as that proposed for example by Becker.

We should focus our attention not on the unorganized flow of immediate religious experiences, but rather on their fundamental organic character as revealed to the consciousness of the individual in the moments immediately following the experience. At this point the experience is significant in that it awakens consciousness and becomes the point of departure for a 'conceptualization' which seeks to comprehend the essence of the experience.

The 'average' interpretation of the experience of the sacred is the attribution to the sacred object of a quality that is different from that which it previously had. In the 'limiting case' the new characteristic often corresponds to a true 'ontological transformation of the object'.[45]

The ontological transformation is a rationalization of the experience of the *wholly other*, and this points to a particular state of consciousness and knowledge which is very difficult to perceive, delimit, and define. From the philosophical point of view the problem of the essence of the experience of the sacred remains open. It might be an *a priori* category of the human spirit or a reality which is grasped by man by means of special perceptive faculties in a manner not unlike that in which he comprehends other objects of human knowledge. We make no judgment on this question since it is not relevant to our present inquiry.

But whatever view one takes of the essence of the sacred and of the *wholly other*, it is in any case concretely possible to identify a certain contrast between the sacred and the profane in the sense that, defining the sacred as different from the profane, there is a constant tendency for the sacred to encroach on the space reserved to the profane and thus a continuous dynamic antithesis exists between these two aspects of life. This contra-position has led some to define the sacred purely in terms of such a dichotomy, but this is surely not enough.

But parallel to this tendency of the sacred to occupy profane 'space' there is a counter tendency of the profane to resist the encroachments of the sacred. This resistance begins at the very centre of the sacred experience, which tends toward secularization as soon as it becomes historically embodied. But history tends, on the one hand, to promote an increasing secularization of social and individual life, and on the other it offers ever new hierophanic forms thus allowing the emergence of new ways of attributing sacred value to the universe. In the realm of social manifestations of the sacred experience, just as in the realm of individual experience, there is a mixture of psychological aspects, and thus sometimes the sacred, and sometimes the non-sacred, aspects of the internal experience are prevalent.

Naturally, these considerations on the sacred experience as a social fact should lead us to consider the problems of ritual, of doctrine, of mythology, etc., which are intimately involved with the sacred, and we shall deal with them in some detail later on. At this point, however, it will be sufficient to note that the individual experience of the sacred acquires its primary social relevance at the level of ritual. At this level we find manifestations which are often indices of the existence of an experience of the sacred, and at the same time, once the existence of such an experience has been ascertained, they are also indices of the fact that the ensuing social phenomenon is the object of socio-religious inquiry.

These considerations anticipate our conclusions concerning the sociological significance of our present discussion of the sacred. They are mentioned here to show that the analysis 'of the progressive withdrawal of the modality of the sacred from social life', which is the main topic of our third chapter, requires a prior understanding of the sacred and of its potential and actual possibilities for permeating social life.

They also have a further significance: they constitute the first outline of an argument that is intended to clarify the unitary logic of the modalities of the sacred, an understanding of which is indispensable for apprehending their relationships to other aspects of historical development.

We shall see that this connection between the forms of the sacred and historical periods—which we scarcely mention at this point—will reappear in a wider setting and at different levels—sacred, mythical, and ritual—and that these different levels will require different interpretations. In this way the apparent dialectical unity becomes two-fold, according to the forms of the sacred that are being considered. These forms can be studied historically in the course of their emergence by referring to the experience which expresses itself in hierophanic manifestations, or they can be studied at the mythical-symbolic-ritual level, since myths, symbols, and rituals may be regarded as means for the communication of experience of the *wholly other* and as stimuli for its repetition.

This variety of levels at which the sacred experience manifests itself, as well as its own essence as a composite of historical, cultural, psychological, rational, and irrational aspects of being, each with its specific characteristics, is one reason for the diversity and multiplicity of experiences of the sacred. 'Everything that man has used, felt, encountered, or loved could become hierophany.'[46] From seasons to rhythms, from gestures to dances, games and mani-festations of physiological life, nothing escapes, or has escaped in the past, from being a vessel of the sacred. In different individuals, in different social groups, settings, or cultures, the sacred has ex-pressed itself in different sets of events, psychic forms, and objects. The multiplicity of manifestations of the sacred, particularly as they find systematic expression in sets of beliefs, makes such sets of beliefs into a more or less deformed projection of the cultures in which they are expressed. Thus, in a certain sense, the history of these manifestations of the sacred is a projection or a manifestation, in the dimension of the sacred, of the history of human society at large.

An object becomes sacred to the extent that it incorporates something different from itself. This diversity finds expression also in the object's assimilation of the experience of some or all of the other characteristics of sacredness which we have mentioned: the tre-mendous, the portentous, the fascinating, etc.

But whether or not these factors are present, in a genuine sacred experience there is always a wide difference between the hierophanic object and that object before it became endowed with sacred quality and so, there is also an analogous difference between the hierophanic object and all objects which have not become designated as sacred.

There are many examples of this dialectic. Among primitive peoples whatever appears unusual, singular, horrendous, frightening, outside the pattern of habit and social life, becomes transferred into the sphere of the hierophanic. Whatever is in some way 'perfect' is also considered to be hierophanic, 'in that perfection is not of this world'.[47] The dialectic of taboo clearly exhibits the break in ontological level which is typical of the hierophanic world. Things which are contaminated or consecrated by taboo are forbidden to profane experience. Again, a series of breaks occurs at the ontological level connected with the concepts of force and of efficacy, as in the case of hierophanies of power.

There is also a typical break of ontological level which tends to compress the whole into one fragment of reality, 'to unify creation, thus abolishing multiplicity, and transforming the fragment into a kind of image of the world.' According to Eliade, this need to identify the whole of reality with one of its parts, is 'an expression of man's desire to see himself, always and effortlessly at the centre of the world, to rise naturally and easily above the human condition, and to reattain the divine.'[48]

There are many other examples, but one point to note is that there is a dynamic decay and growth of hierophanies. New hierophanies always tend to reduce the importance of previous ones, to push them to the background or to absorb them. Above all

> the paradoxical act of incorporation, which makes possible every kind of hierophany, from the most elementary to the supreme incarnation of the Logos in Christ, is found everywhere in the history of religion.[49]

4. FROM THE SACRED TO THE 'WHOLLY OTHER' AND THE ONTOLOGICAL LEAP

It is now possible to draw some conclusions. For those who experience it the sacred is something qualitatively different from the profane, and thus a leap of ontological level is required to reach the reality to which hierophanic significance is attached. The individual who encounters the sacred experiences, perhaps simultaneously, a series of co-ordinated and consistent psychological episodes which, whatever their intrinsic characteristics, *have the effect, at the moment in which he becomes conscious of the experience, of giving him the sensation of having been in contact with something 'wholly other'*. After the passage from the psychological to the rational and reflective phase, this *wholly other* is usually also seen as something of an ontologically different quality.

Naturally, as we have already emphasized, since these things are experienced by individuals who live in a particular situation, the sacred becomes to a large extent a projection and sacred reinterpretation of the 'cultures' to which it refers, and becomes their ideal synthesis projected outside of time as well as in their own history.

Once the experience is over it receives a more precise form and it is possible to repeat it at any time or place by means of the myths and rituals[50] in which it has become embodied. Once this has occurred, the experience is credited with a logical coherence with respect to the culture in which it arises, and which, in a certain sense, it interprets, and with respect to the history of the culture of the society, or of other cultures with which the experience is connected.

The totality of hierophanies is manifested by the at least partial coherence of the symbols and the 'systems' of symbols in which the hierophanies reveal themselves. Furthermore, these same symbols are connected with the culture of the society in which they are expressed: they participate in its history, and at the same time they contribute to its formation. In many circumstances profane history itself may become sacralized and symbolized, although in ways and to degrees that vary in space and time.

Our preliminary considerations on the psychology of the experience of the sacred acquire consistency and significance only when they are located in a wider historical-religious context, which allows us to discern the analytical unity of the apparently highly diverse and discrete manifestations of the sacred that are embedded in particular cultures or that appear peculiar to certain historical periods.

Common consequences are engendered by the experience of the sacred in different individuals in many divergent cultures and contexts. Above all, there is a shared conceptual meaning of these experiences. Using the contributions of sociology and of the history of religions, in this way we can also determine to what extent these consequences and meanings are a product of the culture or of relationships within and among organized groups, and to what extent they are a product of sacred experience itself.

We should not forget that the history of religion concerns itself at the same time with both religion and history, that is, with the dynamic fact which is both collective and individual. It represents an inexhaustible quarry of documents which allow us to compare the individual psyche with collective behaviour. For this reason, the history of religion provides a source for both psychologists and sociologists. If there are common patterns of sequences, either partial or total, in the history of humanity, and if there is a dialectical connection between historical epochs, then perhaps there will be connections between hierophanic systems and social structures. We may expect to find hierophanic systems that express the character of the existing social and economic structure (or of an earlier social structure, since hierophanies outlast the social structures in which they arise).

We have thus located some indices of sacredness in a psychological context, although we have emphasized that such indices do not necessarily reveal the essence of the sacred. In spite of this, we have pointed out that a conception of the sacred as an *a priori* category is operationally useless on the experimental level. In fact, if the sacred is the object of immediate apprehension by the single individual and is known only in this moment as an immediate, pure, and simple perception, then it is not scientifically fertile in that it cannot be co-ordinated logically with the fundamental categories of socio-religious inquiry. In conclusion, we have seen that the individual can become aware of the experience of the sacred, and that through the *wholly other* (which Rudolf Otto does not adequately appreciate in its psychological sense) it is possible to connect the experience of the sacred, even though it should turn out to be an *a priori* category, with that phenomenal reality which is the object of scientific inquiry. In practice, and we shall see later within what limits and in what ways, the points of contact between reality and the sacred are myth (as a symbolic instrument of knowledge and communication) and ritual. Once man has perceived the logical connection between his internal experience and the reality which surrounds him, he tends to make it known to others, to communicate it on the intellectual and the emotional plane, and to relive it through myth and ritual. At the level of these phenomena, of these indices, however imprecise and indirect, we can thus perceive the existence, growth, and decay of the sacred in social life. Naturally, this transition from the experience to mythical and ritual, i.e. symbolic, instruments for the communication of sacred experience, does not entail that the phenomenon repeat itself in qualitatively and quantitatively identical ways. Indeed this transition, in reproducing the same phenomenon in various ways and with varying intensities, raises a series of rather complex problems which will occupy us in the next chapter.

But these last considerations may raise doubts. The reader may feel that we have contradicted ourselves by proposing an apparently unitary category of the sacred in which, however, the *wholly other* and the ontological leap exclude some aspects of the phenomenology of the sacred. Goody's very appropriate criticisms of Caillois, to which we referred earlier, may with apparently equal justification be made against our own views. For example, it is true that in many cultures there is no clear distinction between the sacred and the profane, in the Western sense of these terms, no distinction between technique and magic, or even between technique and religion, and thus the category of the sacred as the *wholly other* appears at least questionable. These criticisms may be made against those who uncritically adopt the distinction between sacred and profane, but our own reference is to a psychological attitude that is basically common to all men, an expression of human nature rather than of a particular culture: and it is this that makes a unitary judgment possible.

The *wholly other*, as distinct from the concept of the ontological leap, is for the most part safe from Goody's criticism. The psychological aspect of religion, that is to say, the experimental part on which we base our inquiry, is, as we have noted with Bergson, coextensive with our species and thus pertains to our own structure. At this level, the religious conviction (of the *wholly other*) which follows the experience appears in every man apart from, and indeed before, any philosophy, and before any culture, in the broad sense of the term. It is a reality of a vital nature and one which is clearly human. On the other hand, the religious spirit always tends to develop from the internal to the external, from the experience to self-awareness and to philosophy, from psychology to logic, from the *wholly other* to the ontological leap. When the psychological attitude which finds expression in the *wholly other* is conceptualized, it may take the form of the *ontological leap*. This latter concept takes on greater validity and truth the closer we move to European cultural forms. The *wholly other*, however, is in itself bound up with the psychological substratum of the individual, and thus has a greater degree of universality than the concept of the ontological leap.

In conclusion, we must accept these two concepts as important elements of our definition to the extent that they are instruments for expressing, in terms which are comprehensible to Western understanding, immediate psychological experiences which are to be found also in other cultures and which may be accompanied by different experiences, even though they will appear more significant when we are dealing with the ideological and cultural complexes of our own Western world. Furthermore, given its prevalently psychological structure, the concept of the *wholly other* will have a more universal application, while that of the ontological leap will be more restricted, since it has greater specificity and rationality and thus is more closely connected to a spatially and temporally restricted cultural complex, and thus to peoples and cultures closer to our own.

5. THE EXPERIENCE OF THE SACRED AND SECULARIZED RELIGION

By utilizing the concept of the *wholly other* we shall later on be able to respond the more easily to those critics who draw a conceptual distinction between the 'sacred' and the 'religious', and who affirm that it is the former and not the latter that is in a state of crisis. It is clear that the concept of the *wholly other* lies upstream from both. On the other hand, if these essential attributes of the 'religious', the *wholly other* and the ontological leap, are conceptually eliminated, then nothing remains of the psychological content of religion. Thus one who holds that religion is not undergoing a crisis, does so only by using the term 'religion' in a different sense, from that in which it used to be employed. For our purpose here we use the term 'sacred' to define a reality which in its substance more or less coincides with what we have so far been referring to as the *wholly other* in its psychological dimension. Thus the problem of secularized religion will find a place in our discussion, but within a logical and conceptual framework rather different from those adopted by Cox, Luckmann, and others.

To clarify this point we refer to Thomas Luckmann's theses. These are based on a conceptual shift of the individual foundations of the religious phenomenon, a shift similar to that on which are grounded the theses of the sociology and the theology of secularization. Luckmann distinguishes three areas of religious development at the individual level, one of which is particularly relevant to the problem with which we are concerned.

> We shall use three pairs of concepts, each pair consisting of one term that refers to the objective social order and one that refers to the individual. The terms on the structural level are: A) the world view (more precisely, the hierarchy of meaning in the world view), B) the sacred cosmos (i.e., the system of religious representations), and C) the 'official' model of religion (i.e., the constellation of doctrine and ritual that functions, in the context of institutionally specialized religion, as a set of normative expectations). The terms on the individual level are a) the subjective system of relevance, b) that set of subjective notions and values to which the individual attributes 'ultimate' significance and by which he will justify his actions to himself and others, and c) the subjective system of religious representations. [51]

Arguing in this way, what one does in practice is to move from the individual psychological religious experience (of the sacred) to the study of the 'subjective system of relevance.'

In fact if the argument, so to speak, moves continuously back and forth between the 'subjective system of relevance' and the religious experience as a psychologically significant experience, then in speaking of religion one is referring to something that has always exhibited characteristics which permit it to be identified and localized; otherwise the possibility of locating a precise logical category of 'the religious' is denied. Thus it is no longer possible to set limits to speculation, and the term 'religious' may be used within any universe of discourse: it is necessary only that there be a justification for its use and a definition which is purely logical, formal, and internal to the discourse itself. Thus, ultimately, in speaking of religion it is possible, and indeed it often happens, that reference is being made to two universes of discourse, to two realities which have nothing in common.

The refusal to base one's inquiry on religious experience, with the experience of the sacred as its central element, entails the — justified — refusal to identify religiosity and religion in general with official or ecclesiastical religion. But while this is a positive step, its corollary, the refusal to attribute logical and methodological relevance to the analysis of the religious as immediate psychological experience, is less positive and in fact is not even necessary. It often allows us to speak of a secularized religion which lacks the experience of the sacred.

But beginning with a psychological experience, on the other hand, makes possible an experimental and objective approach to the problem and inhibits the construction of explanatory schemes which, though laden with cultural significance, are nevertheless unverifiable, and thus have no place in an internally consistent logical argument.

On the other hand, as we have already said, in many cases it is not necessary to employ the *concept* of sacredness. In many cultures no clear distinction is made between sacred and profane, between sacred and magical, between technique, science, and religion. This is the case within the cultural context in which the experience is located (by outsiders). But the category may be employed, and is thus a second order category, in the context of the psychology of the religious experience.

The situation changes when we begin to refer to a psychological attitude which, as such, is in all its essential aspects part of the inheritance of all men, an expression of human bio-psychical structure rather than of a particularly cultural complex. And it is from this fact that the possibility of a universal judgment arises. Otherwise it would be impossible.

Our discussion may appear to be based on an uncritical acceptance of the category of the experience of the sacred, and may appear to fail to take into account recent criticisms of the meaning, especially the operational meaning, of this concept. But this is not in fact the case. At most, the attack which has been launched against the concept of the experience of the sacred is an attack against a logical, cultural, magical, or theological category rather than against a psychological category. When, in speaking of the sacred, we refer to the psychological substratum which is involved, the concept remains valid even though it has been stripped of the cultural, ideological, and philosophical meanings which it has accumulated over time. Many critics fail to distinguish between the experience itself and the intellectual and cultural edifice which is constructed upon it.

In this way it becomes increasingly difficult to distinguish between secularization, the rejection of the magical use of the sacred, and desacralization, the loss of the capacity for living *a psychological experience of the sacred*. Secularized religion, religion which does not involve magical use of the sacred, has a precise meaning. But it is not equally clear what can be meant by a religion which lacks the experience of the sacred. In fact, such a religion would clearly be a religion deprived of *its basic human and experimental psychological basis*, and thus nothing more than an intellectual attitude which 'by definition' is not religious (cf., for example, deism).

The psychological experience of the sacred in its immediacy is clearly a *prius* which allows for the unification in a single logical class of all 'religious' facts and the various levels that are derivative of them. It is a *datum* which the too often ignored history of religion shows to be present in every religion, apart from its logical, conceptual, philosophical, theological, ecclesiastical, cultural, and cognitive content, all of which derive from this experience, and in turn promote it.

The logical category of secularization, of the religion of secularized society, is thus acceptable when a clear distinction is made between secularization and desacralization. The distinction may be set out as follows:

(1) *secularization* is (a) of structures, (b) of the attribution of sacred significance or manipulatory (magical) value to things, persons, spaces, etc., (c) of the attribution of sacred significance to behaviour (moral, etc.);

(2) *desacralization* is a change in the intensity and the diffusion of the experience of the sacred as a psychological experience of the *wholly other*.

Secularization, so understood, may or may not be accompanied by desacralization, and though they are often found together there is no necessary connection between them. We shall return to these problems in what follows.

2

The Crisis of Religion in Industrial Society

It is necessary to choose discerningly and, contrary to the old order, take the quadrivium before the trivium. There is peril in rhetoric and dialectic, safety in arithmetic and geography. An entire body of episcopal or purely pious literature, and on the other hand a rationalist and impious literature, were both equally unrealistic in assessing the volume and force of Christianity in the nineteenth century. From the elegant Monseigneur Bougard to the ironical Anatole France, with Louis Veuillot in between, nothing but fantasy! Since the passing of that age of oratory, we have learned to add and subtract, and to plot curves and round geometrical forms. Let us say that we are in full training. To learn the dimensions of a religious society, we must use statistics that are comparable, make certain or probable retractions, simplify fractions, and avoid the deception of averages. We must adopt graphic representations that are at the same time exact and 'meaningful'. In short, before even approaching the domain of our real topic, we practise statistics and cartography. I will even say that the invasion of algebraic formulas and square roots cannot but worry slightly an old mathematician who has taken up another interest and who, without renouncing his old loves, insists on putting the sociology of religion among the human sciences.

Gabriel LeBras
(*The Sociology of Religion Among the Human Sciences*)

1. PRELIMINARY CONSIDERATIONS

Yinger[1] has listed four factors that affect the process of socio-religious change: (i) variations in personal religious needs and interests, which arise from basic personality differences in the level of intellectual development, etc.;[2] (ii) variations in political and economic interests; (iii) mobility and social change; (iv) variations that stem from the internal development of the religious system. The transformative influence of these factors destroys existing social and religious patterns, and they stimulate a process, initially slow and partial, but which steadily accelerates, of the decomposition of behaviour and of psychological orientations. The social context of religion was once supportive of it, and the values, actions, and attitudes of lay and religious life were mutually enriching and enhancing. But at a certain point the influence of social life began to be negative for religion, so that (1) Almost all new social phenomena came to have a disintegrative effect on religious life; (2) A steady diminution of the influence of religion on secular life became evident. This was accompanied by the desacralization of society, a process that has not yet reached its culmination.

All this occurs as new social developments disturb the normal pattern of religion, and we are concerned here with the identification of these social factors.[3] We begin with a brief quantitative profile of the way in which these phenomena have taken shape culturally and historically, and we must then attempt to categorize the conditions under which the 'decomposition of religiosity' is most apparent. Once the extent of the phenomenon has been established, and once we have reviewed the *post hoc*, we shall, as far as possible, try to discover the *propter hoc*.

2. METHODS OF STUDYING ECCLESIASTICAL PHENOMENA, AND THEIR LIMITATIONS: INDIRECT AND EXTRA-ECCLESIAL INDICES

We are concerned with the extent to which contemporary society has become desacralized, which means the extent to which human society has lost the sense of the sacred. If the experience of the sacred is the nucleus of the religious experience,[4] then by concentrating on the decay of sacrality we should be able to pinpoint with a certain degree of precision, and in quantitative and qualitative terms, the diminution of religiosity.

The terms of the problem are, even so, far from clear. Methods of study have already been evolved in the sociology of religion,[5] and we must adapt these, and the data and research that has accumulated, in addressing our problem, even though socio-religious research has developed unevenly, indeed almost randomly, and even though its approaches are heterogeneous.

Our discussion will be concerned primarily with the Roman Catholic Church, although, by making forays into other data, we shall hope to extrapolate to other religions. In particular, we shall pay attention to the instruments for 'measuring' the degree of religious impregnation in societies with a Catholic background. To speak of measurement in this context may seem rather foolhardy, since it may be taken to imply that there is a possibility of establishing the intensity and frequency of the experience of the sacred and, as we have mentioned previously,[6] of the religious experience. We have, indeed, no *direct* measure of the intensity of the experience of the sacred, but we may identify those elements that may be assumed to be indirect indices (that is, external to the individual psyche) of the level of sacrality. In broad surveys one can inductively establish the intensity and the diffusion of religiosity in external manifestations such as religious practice and religious attitudes, and to these issues we shall give some attention.

Since our purposes are more synthetic than analytic, we must make use of data collected by others. These data are necessarily heterogeneous. They were gathered in different times and places, based on different conceptions of sacrality and religiosity, and dependent on the divergent importance attached to particular indices in different religions (consider the different significance attached to church services by Catholics and Protestants, for example). None the less, some uniformity can be discovered, and although we shall not analyse the differences in these procedures in detail, we shall indicate them briefly *en passant*. First, however, we must seek to relate religious phenomenon to the dynamics of religiosity in social life, and to do this, to determine the degree of sacredness within social life, we must first determine the level at which the research and the measurements should be carried out.

As we have seen, the experience of the sacred is the focal point of religious experience as a whole, including also the related rituals and myths. Religious experience centres around the experience of the sacred, and is in turn the fulcrum of a series of social relationships that arise in support of them.

Thus we may speak of religious society:

(1) Where there is a hierophany on which the experience of the sacred is focused. This occurs in at least two situations: (a) when there is an experience of the *wholly other* which the individual regards as a real ontological transformation of the fact, act, object, or space, on which the experience is focused. Thus, a stone or a tree which is the focus of a sacred experience is no longer regarded as just a stone or a tree, but, say, as the embodiment or manifestation of a god; (b) when the experience is not credited with this type of meaning, but when none the less the experience has a powerful effect on the subject.

(2) Where there is a generically religious experience, again connected with a sacred hierophany. This happens in at least two cases: (a) when there are facts or acts (basically rituals), related to doctrine or myth, which arise from, or give rise to, a sacred hierophany; (b) when there are group acts or facts which, although they are not themselves rituals, are intended to intensify, diffuse, and facilitate the experience of the sacred, i.e. facts and acts which, although not themselves proper experiences, are meant to encourage and strengthen the phenomena described in (1) and (2).

These categories *all refer to the experience of the sacred*, the centre of the religious experience, which in turn is the core of socio-religious structures. Thus it is not possible to determine *a priori* where a given social fact or act is religious or religiously relevant. This can be established in individual cases by analysing data and documents, by surveys, and by the use of analytical procedures. Our categories are neither definitive nor exhaustive, but in a considerable number of cases they do supply the first methodological equipment for approaching social facts which, on the basis of these categories, can be defined as clearly religious. Some other social facts can be discarded as clearly not religious. But it is necessary to bear in mind the existence of a shadowy area where facts are mixed, uncertain, and not easily labelled.

Both at the centre and the periphery of the sacred, there are myths and rituals in which sacredness is expressed, and an organization which is the carrier and protector of these myths and rituals. This being so, the first analysis is of myth and ritual, and only in the second place of organization, since this is only secondarily and not immediately connected to the experience of the sacred.

Yet myth and ritual do not form an integral part of the essential nucleus of the sacred experience. They are themselves an index, a more or less peripheral expression, a symptom, of the existence of an experience of the sacred. Myth and ritual either flow from or elicit that experience; whoever wishes to live the experience turns to them, even though there is no certainty that myth, ritual, and experience will occur simultaneously.

For these reasons the criteria for classification of the degree of sacrality of a society seem at first sight to be rather problematic, since for the purpose of field analysis the choice of indices of sacrality is left to the individual researcher.[7] The criteria of his choice will vary according to custom; to the stratification of the society into classes, races, and folklore substructures; the popular religiosity of the milieu, the scientific orientation of the researcher, and so on.[8]

An analytical morphology of religiosity, culturally and historically, is essential for the development of techniques of measurement, and it has been developed by various authors. Some of them have emphasized, for example, the importance of geographical determinants for this morphology.[9] But none of these theories have reached final results, however similar the positions of these writers with regard to the construction of analytical procedures.

This measure of agreement is great enough to facilitate synthesis and theory construction. This is so because the indices used for analysis are projections of the ritual, liturgical, and symbolic universe of religions, which is in itself coherent, if only because, apart from any other considerations, it arises from a constant and deep felt common need to mould the individual for religious purposes.

We must expect to find connections between, on the one hand, human personality and types of experience of the *wholly other*, and, on the other hand, the type of religious practice, ritual, and liturgical manifestations both official and spontaneous. From such connections we discover the sense of the sacred that exists within a given society. This leads to a paradoxical situation. Because the sociology of religious practice is basically a sociography, which has always operated without much attention to basic methodological questions, we would expect to find it in a state of confusion and chaos. Yet it presents a fairly coherent picture, and among the sociographic studies issuing from the various schools of sociology this is the one the data of which may almost always be useful at a theoretical level.

Research which would otherwise be insignificant acquires a certain importance simply because it is, so to speak, set within the liturgical universe. Because of this, indices are suggested, not by the usual preliminary methodological considerations, but by centuries of psychological analysis of religious behaviour. [10]

For a long time it has been possible to discern a certain convergence of ideas, especially with reference to the fundamental acts of religious life. As we have remarked previously, the study and measurement of religious 'practice', as a synthetic expression of the vitality of ritual and myth and thus indirectly of the sacred, provides one of the criteria of analysis of the religious vitality of a people, at least within a certain religion. [11] Naturally, the measurement of practice in turn amounts to distinguishing between those who do and those who do not practise. From a microsociological point of view, this is not a particularly meaningful distinction, although, at least until recent times, it has been fairly fruitful if employed in the context of an inquiry with broader perspectives. This distinction between practising and non-practising, i.e. between those who are and those who are not attracted to myth and ritual, seems, in fact, to be a particularly fruitful one *in certain societies and in certain historical periods.* But we must remember that a measurement of 'practice' is a measurement of the intensity of religiosity only *within certain precise limits.* This is because, for every practising individual or group, their practice marks the extent to which the relevant expression of the sacred is approximated, and also because different practices are in some way connected with different types and different degrees of religiosity.

From the scientific point of view, however, the use of external indices for the measurement of experience and thus of individual religiosity is not entirely satisfactory.

Apart from other difficulties, we must consider the fact that there are different types of experience. In the first place there is the primary, authentic experience of the mystic or of one who suddenly 'feels' the existence of the sacred and is, as we say, 'converted' or 'reborn'. Then there is the secondary experience of one who, through ritual and symbol, relives his own or others' primary experiences, but in the form of habitual practice rather than of blinding illumination. Something of this sort happens on the human plane when love changes to affection. Finally, there is the tertiary experience of sheer habit which is nearly or wholly colourless and in many cases amounts to no more than a simple act of will which leads to a 'practice', a participation in a ritual from which the content of sacred experience *may* be completely absent. In the face of these difficulties, the material at our disposal and the indices with which we may work appear to be quite inadequate to the problems of measurement.

In conclusion, it is difficult to be certain that there is a convergence between external expressions and intimately felt religiosity. Furthermore, should we wish to analyse the religiosity of a single individual, we should look upon the procedures of analysis of practice as purely auxiliary tools. If we were to study the religiosity of a small group we should try to study a large number of external expressions in order to understand the intimate religiosity with greater precision. In a wider setting, but within precise spatio-temporal boundaries, the few basic indices generally used by sociologists of religion are sufficiently reliable indicators.[12]

But there are other reasons for exercising great caution in using rate of religious practice as an index of the sense of the sacred. Religious practice is influenced by the positive or negative judgment of others, as well as by a number of other external factors which might all be classified under the heading of social control. But even if the duty and the desire to act, in this case to practise religion, is integrated into experience, so that whether one practises or not depends on the above conditions, these considerations do not disqualify religious practice as an index, so long as a sufficiently wide setting is taken into account. Although a subject's religious practice is related to the adaptation of his attitude to a social situation, it is the subject who interprets this situation according to *his* feelings and *his* sense of the sacred. This interpretation is influenced by the sense of the sacred of others with whom the subject shares human ties and who exercise constant social pressure on him. From this we can conclude that, by and large, religious behaviour probably represents a strengthening of the psychological attitudes typical of the milieu.

In areas with a low rate of religious practice the sense of the sacred will be stronger than is suggested by the practice rate, while in areas with high practice rates the contrary will be true. But for the purpose of our argument, such distortions may well be tolerated as long *as we limit our discussion to institutionalized organized religion and ecclesial religiosity.*

Since we do not have a complete set of data regarding the world's religions, we must limit our considerations mainly to data relative to Catholicism and Protestantism. With its 900 million adherents, practising and non-practising, Christianity represents a large enough sample for preliminary discussions.

However, even among students of Christianity, there is not general agreement about which rates to consider as the parameters against which to measure religious practice and, indirectly, religiosity.

Our list of the generally accepted principal indices begins with practices which seem, at least at first glance, to indicate greater religiosity, and proceeds to practices which may continue after those considered earlier in the list have been abandoned, and which indicate a lower degree of religiosity. When these practices disappear, a more irrevocable abandonment of organized religion is indicated. Naturally this way of organizing the list involves some possibilities of error of the sort we have mentioned above. [13]

Divine Service. As Chelini and Gonzáles [14] assert, presence at the Catholic mass, or at the divine service of other religions, is an external index which still marks a fairly high degree of religious involvement. As Gonzáles points out, attendance at mass presupposes constant attention, week by week, to religious phenomena, a continuous act of will, and a degree of continuous commitment.

Easter Communion also involves a strong commitment to religion although when not accompanied by attendance at mass it indicates a weaker commitment, unless other internal manifestations of religion are present (such as meditation, private prayer, mental prayer, etc.). It is generally held that, by and large, those who abandon Easter communion also abandon these internal practices. On the other hand, it is possible that communion constitutes an index of a more authentic religiosity than does attendance at mass, which is more likely to be a matter of conforming with the standardized rhythms of social life.

Principal Rites. If Easter communion is abandoned the next in-

dication of diminished commitment is the total or partial abandonment of the three great solemn rites of Christian life: *baptism*,
religious marriage, and *religious burial*.

Baptism is the least emphatically religious act of these three. Often
those who are somewhat religious fail to baptize their children or do
so very late, while many others who have lost their sense of the sacred
or of the sacred significance of the act itself may baptize their
children out of habit, giving the ceremony an almost folkloristic
significance.

The abandonment of the 'religious wedding' implies rather more,
even though, as we shall see later, this is often conditioned by moral
factors which have little or nothing to do with the intensity of
religious commitment. Finally, 'civic burial', whether at the wishes of
the relatives or of the deceased, represents a more complete and
usually a very sincere break with religion, since it seems unlikely that
many would take an ambiguous attitude towards death. Who would
refuse a religious burial if he had a hope, however thin, of some kind
of future life? Most survivors would find it difficult to refuse a
religious burial to their kinsfolk.

Additional Indices. The explicit profession of militant or non-
militant atheism is of course an important indicator, although we
consider as atheists primarily those who deny the existence of God.[15]

For our purposes, it is not necessary to employ Jacques Maritain's
distinctions between practical atheism; absolute atheism (the denial
of the existence of God); negative atheism (a simple rejection of the
idea of God); and positive atheism (an active struggle against the
idea of God),[16] useful as such a classification may be. The
sociologist's concern is the range of attitudes, social problems, and
relationships between groups and social classes, which manifest some
degree of disaffection with regard to religion and the sacred interpretation of life. When the process of detachment and the
rejection of the sacred and the religious is marked, this disaffection is
expressed as atheism — a particular orientation which arises in
certain psychological, social, historical, and political circumstances.

When we look at the psychological structure of individuals,
however, and at their social and cultural contexts, what Jean Lacroix
has to say becomes very relevant. 'One might suggest, schematically,
that there are in the first place problems suggested by man (by
society) which beset his existence, and that then there is the refusal of

God as an indispensable element for the solution of these problems.'[17] Lacroix has Marxism in mind which includes atheism as part of its solution to society's problems. But on other levels, industrial society everywhere poses problems analogous to those which, on the political plane, call for, or might call for, the abandonment of religion.

It is as true as ever that 'discussing atheism can no longer mean [discussing] an abstract conception relative to which it is sufficient to establish its incoherence or lack of foundation: to discuss atheism means rather to return to the contemporary situation of man. Atheism is a lived system of values.'[18] The justification of atheism based on a kind of common sense or some sort of philosophy are important and deserve attention but our interest is mainly in atheism as a system of lived values.

For sociology, for psychology, and for all the disciplines that analyse human attitudes and experiences, it is essential to study the circumstance when religious experience does not occur, which is the criterion of almost every form of practical atheism. Atheism, since it is negative, is not directly experienced — what occurs is that man no longer experiences as real the religious intimations of the surrounding environment. Thus atheism, in going beyond a simple practical response to a speculative attitude, seems to be the growing awareness of the absence of religious experience, and hence it constitutes a denial of sacred values, and a struggle against those who live by them. This is the limiting position of positive atheism as discussed by Jacques Maritain.

But apart from the positive and negative indices of which we have spoken (religious practice and atheism respectively), we may also use other kinds of documentation, such as so-called 'personal documents' concerning individual religious experiences, since these documents are like photographs, however distorted, of certain milieux. Questionnaires, interviews, public opinion polls, tests — all may, in varying measure, throw light on the overall picture.

For the past, we can avail ourselves of documentation which does not differ so much from that of our own times, for how shall one regard episcopal inspections, if not as surveys? Furthermore, they are surveys which have been repeated with great regularity for centuries by interviewers (the parish priests) who are specialists and, within certain limits, reliable. For the past as well as for the present, we shall use supplementary documentation concerning the history of religious associations, saints, lay movements, and so on, but we shall only occasionally refer directly to this historical documentation, assuming some acquaintance with basic historical data from the history of religions (and especially of the Christian religion).

Of course this documentation *cannot provide an exact measurement of the religiosity of various societies in space and time.* Even if it were possible to use on a vast scale, indices and sophisticated methods of analysis such as those proposed by Isambert and Maître[19] and even if we could measure exactly some religious attitudes from certain points of view, we could still not measure with equal precision the degree of religiosity of the society under study. Studies conducted so far—however rough, imprecise, and distant they are from the intimate reality of society—do, however, lead to results that are sufficient for our purposes.

The measuring devices of which we shall avail ourselves allow us to approach mainly the components which we have seen to be external mythical-ritual expressions of the religious experience. Attendance at mass, observance of Easter, etc., are a substratum and an expression of an ontological discontinuity, of a *wholly other* which is seen to be such by those who live the experience. But they are expressions that are by and large proportional to the frequency, in space and time, of participation in these ritual celebrations. As we have seen, perhaps those who live the experience do not all or always live the life of the *wholly other*, but in the majority of cases a cessation of ritual participation is a concomitant of the decline of religious experience, within the limits discussed in the next section.

3. THE CURRENT STATE OF IRRELIGIOSITY AND THE
PROBLEM OF EXTRA-ECCELESIAL AND SECULAR RELIGIOSITY

It must be emphasized from the outset, that the discussion of religiosity does not end with the discussion of religious practice and the various other indices which occupy us in this section. We have still to face the problem of determining the existence, intensity, and frequency of extra-ecclesial and secular religiosity. The interdisciplinary approach, heralded by Gabriel Le Bras, has broadened the intellectual perspective of the sociology of religion, and freed it from the slavery of counting practitioners — an early tendency which some regarded as a trivial exercise, [20] the sociography of religious practice.

Obviously this is not a matter of simply widening the field of religious facts to be studied, but involves a relevant qualitative leap. Apart from religious practice there is the question of the type of religiosity which is taking shape outside organized churches, beyond *Kirchlichkeit*, and of the characteristics assumed by religion once it is affected by the world of technology, by the new image of God, by the extra-ecclesial locus of this religiosity, and so on. This field requires new techniques of measurement and analysis. The present argument lies within the framework of this 'second development' of the sociology of religions.

The perspective from which we have been looking at the problem of the crisis of religion lies to a great extent, if not completely, within the framework of ecclesial societies. The crisis is thus observed mainly at the institutional level, as an immediate reflection of the individual's personal crisis. In short, *the argument developed in the second section goes from the religious experience to practice as an institutional fact.*

It is clear that if religiosity is identified with ecclesiality, then the ecclesial crisis becomes the crisis of religiosity, and thus one must conclude that modern society is unreligious. [21]

Behind this argument, naturally, lies a series of hypotheses (which we will not discuss here) which must be challenged, implicitly or explicitly, by those who refuse to accept the fixed equation religiosity = ecclesialism. One of these assumptions is that the religious needs of the individual in our society have been historically satisfied only by the church, that the objective dimension of religiosity is identified with religious behaviour as a social fact.

The tendency of the sociology of religious practice to start from the formula, religion = ecclesialism, must not be completely and uncritically accepted. Here we agree with Luckmann, as long as his argument is not seen as a complete dismissal of the results of studies of ecclesial religiosity. Essentially, his thesis must be understood as an integration of, and addition to, what has been done so far.

Although it is true that organized religion does not necessarily have the power to encompass all religious experience, on the whole it did achieve this until recently and it does so in some measure today.

In a society in which churches and new religions which are potentially organizable into churches have a strong symbolic value in contrast with the profane, the individual tends to attach his religious 'calling' to them, as the data of the sociology of religion demonstrate. There is thus a fairly consistent and wide coincidence of religiosity and ecclesialism (taking this latter term in the widest sense).

However, as the symbolic value of the churches gradually diminishes and religion becomes more privatized, circumstances give rise to a non-ecclesial type of religiosity. In a word, it seems that *as religious practice diminishes, religiosity diminishes to a lesser extent than practice itself*. Thus, as the crisis of the churches advances, what was originally and apparently a marginal phenomenon becomes more and more relevant.

Thus it is clear that as secularization advances in industrial and post-industrial society,[22] the traditional 'sacred cosmos' loses its significance as the index of a religiosity bound up with the experience of the sacred. This is *because of the high degree of subjectivization of models of belief*. Thus, as Luckmann argues, it becomes difficult to measure religiosity and at the same time 'count the believers' in terms of 'conformity with and deviation from the "official" model'. But these considerations seem only to support the conclusion that it is not possible to distinguish between belief and non-belief, and that it is thus equally impossible to establish whether or not religion is undergoing a crisis. The correlation of the models of belief typical of industrial society, however subjective and variable they may be, with the existence or non-existence of an experience of the sacred does still allow us to study the religious situation in society. However, it is necessary to construct new logical and conceptual models which are no longer concerned with distinctions among those who believe in something endowed with mutually consistent attributes (for example, those who believe in God, in more than one god, in a sacred cosmos, etc.). Instead it is a problem of grouping together a number of conceptual 'translations' which may contradict one another but which belong to a single type of psychological experience. Unless these considerations are taken into account, it is possible that a single concept, as employed in the sociology of religion, might include phenomena that from a psychological point of view are not always religious. For example, an experience of the sacred may conform to social and cultural conceptions of what is religious or it may not, whilst still remaining an experience of the sacred. Today, however, in the light of the sociology of religion's most recent critical analyses, it seems more logical to accept conceptual contradictions while maintaining the unity of experience, in order to view as religious a reality which is the object of socio-religious analysis. Thus we can call believers those who have any concept, whatever its type and content, which is related to the experience of the sacred. Socio-religious study within industrial and post-industrial society is concerned with religiosity, seen as a flow of experience of the sacred. This experience is part and parcel of society, and is variously conceptualized both socially and individually. These conceptualizations are potentially contradictory in space and time. As a function of this different situation, variations in behavioural patterns will also be found.

The problem of the measurability of religiosity in advanced societies and of its appropriate indices appears in a new form and challenges the methods used until recently in the sociology of religion. In the next section we will refer only marginally to the problem of extra-ecclesial religion and its indices: we shall return to it later.

4. THE CURRENT STATE OF IRRELIGIOSITY: A FEW FIGURES

Although based on the indices to which we have referred, the figures presented in the following pages are intended to offer some points of departure for analysis based on samples sufficiently broad to orient the student. In many cases documentation is less than adequate, but we begin with France, since the figures for this country are the most complete and elaborate. We then turn to other countries, and with respect to Protestantism deal mainly with Great Britain and the United States. We conclude with Italy, even though the data are few and inadequate.

France

A few years ago Boulard suggested that, for the entire country, out of 31,700,000 Frenchmen over the age of fourteen years, 10,500,000 (34.2 per cent) participated in Easter communion.[23] Among those over twenty-one years of age, the percentage dropped to about 30 per cent. The proportion of Frenchmen who, in spite of having Catholic parents, remained unbaptized was, according to Boulard, 3 per cent. The highest figures for this category were to be found in southern central France, where in some regions the percentage of non-baptized reached 60 per cent. Partial research conducted before and after *La Croix* published this synthesis (1953), confirmed these conclusions, focusing on the fact that the proportion of practitioners was lower in the large cities than in the country and in small urban centres. In Paris, for example, the proportion of practitioners varied between parishes from 4 per cent to 20 per cent.

Chelini has synthesized the data collected by various studies on the Jura, Grenoble, Marseilles, Vienne, St. Étienne, Toulouse Nancy, Paris, Lyons, Lièges, Strasbourg, Libourne, Autun, Le Puy, Lille, Arles, Bordeaux, Dijon, Langres, Versailles, Landerneau, Vendenheim, and Lampertheim.[24] These are shown on page 51. By and large these and other surveys indicate that the larger urban centres show a lower level of practice than do smaller towns and rural areas, and that there is a lower level of practice among the working classes. Studies confirming the above results have been made also at Nice, Rouen, Roanne, Metz, Poitiers, Rive de Gier, Annecy, and in various other centres.[25]

One of the most interesting studies is that conducted in the diocese of Coutances (Normandy) with Boulard as scientific consultant.[26] In the southern part of the diocese the percentage of those observing Easter communion varied between 74.7 per cent and 71.7 per cent of Catholics; in the centre the variation was between 62.5 per cent and 55.8 per cent; in Presqu'île between 45.6 per cent and 45.5 per cent; at Cherbourg the percentage fell to 26.1 per cent. This is one of many examples of lower levels of practice in the urban centres compared with less urbanized areas. Dreyfus reports on a similar situation among the Protestants in Alsace,[27] with an average participation of 10 per cent in the urban centres and of 25 per cent in the countryside. More precisely, Strasbourg had a regular practice rate of 10.3 per cent; the banlieu had a regular rate of 11.8 per cent; and the countryside had a regular practice rate of 28 per cent. The percentage of the faithful attending church on the more important religious occasions were 30 per cent, 25.8 per cent and 52 per cent respectively. Thus, the Protestant situation was here analogous to the

Catholic. In the particular case of Alsace, however, we note that average practice among Catholics was much higher. In the Jura, too, there was a one to three ratio between the per cent of rural practitioners (34 per cent) and that of urban practitioners (13 per cent).[28] Clearly, it would be imprudent to generalize too readily about differences between city and country rates of practice, on the basis of these data, but the indications cannot be entirely dismissed.

City	Date of inquiry	Total population	% attending mass of the Roman Catholic population	% of Roman Catholic adults attending mass
Dôle	15 Oct. 1950	17,135 inhabitants in 1946	20.66	13
Grenoble	11 May 1952	130,000 total in 1952	13.08	
Vienne	26 Oct. 1952	24,758 total in 1952	23.22	
Marseilles	8 May 1953	650,000 total in 1953	13.20	11.4
St. Etienne	8 Mar. 1953	180,000 in 1953	28.5*	24.1
Toulouse	15 Mar. 1953	276,000 in 1953	15.05	11.4
Nancy	15 Nov. 1953	165,000 total in 1953	25/26	
Paris	14 Mar. 1954	5,000,000 in the diocese in 1954	12/13**	
Lyons	21 Mar. 1954	484,710 city 1954 713,720 total	20.09	
Liège	10 Oct. 1954	156,000 city in 1954	21.84	18.20
Strasbourg	14 Nov. 1954	112,500 'intra muros' 146,500 suburbs 159,000 total	39.93 33.45 36.09	
Libourne	6 Feb. 1955	19,474 in 1955	17.99	9.12m 16.81f
Autun	20 Mar. 1955	14,399 in 1954	28.31	
Le Puy	10 Mar. 1955	30,744 in 1955	55.9	42.8
Lille	23 Oct. 1955	194,827 in 1955	18	12.7m 21.9f
Arles	27 Nov. 1955	26,481 in the 5 parishes of the city of Arles in 1946	12.04***	9.8
Bordeaux	27 Nov. 1955	257,946 city 199,055 suburbs 457,041 total in 1955	20.63 11.75 16·8	13.17 8.86 10.51

* Over 13 yrs. old.   ** Of total population.
*** Over 12 yrs. old.

Chelini, warning against over-simplification, introduces the following distinctions:

(a) religiously 'good areas', in which the city has a rate of practice which is high but still lower than that of the surrounding countryside;

(b) religiously 'bad areas', in which the city has a practice rate which is not much lower than that of the surrounding rural areas;

(c) religiously 'indifferent areas', where the practice rates in the city and in the countryside are approximately equal.

Irreligiosity seems to proceed from the city to the countryside, and, once it has become fairly widespread, there is little difference between city and countryside. In general, according to Chelini, practice in agricultural areas covers a range between 0 per cent and 100 per cent. This happens, we think, because the less 'acculturated' populations tend to polarize their psychological states and conflicts more easily.

While there are sufficient data concerning participation in Easter communion and attendance at mass, fewer, although fairly indicative, data are available concerning the principal religious rites. Chelini reports that in a parish in Marseilles[29] the percentage of baptized is 90 per cent, while in Paris[30] between 1930 and 1944 this figure drops to an average of 76 per cent (72 per cent for the centre of the city). In some regions of France there are areas with extremely low rates, as Le Bras[31] has clearly shown. To give an example chosen at random from the many published by Le Bras for various periods: in 1937 in the diocese of Limoges, 'doyenne' of Saint-Sulpice-Les Champs, of the total number of births, 75 per cent were non-baptized, and 70 per cent of funerals, and 80 per cent of weddings, were civil.[32]

From Chelini we derive the following table:

Religious practice among Roman Catholics

	Baptism*	First Communion	Religious weddings	Religious funerals
Liège (1954)	95%	75%	70%	80%
Paris (1930–43)	80%	—	43%	64.5%
Marseilles (1945)	90%	—	72%	72%
Dole (1949–1950)	83.5%	90%	80%	90%

(* = percentage of live births to nominally Catholic parents)

The percentage of those not professing any religion in Auxerre in the late 1940s went from a maximum of 25 per cent among agricultural workers to a minimum of 10 per cent. Sixty-six per cent of the population were practising, and among these 22 per cent regularly attended church.[33]

These are all limiting cases, of course, or cases dealing with small geographical areas. With respect to the high percentage of civil weddings, we must remember that their number is not always a reliable index to ecclesiastical religiosity of a country. Civil weddings are more frequent in the city than in the country.[34]

The answer to the problem posed at the beginning of our study appears to be much the same throughout France: in all geo-social areas, urban or agricultural, industrial or non-industrial, there is an ongoing process of religious decay, although this process is variously distributed in intensity according to a wide range of factors and circumstances.[35] Furthermore, this crisis grows rather than recedes over time.

United States

In the 1950s, three quarters of Americans thought of themselves as active members of some church.[36] Little change appears to have occurred between 1939 and 1954 with respect to church attendance either, weekly attendance remaining at between 36 per cent and 46 per cent, according to Gallup surveys.[37] Other indications led observers to consider that there had been a decline in religiosity in the United States, for example as assessed by the proportion of space devoted to religious articles in the press, the degree of interest expressed in the church in general.[38] Even in the 1950s, as many as 21 per cent declared that they did not belong to any church, and in a different survey 27 per cent said that they were not active members of any church.[39] There were marked but expectable differences between Catholics and Protestants with respect to Church attendance, as the results of data collected in a University of Michigan survey in 1957 and 1958, indicate. (See p. 54.)

These figures do not include people who do not belong to any church, of course.

Frequency of church attendance by sex and denomination (in %)[40]

Religious group		number	regu-larly	often	rarely	never	TOTAL
Protestants	male	1883	30	23	37	10	100
	female	2302	46	23	25	6	100
Roman Catholics	male	584	67	14	14	5	100
	female	686	75	13	9	3	100
Jews	male	79	19	20	43	18	100
	female	109	8	22	57	13	100
Baptists	male	394	35	29	28	8	100
	female	545	47	30	18	5	100
Methodists	male	324	25	29	36	10	100
	female	406	43	27	22	8	100

The persistence of high figures for church membership and church attendance in the United States during the 1950s, led some writers to the conclusion that America was experiencing a religious revival. The argument which ensued turned in part on the adequacy of early statistics, and the extent of religious practice in the nineteenth century. Jean Chelini saw that development as evidence to counter the thesis of the decline of the sacred advanced in the first edition of this book.[41] Whatever may have been believed about religious revival in the United States in the late 1950s, it has since then become clear that a process of religious decline has occurred since that time. This emerged from Gallup polls in 1958 and 1966, as well as from the variety of surveys and more limited studies. To take only one, a questionnaire distributed to students entering Haverford College in 1948 and 1968 gave striking results:

	1948	1968
believe in God	79%	58%
believe in a life after death	46%	34%

Weekly church attendance among these young people had also declined by 11 per cent during this same period.[42] More generally, this process of decline had also become evident to the American public at large. In a poll conducted in 1957, only 14 per cent of Americans felt that the Christian religion was losing influence, but in 1967 this percentage had risen to 57 per cent.[43] Perhaps the most well informed sociologists of American religion also concluded, in 1968, that the abandonment of religion had become apparent at all levels in the United States from the late 1950s.[44]

Latin America

Although few surveys have been conducted in Latin America, it is clear that the rate of religious practice there is low. There are some similarities with the situation in Europe, but in Latin America in general a far smaller percentage of the population attends mass and Easter communion. Thus in Chile, a parish is considered to be one of the better ones, if it attains 10 per cent attendance at mass, and even in practising areas the average is only one communion per year per parishioner.[45] Practice has probably never been high, but an increasing proportion declare themselves to be non-Catholics. In 1907, 2 per cent made that declaration; 5 per cent in 1920; 11 per cent in 1940; 12 per cent in 1952; and 14 per cent in 1965. Of course, some of these belong to Protestant organizations which have certainly grown in Chile. Among university students in the 1960s, as many as 18 per cent declared themselves not religious, with 67 per cent affirming themselves Catholics, 6 per cent as Protestants, and 9 per cent as having no opinion or following some other religion. Attendance at Easter communion varies geographically, with the central areas showing between 16 per cent and 25 per cent; the north between 4 per cent and 10 per cent, and the south about 10 per cent. In some parts of Santiago, however, the figure falls as low as 1 per cent.[46] The religious crisis has also affected religious callings. Whereas in 1750 there was estimated to be one priest for every 779 inhabitants, the ratio had fallen in 1845 to one for every 1,548, and in the early 1960s was one for every 2,783 Catholics, and one for every 3,127 inhabitants.[47]

In Brazil, remarkable religious diversity and the existence of vigorous movements does not conceal the fact that the Catholic church maintains only a low level of practice. Taigo Colin wrote of certain parishes in Rio de Janeiro:

One can guess the answer if it is realised that the majority of communions are taken by the very small number of the faithful, found everywhere, who take communion frequently. In these parishes, similarly, the number of those who do not take Easter Communion is many times the number of those who do their religious duty at Easter.[48]

For a particular parish Colin found that no more than 53 per cent participated in the principal rituals of Christian life; 31.2 per cent attended mass and Easter communion, but 68 per cent belonged to Catholic associations.

Elsewhere in Latin America the situation is often even less satisfactory to the Church. Thus in one diocese in Uruguay in 1961, over 31 per cent of the population has not been baptized.[49] In the cities of Peru and Venezuela, attendance at mass varied between 10 per cent and 30 per cent, although there is some evidence that attendance at mass has increased in Peru.[50] About 98 per cent of Venezuelans were baptized in the 1960s, but the practice rate was only 12.7 per cent in Caracas, and considerably lower in Llanos and the eastern regions of the country, but rising to 70 per cent in the Andean section of the country.[51] In Columbia, 95 per cent of the population professed to be Catholic, yet only one third of those baptized took their first communion, in the 1960s. Attendance at mass varied between 12 per cent and 15 per cent, although about 50 per cent of the population received last rites.[52] In Mexico, 94 per cent of the population were estimated as having been baptized into the Catholic Church in the 1960s, but religious marriage accounted for only 67 per cent of all marriages. Attendance at Sunday mass was very variable throughout the country, attaining almost universal participation in six dioceses, but being between 5 per cent and 25 per cent in twelve others, and between 30 per cent and 60 per cent in another sixteen.[53] Low rates of practice might not always reflect a deliberate decision not to participate. In parts of Latin America, opportunities for participation are sometimes limited, but it is also true that there has been a considerable growth in the number of Protestants since the Second World War—it is estimated that the increase was from 3,171,900 in 1948 to 7,710,000 in 1961.[54]

Clearly, in many parts of Latin America, the processes of industrialization that may be regarded as having influenced religious life in Europe have not been operative, or have been operative for a much less long period of time. There are also different cultural meanings attached to religious participation, and many people who do not participate in mass, none the less take part in religious processions, and may manifest a strong sense of the sacred, which may manifest itself in ways that are incomprehensible to the average European.

Europe

On the evidence available, religious practice in Austria has not, apparently, been at a very high level.[55] To mention one example: in the city of St. Pölten, with 30,709 inhabitants and a high industrial density, in 1957 the level of practice was 33.3 per cent.[56] In Austria generally the percentage of Easter communicants was 46.5 per cent; those attending mass constituted 34.5 per cent.[57] Other figures show little variation from those given in greater detail for France. The same may be said of Belgium, studied by Collard and others[58] in a survey which resulted in a detailed map of religious practice, but which unfortunately is no longer up to date.

The data on Germany are of special interest, given the high level of industrialization of that country. Our figures are from the detailed and precise work of F. Groner.[59]

In 1948, 60.7 per cent of obligated German Catholics attended mass: the percentage attendance in the total Catholic population was 47.3 per cent as opposed to 56.3 per cent in 1935. In the same year 66.9 per cent of those obligated took Easter communion: for the total population the figure is 52.7 per cent in 1948 and 56.3 per cent in 1935. The average annual communions per Catholic dropped from 14 per cent in 1936 to 12.7 per cent in 1948.

The number of Catholics who participated in spiritual exercises fell from 6 per cent in 1938 to 2.5 per cent in 1949. The number of mixed marriages rose from 11.3 per cent of marriages registered in 1919 to 29.5 per cent in 1948: 30 per cent of Catholics entered mixed marriages, and *of these*, 30–40 per cent did not marry in church. Groner observes that man no longer regarded religion as the most important issue when considering the establishment of a new family. More recent statistics on ecclesial religiosity in Germany indicate a marked decline in religious involvement.

Sunday religious practice in Western Germany, 1956–1963

| | Attended mass | | Population (1963) |
City	1956	1963	in thousands
Osnabrück	59.1	49.5	141
Münster	52.1	46.9	190
Regensburg	46.8	42.0	125
Hagen	45.2	33.6	199
Aachen	43.6	38.7	174
Bottrop	42.4	32.6	112
Recklinghausen	41.6	35.1	130
Freiburg	40.0	35.2	150
München-Gladbach	40.0	37.5	153
Essen	39.8	33.9	729
Bonn	39.6	35.1	144
Herne	38.6	29.0	111
Gelsenkirchen	38.4	34.3	381
Augsburg	38.1	35.9	211
Wanne-Eickel	37.8	29.6	108
Kassel	37.2	29.6	212
Remscheid	36.3	32.0	129
Oberhausen	35.4	29.7	260
Stuttgart	35.2	27.6	641
Mühlheim/Ruhr	35.0	28.5	190
Dortmund	34.9	28.7	651
Wuppertal	34.7	1.9	423
Düsseldorf	33.8	30.0	704
Krefeld	33.6	28.8	217
Ludwigshafen	33.2	26.6	172
Mainz	33.0	27.3	139
Bielefeld	33.0	33.6	173
Offenbach	32.4	30.4	118
Karlsruhe	32.2	26.4	250
Oldenburg	32.1	36.3	126
Bremen	31.9	27.6	578
Solingen	31.8	31.0	172
Duisburg	31.6	25.7	501
Hannover	31.3	32.7	571
Kiel	31.3	29.7	271
Brunswick	30.9	31.1	241
Cologne	30.7	28.5	832

City	Attended mass 1956	1963	Population (1963) in thousands
Mannheim	28.9	24.6	321
Saarbrücken	28.2	26.9	133
Darmstadt	27.1	26.4	140
Nuremberg	26.7	25.6	466
Frankfurt/Main	26.3	22.8	694
Hamburg	26.3	22.9	1,851
Lübeck	26.1	23.7	237
Bremerhaven	26.0	21.6	143
Munich	25.2	23.0	1,157
Wiesbaden	24.8	22.6	258

Source: *Angaben der Amtlichen Zentralstelle für kirchliche Statistik des Katholischen Deutschland; Statistisches Jahrbuch für die Bundesrepublik Deutschland*, 1964. Cf. Greinacher, *Die Kirche in der Städtischen Gesellschaft*, Matthias-Grünewald, Mainz, 1966.

In 1957, in Germany the level of Catholic practice was lower in the large cities than in the smaller ones, and was lower in the cities than in the country, as is shown by the following table:[60]

Sunday church attendance in West German cities (1957)
(percentages of Roman Catholic population)

Cities with more than 200,000 inhabitants

City	Attending mass	City	Attending mass
Essen	39.8%	Hannover	31.3%
Gelsenkirchen	38.4%	Kiel	31.3%
Augsburg	38.1%	Brunswick	30.9%
Oberhausen	35.4%	Cologne	30.7%
Stuttgart	35.2%	Mannheim	28.9%
Dortmund	34.9%	Nuremberg	26.7%
Wuppertal	34.7%	Frankfurt am Main	26.3%
Düsseldorf	33.8%	Hamburg	26.3%
Karlsruhe	32.2%	Lübeck	26.1%
Bremen	31.9%	Munich	25.2%
Duisburg	31.6%	Wiesbaden	24.8%

Sunday church attendance in West German cities (contd.)

Cities with between 100,000 and 200,000 inhabitants

City	Attending mass	City	Attending mass
Osnabrück	59.1%	Remscheid	36.3%
Münster	52.1%	Mülheim (Ruhr)	35.0%
Regensburg	46.8%	Krefeld	33.6%
Aachen	43.6%	Ludwigshafen	33.2%
Hagen	45.2%	Mainz	33.0%
Bottrop	42.4%	Bielefeld	33.0%
Recklinghausen	41.6%	Offenbach	32.4%
Freiburg	40.0%	Oldenburg	32.1%
München/Gladbach	40.0%	Solingen	31.8%
Bonn	39.6%	Saarbrücken	28.2%
Herne	38.6%	Darmstadt	27.7%
Wanne-Eikel	37.8%	Fürth	23.7%
Kassel	37.2%	Bremerhaven	26.0%

Average:

Cities between 100,000 and 200,000 inhabitants	39.0%
Cities over 200,000 inhabitants	31.6%
West Germany as a whole	48.4%
All cities of more than 100,000 inhabitants	33.7%
All of Germany except for large cities	52.4%

The development of religious practice between 1946 and 1960 is shown in the table on p. 61.

Thus, after a postwar revival practice declined slowly but regularly.[61] But Greinacher's synthetic picture of the development of the situation between 1915 and 1960, a period of 45 years, documents a very minor decrease in participation in Easter communion; especially between 1948 and 1960 there are no significant changes.

But decline has persisted during the sixties, and is more pronounced in East Germany. One index of the religious crisis in East Germany is the decline in the number of baptisms and confirmations. For example, in Leipzig in 1949 there were 5,700 baptisms, while in 1960 there were only 1,400. In 1949 there were 6,200 con-

| | Percentage of total number of Catholics | | | | Average number of communions per Catholic | |
	Taking Easter Communion		Attending Mass			
Year	Germany	Federal Republic	Germany	Federal Republic	Germany	Federal Republic
1946	48.8	—	45.1	—	12.0	—
1947	51.0	—	46.4	—	12.1	—
1948	52.7	—	47.3	—	12.7	—
1949	53.8	56.3	48.7	51.1	12.8	13.4
1950	54.2	56.2	48.7	50.7	12.9	13.4
1951	54.2	56.0	48.3	50.1	12.9	13.3
1952	54.1	55.9	48.2	49.9	12.7	13.1
1953	53.9	55.5	48.1	49.7	12.5	12.8
1954	53.7	55.2	47.9	49.4	12.4	12.7
1955	53.1	54.4	47.2	48.6	12.0	12.3
1956	52.7	53.9	46.6	47.9	12.0	12.2
1957	52.5	53.7	46.4	47.6	12.1	12.3
1958	52.2	53.4	45.9	47.1	12.3	12.4
1959	52.0	53.1	45.6	46.8	12.4	12.5
1960	51.3	52.4	45.2	46.3	12.5	12.6

firmations; and between 1954 and 1958 this number decreased to about 3,500; in 1959 to 840. The same thing happens with respect to church membership. In Böhm there were 7,000 registered parish members, while in 1965 there were only 3,500. But we must not forget the influence exercised on these developments by 'social control', and by escapes to the West. [62]

Statistics for 1958 concerning Protestant churches and sects show, among other things, a high percentage of unbaptized live births for the Communist Republic: in German Pomerania, 12.3 per cent; in German Silesia, 9.5 per cent; and in Anhalt, 9.8 per cent; while the highest percentage in the Federal Republic was in Bavaria with 8.7 per cent. The percentage of men taking communion varied from 28 per cent in Saxony to 41 per cent in Schaumburg-Lippe. These percentages have since declined further. [63]

We now come to Great Britain, which differs from the rest of Europe in having virtually no peasants. Our knowledge of religious practice and mentality in Great Britain is limited, and often based on local surveys, journalistic inquiries, and sample surveys. Ward summarizes the state of religious practice during the fifties on the basis of various surveys (see page 63). [64]

The general pattern in England is one of decline. Easter day communicants in the Church of England fell from just under 10 per cent of the population aged fifteen or more in the period just before the First World War to 6.5 per cent in 1960, and 5.6 per cent in 1968. Although between 10 and 12 per cent of the population of England and Wales attended church on an ordinary Sunday in the late 1960s, this figure was so high only because of the high attendance of Roman Catholics, who were, of course, under obligation to attend. Even Roman Catholic attendance has fallen however, by about 6 per cent between 1966 and 1969. [65] The evidence available about belief indicates the same general trend. Whereas a Gallup poll reported that in the 1950s about 78 per cent of the English believed in God, in a survey published in 1974 only 64 per cent confessed to this belief. In the late 1960s, a survey indicated that 54 per cent of people questioned believed in heaven, but in 1974 only 39 per cent believed that there was life after death, while 35 per cent positively disbelieved. [66]

Membership in the Church of England is not easy to assess, but the indications are of steady decline throughout the twentieth century, when the experience of the Baptists, Congregationalists, and Methodists in England and Wales was very much the same — the Congregationalists falling from 440,000 in 1935 to fewer than 200,000 when they joined the Presbyterians to form the United Reformed Church in the early 1970s. Whereas in 1899, nearly 68 per cent of weddings took place in Anglican churches and only 15 per cent in civil registry offices, by 1973 the Anglican share of weddings had fallen to 36.5 per cent, and that of civil marriages accounted for 46.6 per cent of the total. Baptisms also diminished, and only burials continued as frequently under religious auspices as in the past. [67] Consistent with these developments, there has also been a diminution in England and Wales, as elsewhere, in the number of men offering themselves for religious vocations, in the Anglican, Catholic, and Nonconformist churches. The annual intake of clergy in the Church of England fell by 50 per cent from the early 1960s to the mid-1970s. [68]

Sunday service — the results of some surveys

Survey	Percentage of adults who claim to attend church:	
	one or more times a week	never
News Chronicle — national survey	14	—
News Review — national survey	14.4	4.9
Institute of Public Opinion — national survey	15	—
questionnaire survey by Gorer	15	39.5
interview survey in Derby	13	27
interview survey in a zone of London	11	61
survey of young housewives		
London	14	69
Leeds	18	56
Birmingham	13	64
York census	13	—
High Wycombe census	10.5	—

There are marked differences among the various denominations.

Survey	practice in %		
	Church of England	Free Churches	Catholic Church
News Chronicle	9	20	44
News Review	7.9	14.2	52
Derby	7	23	51
Youth and Religion survey of urban youth between 15 and 24 years of age			73

The figures for those who never attend church are no less significant.

Survey	Church of England	Free Churches	Catholic Church
News Review	52.2	41.4	23.5
Derby	28	19	14

The situation in the Netherlands seemed to be better a few years ago.[69] In Friesland, the region with the lowest practice rate, the percentage of Catholics who did not take Easter communion was 23.5 per cent, but for the entire region the number of those who did not belong to any church was 22.4 per cent. In the capital, Groningen,[70] those who did not profess a religion were 43 per cent (1947): this figure was surpassed only in Amsterdam[71] and then only slightly. The general situation is reflected by figures which show that those without any religion has risen from 0.31 per cent in 1897 to 17.04 per cent in 1947 and to 18.4 per cent in 1960.[72] Apparently the great majority of the non-religious are of Protestant origin. The situation in the Netherlands shows a continuing change between 1948 and 1970.

There is no lack of figures showing a further decrease in religious practice in the last two decades. Steeman provides figures for Catholics in several Dutch cities:[73]

Year	Amsterdam	Rotterdam	Utrecht	Maastricht	Tilburg
1948	52.9				
1950			67.1		
1951		47.8			
1956				56.8	
1958					72.4
1966	39.4	34.2	48.8	49.9	63.0

The table opposite showing the decrease in the number of communicants is also Steemann's.

For the whole of the Netherlands, Catholic religious practice as measured by mass attendance is 63.6 per cent, excluding those who attend mass in institutional settings. These data are from surveys of 16

The number of Catholic communions distributed in parish churches and auxiliary churches according to church statistics 1955–65

	TOTAL	per R.C. of 7 years and over
1955	120,947,000	33.0
1956	121,588,000	33.2
1957	124,043,000	33.5
1958	125,856,000	33.2
1959	123,657,000	32.1
1960	121,975,000	31.5
1961	121,676,000	30.6
1962	112,659,000	27.9
1963	108,194,000	26.2
1964	106,433,000	25.4
1965	122,680,000	28.6

and 23 January 1966. Steemann's comparisons with former surveys show that there has been a decrease in mass attendance, usually the greater the longer the time interval between the two points of comparison.

There is no reason to believe that the increase in the number of non-religious is a phenomenon which is characteristic only of England, the Netherlands, and Protestant countries in general. The Austrian census of 1951 showed that there were 264,014 non-religious individuals, a figure equal to 4 per cent of the entire population; but perhaps many of these are 'denominationless' Protestants. (If children and those otherwise incapable of understanding are excluded, the percentage is of course higher.) In 1947, when the communist regime had already been established, Czechoslovakia had 820,000 non-religious persons out of a total of 12,604,000 inhabitants (6.5 per cent). This situation persisted certainly up to 1967.[74] The number of priests has decreased in Czechoslovakia primarily for political reasons. Before the war the number of seminarians varied between 900 and 1,000. During the summer semester of 1967 there were 169 seminary students, 83 at Litomerice in Bohemia, and 86 at Bratislava in Slovakia. It is enough to consider the difference in church membership between 1930 and 1967 (see p. 67).[75]

Sunday mass attendance in several cities of the Netherlands, in comparison with the results of earlier counts (percentage of Roman Catholic under obligation)

	Earlier count			1966	
	year	% mass attendance	No. of parish-ioners	Abs.	%
Large cities					
Amsterdam	1948	52.9	210,969	82,981	39.3
Rotterdam	1951	47.8	169,724	57,571	33.9
Utrecht	1950	67.1	87,317	43,480	49.8
Arnhem	1956	52.0	47,331	21,596	45.6
Medium cities north of the Moerdijk					
Schiedam	1956	47.6	24,228	11,401	47.1
Delft	1958	64.9	26,110	14,732	56.4
Vlaardingen	1962	52.2	10,569	5,210	49.3
Amersfoort	1963	56.7	18,089	9,854	54.5
Hengelo	1961	79.1	24,245	18,225	75.2
Deventer	1961	69.2	13,173	9,606	72.9
Alkmaar	1864	70.2	18,000	13,686	76.0
Zaandam	1962	54.4	10,222	5,425	53.1
Beverwijk	1962	64.3	17,541	11,281	64.3
Cities south of the Moerdijk					
Tilburg	1958	72.4	113,902	71,845	63.1
Maastricht	1956	56.8	77,447	38,605	49.9
Small cities north of the Moerdijk and in the province of Zeeland					
Alphen a/d Rijn	1962	66.9	6,209	4,315	69.5
Vlissingen	1963	43.2	5,267	2,062	39.1
Middelburg	1963	54.8	2,667	1,241	46.5
Goes	1963	69.3	3,232	1,933	59.8
Kampen	1961	67.4	2,973	1,928	64.9
Zierikzee	1963	67.1	820	532	64.9

Church membership in Czechoslovakia

	1930 %	1967 %
Roman Catholics	73.5	50.5
Czechoslovak Church	5.3	4.4
Protestants	7.7	7.4
Orthodox	1.0	0.6
Greek Catholics	4.0	—
Other denominations	—	1.1
No denomination	5.8	36.0

In Yugoslavia, the 1953 census showed 2,127,875 non-religious individuals (as against 100,000 before the war), which represents 12.1 per cent. More exactly, the 1953 census showed that in Yugoslavia 12.1 per cent of the population declared themselves to have no religion. Again, these are mainly persons who are involved in the communist political apparatus. To be exact, the 1953 census shows the following proportion of those declaring themselves to have no religion: Serbs — 15.8 per cent; Croats — 10.1 per cent; Macedonians — 15.8 per cent; Montenegrans — 39.5 per cent; Slovenes — 10.3 per cent; others — 4 per cent; the country as a whole — 12.6 per cent.

It appears that the percentage of atheists was higher, the lower the socio-cultural level of the various ethnic groups, and this fact merits further inquiry.

Among men the percentage of atheists was 16 per cent, and among women 9.4 per cent. The differences between men and women and the absolute percentages of atheists (or at least those without religion) were much higher in Montenegro, where the culture was, and in part still is, less developed, and thus where the clash between industrialization and political development, on the one hand, and pre-existent cultural structure on the other, has been greater. We already know rather well that the idea that 'religion is woman's business' is widespread in a certain type of Mediterranean culture (and not only there) of which Montenegro is an example. An attitude of this type is a vehicle for the spread of atheism.[76]

We have later reports from Catholic sources which more or less confirm the official trends revealed by Yugoslav reports. For Ljubljana in particular,

> Statistics for the year 1965 show that about 26 per cent of Catholics regularly attended mass. Out of 100 Catholics who attended mass 23.3 per cent were men, 61.1 per cent women, and 15.6 per cent children. We must not forget that these include inhabitants of peripheral areas which we have been unable to distinguish statistically from the others. The statistics also show that in Ljubljana one Catholic in six goes to communion. This would not be bad were it not for the fact that many of those who go to communion come from the countryside. The situation is worse so far as attendance at catechism instruction is concerned. According to the statistics, during the scholastic year 1965–66, only 3,938 school-age children attended instruction; this corresponds to 25 per cent of the Catholic boys and girls who live in the parish of Ljubljana.

In Croatia apparently 90 per cent of the population are willing to have the priest enter and bless their houses. [77]

In Bulgaria, only 26.65 per cent of the urban population, and 41.56 per cent of the rural population were found to be 'religious' in the mid-1960s — that is, about one third of the total sample of 40,000 interviewed individuals. [78]

The situation in Poland also appears to have been one of a decline in religious commitment, at the levels of both ideology and practice, occurring so rapidly that it was measurable in the differences in the findings of two surveys conducted at an interval of only three years, in 1958 and 1961. The table opposite gives information about attitudes towards religion in those two surveys. [79]

During the same period the number of those who thought that it was worth while to risk one's life in the defence of religion decreased from 50 per cent to 32.3 per cent. The process of desacralization, however, eventuates in an equally rapid decline in interest in the political ideals of Polish society.

Attitudes towards religion (in percentages)

Which of the following best represents your attitude to religion?	1958	1961	difference
sincere believer who practises regularly	7.4	4.9	−2.5
believer who practises regularly	25.3	13.7	−11.6
believer who practises irregularly	34.6	34.2	−0.4
believer who does not practise	6.3	12.3	+6.0
agnostic	7.4	8.1	+0.7
non-believer who practises	4.1	4.9	+0.8
non-believer who does not practise	10.4	14.9	+4.5
declared opponent of religion	1.9	3.2	+1.3

A survey of a sample of 733 young people, almost all of whom were between eighteen and thirty years of age shows:

agnostics	7.4%
have no interest in religion or no definite opinions	2.3%
non-believers but practises for the sake of others	5.6%
non-believers who do not practise	12.3%
declared opponents of religion	3.1%
TOTAL	23.3%

Considering the fact that the social milieu certainly exercises some influence on the answers, the percentage of atheists may be overstated.[80] In another poll of Polish youth, Maître discovered that his respondents classified themselves as Catholics — 78.3 per cent; Atheists — 4.3 per cent; have no interest in the question — 5.3 per cent; no opinion — 11.9 per cent; others — 0.2 per cent.[81] Between 70 per cent and 80 per cent of Polish Catholics are assessed as practising Catholics, and the number of Polish clergy has increased considerably in the postwar period.[82] This assessment of the overall strength of religious practice in Poland is confirmed by other surveys.[83]

The situation in Hungary appears to be not very different from that in Poland. [84] A survey conducted among students of the 'senior-classes' (seventeen-year-olds) in Hungarian schools in 1967 [85] has yielded the following results:

Distribution of the sample of Hungarian youth according to religious thinking

Classification	%
religious	14.0
categorically atheist	42.5
inconsequentially atheist	14.5
undecided	26.5
traditionally religious	2.5

Distribution of the sample of Hungarian youth according to religious behaviour

Classification	%
practising	60.2
non-practising	39.8

The abandonment of religious practice in Rumania is fairly advanced. Briefly, we may report an extract from *Glas Koncila* for 28 March 1967:

> Orthodox believers go to church in great numbers only for the major religious occasions. On Sundays and other holidays the church is attended by a large number of old women who write little prayers on pieces of paper which, according to local custom, are found on church pews. The Catholic believers are truly made of gold—in a country where, since the war, the chalices have been made of wood. In Bucharest there are seven Catholic churches, all of them full—especially on Sunday.

Obviously, in East European countries political factors have affected both religious practice and the extent of atheism. But what of countries which, at least nominally, are solidly Catholic—such as Spain and Portugal? [86]

Although the data are incomplete, they are sufficient to show the symptoms of advanced deterioration of ecclesial religion. It is enough to refer to the results of surveys done in the areas of Lisbon, Bilbao, Madrid, and Santander even though they are somewhat out of date.[87]

In 1956, in the archdiocese of Lisbon, central Lisbon showed a practice rate of 17.9 per cent of those under obligation to attend, and in the rest of the area studied, a rate of 16.7 per cent. Elsewhere, apart from the coastal region, which showed a fairly high rate (between 46 per cent and 34 per cent), the situation was, if variable, not one giving much encouragement to the Church. Along the Tagus, the rate of practice had fallen to 10 per cent; in a number of parishes the rate among men varied from as little as 2 per cent to 5 per cent. Here, too, as is usually the case in the areas of low religious practice in Catholic countries, larger percentages practised in the cities than in the countryside.[88] Similar findings for the same period, cited by Querido, give for Lisbon a total practice of 17.2 per cent (9.4 per cent of men and 20.3 per cent of women, with 30.8 per cent of children between seven and fourteen years). Among the rural population of the diocese, practice reached 38 per cent in the extreme north, and fell to figures as low as 1.2 per cent of men and 5.8 per cent of women in some areas of the south. In the diocese of Faro, the practice rate is 15 per cent in the city and 8 per cent in the countryside. With respect to the sacraments the situation is no better: there are dioceses in the north of Portugal where 97 per cent of weddings take place in church and areas of the south where the percentage of Catholic weddings is less than 50 per cent. (In Odemira, for example, 80 per cent of the families do not belong to the church.) Querido, in synthesizing the data, indicates that the cause of this situation is to be found, not in technological-scientific progress, but in the political situation and in poverty which acts as a vehicle for irreligious ideas formed elsewhere. In Beja, in the south of Portugal, Sunday practice is 2.7 per cent. Twenty-five per cent of the population state that they have no religion, while in some areas 85 per cent of births are illegitimate. This last figure seems to indicate that the situation is connected with factors of a moral rather than of a technical-industrial character. At the beginning of the 1960s religious practice had begun to decline even in the northern, most religious areas of Portugal.

There had also been a marked reduction of practice in the Spanish diocese of Bilbao. Over ten years ago, throughout the diocese an average of 284,634 persons attended mass, 55.8 per cent of those under obligation. Industrial parishes showed an overall percentage of 43.82 per cent; in areas of high industrial concentration this percentage dropped to between 35.07 per cent and 20.18 per cent. Practice rate was lowest in mining areas. In predominantly agricultural areas practice was 60.65 per cent, with maxima of 84.09 per cent and 79.75 per cent over the total population. In Madrid, in the 'Barriada' Pacifico, the percentage of those taking Easter communion was 53.65 per cent, in the early 1960s. [89]

R. Duocastella summarizes the Spanish situation in the data reported in the table below, which were tabulated on the basis of most of the surveys which had been conducted. His analysis concludes by underlining a certain lowering of the level of religious practice (and of religiosity as shown by other indices such as religious vocations, etc.), which began in the fifties after an overall improvement during the preceding decades. [90]

Sunday mass attendance and participation in Easter Communion *
Diocese

(1) *Cantabric region*						
Oviedo		1951	1	1640 (14 years +)	83.7	97.2
mining area		1963	17	112,178	22.8 (b)	
Santander**	3/4 rural	1959	574 (100%)	304,923 (100%)	48 39.8–60.1 (a)	—
(2) *Basque provinces and Navarra*						
Bilbao	2/5 rural	1952	94 (100%)	354,784 (100%)	55.8 55.6–69.3 (a)	62.7
San Sebastian	1/2 rural	1946	87 (100%)	395,000 (100%)	79 76.5–83.5 (a)	
Vitoria	1/3 rural	1962	397 (100%)	135,000 (100%)	85.2 84.2–86.3 (a)	91.5
Navarra	3/4 rural	1960	605 (100%)	409,000 (100%)	90	97.5
(3) *Catalonia*						
Solsona		1962	1	2,465	49.4	
Lerida (semi-rural)		1951	3	7,170	25	
Barcelona (rural area)		1952	5	3,438	32.6	47.5

(4) *Castile and León*

León	1951	11	5%	66–83 (a)	88.0
Valencia	1951	4	3%	78–85 (a)	90.0
Burgos	1951	21	5%	69–78 (a)	90.0
Zamora	1951	4	4%	78–88 (a)	99.0
Avila	1951	8	5.25%	53–57 (a)	82.0
Valladolid	1951	5	2.4%	49–58 (a)	81.0
Salamanca	1951	8	3%	51–67 (a)	94.0
Soria	1951	8	5%	62–79 (a)	97.0
	1961	136 (65%)		58–76 (a)	65.0
Logrono 3/4 rural	1951	11	13%	34–56 (a)	65.0
2/5 urban	1958	(100%)	229,874	61.3	—
Ciudad Rodrigo (rural)	1951	100%	70,966 (100%)	49.1 42–45 (a)	

(5) *Central region*

Madrid (rural area)	1945	100%	304,000	30.6	37
Toledo (rural)	1951	1	3,500	6 (c)	
Cuenca (rural)	1963	100%		La Alcarria 30 La Sierra 40	27 40
Albacete	1958	1	210,034	18	16.6

(6) *Eastern region*

Valencia (rural)	1959	100%	244,802 (100%)	34.5	29.8
Majorca	1957	108	342,417	68.2	81.7

(7) *Southern region*

Badajoz (semi-rural)	1950	1	1,783	15.1	43.8
Seville (semi-rural)	1961	1	41,126	12.1 12.0–88 (a)	6.6

*The figures in the table concern only the rural population.

**S. Odriozola, 'La Asistencia a la misa en la diocesis de Santander', *Boletín Oficial Obispado*, 1950
(a) Percentage of men and of women
(b) Among those under obligation
(c) Among those over 15 years of age.

These few figures seem to confirm the conclusions of Noirmont and others,[91] who consider that the Spanish working classes, and particularly the miners, are becoming dechristianized. Duocastella's research on priestly vocations and the number of priests reveals that in 1769, out of a total population of 9,308,804, there were 65,825 priests: one priest for every 142 inhabitants. In 1957, after an almost uninterrupted decline in their numbers, there were only 23,372 priests in a population of 29,546,384: one priest for every 1,264 inhabitants.[92]

The most recent assessments of religious practice in Spain show a picture that is relatively little altered. In 1967 it was estimated that 33.3 per cent of those under obligation in Vitoria, actually practised; in Nalon (Asturias) 18.8 per cent; in Granada, 36.0 per cent, in Ciudad Real, 27.8 per cent. In 1968, 47 per cent were found to be practising in Mieres (Asturias); 54.1 per cent in Salamanca. In Menorca in 1972, the practice rate was 54.08 per cent.[93]

Scotland has always shown rather different religious dispositions from those prevalent in England, and up to the late 1950s, 70 per cent of Roman Catholics in Scotland were still practising. The proportion of Catholics to members of other churches has steadily increased in Scotland for several decades. Thus, in 1878, only one-twelfth of the population was Catholic: by 1954, the proportion had risen to one-seventh. High Catholic practice was accompanied in that country by relatively high figures for the Protestant majority, and in the late 1940s and until 1956, the communicants among members of the Church of Scotland constituted also about 70 per cent.[94] Up-to-date figures for this country are not available.

For a long time Ireland displayed immense stability with respect to religious commitment, compared to decline in most other countries.[95] Very high practice rates persisted among the more than 90 per cent of the population who were Catholics. Studies have been few, perhaps because the uniformly high rate of practice presents no problems for the Church, and consequently prompts no particular sociological inquiry. Until the early 1960s, there was no marked change in the number of vocations, but from 1961 onwards there was evidence of change, and from the mid-1960s a discernible decline became apparent in the vocations for the secular priesthood, the religious orders, and even in the sisterhoods.[96]

Switzerland has also enjoyed a comparatively high rate of religious practice in the past, but since the late 1950s the limited amount of information available has presented some evidence of decline. As elsewhere, the rate of practice among Protestants in Switzerland is lower than that among Catholics, due no doubt to the lower significance that Protestants attach to Sunday worship.[97] Thus, in the canton of Freiburg Catholic practice varied between 84.2 per cent and 98.5 per cent: for Easter communion the average was about 95 per cent. The practice rate among Protestants was 33 per cent. But even in Switzerland remarkably low figures can be found. In Geneva practice among Protestants over fifteen years of age varied in the early 1960s between 6 per cent and 7 per cent, with minimum and maximum points of 3.69 per cent and 23.56 per cent according to the parish. [98]

Naturally, we cannot overlook the Soviet Union where, after forty years of struggle against religion, the practice rate was 25 per cent, as against 60 per cent in the period preceding the revolution. These figures were supplied by the Metropolitan of Moscow, but it is difficult to assess their reliability. A bare percentage does not say much about the 'basic' religiosity of the Soviet Union. Recent information supplied to us on a personal basis by Italian students returning from Russia (1969) suggests a basically stable situation.

When they gained power, the Bolsheviks worked to spread radical atheism: the anti-religious struggle was accompanied by mass conversions to atheism. Although there was certainly 'pressure' from above, the fact that previously the Orthodox church and its ministers had often been under considerable attack from the popular masses indicates that Marxism found the people already well-disposed towards its anti-religious propaganda. The fact that, with popular support, in many villages the churches were closed and converted into clubs, schools, etc., indicates that at least some strata of the Russian population were already predisposed to religious indifference, where they were not actively hostile.

The rapid expansion of the Society for the Promotion of Atheism is particularly significant. The association was created in 1925, and by 1929 it already had 9,000 cells with about 500,000 members. In the meantime the union had become the 'Union of Militant Atheists', but without any significant changes in its goals and policies. Membership increased rapidly in a few years, and the number of cells increased from 9,000 to 70,000. In 1932 there were $5\frac{1}{2}$ million members over the age of fourteen, (70 per cent of them men, the remaining 30 per cent of them women). Young people between the ages of fourteen and twenty-two comprised 45 per cent of the membership; another 45 per cent were between twenty-three and forty-five, and only 10 per cent were over forty-five. A children's branch had 2 million members under fourteen years of age.

But apart from this 'active' profession of atheism, which was influenced by various factors and which thus does not present a true picture of the state of basic irreligiosity, what was the situation of religious practice as revealed by the usual indices?

In 1935, Hecker asserted that at least half of the population had already, *de facto* or *de jure*, abandoned more or less completely any relationship with the churches. The situation of religion was thus not catastrophic, and not in fact much worse than in various countries where there had been no anti-religious campaign.

If we remember that in 1935 the Soviet government still refused to print or import religious books, that seminaries and other institutes for the formation of priests had been suppressed; that the churches were forbidden to engage in charity work or to organize leisure time activities for the believers; that the children of priests were barred from institutes of higher education; that the priests and the religiously active in general were often deported without apparent reason; and that even religious practice was viewed with suspicion — then a practice rate of 50 per cent must be considered truly remarkable. One should also remember that the changes in religious legislation which were introduced in 1929 still made public religious propaganda a crime (except for sermons, which are well known to have little effect).

However, from the beginning of Soviet communism, unlike their counterparts in the West, those Russians who abandoned religion did so in a rather radical way. This is shown by the figures concerning weddings, funerals, and baptisms. According to the Webbs' data, in 1927 and 1928 the percentages for the city of Moscow were as follows:

	Without rites		With rites		Unstated	
	1927	1928	1927	1928	1927	1928
births	33	38.1	59.7	57.8	7.3	4.1
funerals	30.1	30.3	66.8	65.7	3.2	1
weddings	81.6	86.3	15.6	11.8	2.8	1.9

It is difficult to say how accurate these figures are but even if the percentage of error were 50 per cent, our argument would not be changed. For many men in the Soviet Union, religion was already dead at the beginning of the 1930s. It is sufficient just to look at the figures for non-religious funerals, which, from the considerations presented at the beginning of this chapter, we know to be the most significant.

Even the most recent data are quite inconsistent. In 1957, the ecclesiastical hierarchy estimated that 50 per cent of the Russian population was Christian. In 1960, Davis estimated that three or four million people attended church on Sundays. But others, basing their estimates on the number of candles sold, hold that this figure varies between 20 and 30 million persons a year. This estimate was repeated in 1959 with the same results (20–30 million candles sold), for a total of about 50 million persons. When the Patriarch of Moscow entered the World Council of Churches he claimed to represent 140 million people, although the Council estimated the number of members of the Russian church at 30 million. In *The New York Times* of 6 July 1962, Martin Niemöller maintained that 130 million Russians 'belong to the Orthodox Church'. Clearly, then, there are wide divergences in the estimated numbers of Christians in Russia.

Because of prevailing pressures against religious practice, the number of individuals who preserve a sense of the sacred must be larger than the number of practitioners. However, in spite of the poor reliability of many figures and although there is a tendency for real religiosity to be hidden (rather than of a pretence to a religiosity that does not exist), a vast process of religious impoverishment is at work in 'Holy Russia', and this impoverishment is great both in extent and depth.[99]

In the Scandinavian countries, too, the level of desacralization is very high, as is shown by various surveys,[100] some of which were carried out in the sixties. At the end of the nineteenth century on an ordinary Sunday, 17 per cent of Swedes attended services in the 'state church': this percentage decreased to 5.7 per cent in 1927 and to 3 per cent in 1960. Today, 2 per cent of the population attend the Lutheran church *every* Sunday, and to these must be added another 2 per cent who attend the 'free' churches. Another 23 per cent go to church at least once a month, and another 25 per cent go occasionally. Twenty-three per cent of the population declare themselves to be non-Christians but allow their children to practise; 19 per cent are indifferent, and 6 per cent atheists.

However, according to Gustafsson, since the beginning of the century the percentage of those who belong to sects has risen from 4 per cent to 5.3 per cent of the population over eighteen years of age. In fact, Gustafsson emphasizes at the beginning of his study that only 1 per cent of the Swedish population is 'aus der Kirche ausgetreten' — that is to say has deliberately renounced church affiliation. As against this 1 per cent outside the church in Sweden, stands 3.8 per cent in Norway — but there too the average rate of practice was low, at 2.7 per cent. In both countries the percentage of non-religious funerals is insignificant.

As usual, however, the figures we have available are not always consistent among themselves. In a survey of young people in Sweden by Karin Busch in 1969, the question 'Do you believe in the existence of a God who affects your own life?' was asked. This is a rather restricted question compared with the usual 'Do you believe in God?', 17 per cent answered yes, 30 per cent said it was possible, and 53 per cent answered negatively. In 1954, with respect to the same question the figures had been 49 per cent, 31 per cent, and 10 per cent respectively. This is a marked increase in indifference in the space of only fifteen years.[101] The bulletin of the Stockholm Institute of Sociology of Religion has published data about religious practice in Stockholm, a city with a population of 803,600 inhabitants in 1963. 20,757 citizens were practising, that is about 2.6 per cent of the population. Taking into account a number of factors which we shall not discuss here, one might arrive at a figure of about 5 per cent of *nominally* committed Christians.

B. Gustafsson furnishes similar data for Sweden as a whole: average Sunday church attendance — 5.3 per cent; baptisms — 87 per cent; confirmations — 88 per cent; religious weddings — 92 per cent; religious funerals — 96 per cent. Although more than 90 per cent of the Swedes declared themselves members of the Lutheran Evangelical Church, the percentage of those who believe in God is low especially among young people.

Since the Scandinavian countries are Protestant, one must also take into account those who listen to religious services on radio or television or who participate in religion at other levels. In Norway, where actual practice in 1956 was 2.7 per cent, when these other possibilities are taken into account 76 per cent of the population was found to be involved.[102]

In Denmark systematic church attendance is very low: 1.7 per cent in 1964 in the capital. Practice has decreased everywhere: in the diocese of Aalborg, where practice was, by Danish standards, rather high, it fell from 10.5 per cent to 4.7 per cent between 1927 and 1967.

Research done in 1966 by Kuhl and others shows, however, that only 31.4 per cent *never* go to church. 30.5 per cent go on major religious holidays; 20.5 per cent go 'sometimes'; 5.3 per cent go at least twice a month; and 2.8 per cent one or more times a week. Furthermore between 16 per cent and 44 per cent of the sample listened to religious broadcasts, with percentages varying, as usual, according to whether the area was rural or urban.[103]

In Finland, 91 per cent of women and 64 per cent of men were found to believe in God or in some superior being. Although church attendance is low, there are other very widespread forms of involvement in religious activities, which sometimes include 50 per cent of the population.[104]

Italy

Until now there have been very few depth studies of religious practice in Italy, and we know much less of the Italian situation than of that in France, Belgium, the Netherlands, and even Germany. But for a general orientation we may refer to the Doxa survey of 26 February 1962 which appeared in number 3–4, 1962 of that polling firm's newsletter. The survey concludes by observing that 53 per cent of adult Italians 'go to church'.

In particular, of 100 interviews:

	TOTAL	men	women
had been to church on the previous Sunday	53	45	61
had not been to church on the previous Sunday	47	55	39

Furthermore, from 100 interviewed from the indicated social classes:

	Upper and upper-middle	Middle and lower-middle	Lower
have been to church on the previous Sunday	52	53	54
have not been to church on the previous Sunday	48	47	46

By sex we have the following data:

men

have been to church on the previous Sunday	45	45	43
have not been to church on the previous Sunday	55	55	57

women

have been to church on the previous Sunday	62	59	62
have not been to church on the previous Sunday	38	41	38

From 100 interviewed from communities having a population of:

	less than 10,000	10,000– 50,000	over 50,000
have been to church on the previous Sunday	60	53	43
have not been to church on the previous Sunday	40	47	57

Burglassi[105] has recently provided an exhaustive synthesis of the Italian situation. The first large-scale field survey was conducted by Aldo Leoni in the region of Mantua,[106] and covered 370,869 persons. This showed an average rate of practice of 37 per cent of those under obligation to attend mass (rural parishes). The practice rate varied from an average of 47 per cent in the upper region to an average of 26 per cent in the lower region. The percentage of Easter communicants varied between an average of 69 per cent in the upper region and 51 per cent in the lower region. Against this, in 1880–2, when the first usable data were collected, practice varied between 82.3 per cent in the upper and 77.6 per cent in the lower region. During the same period, participation in the mass in the city of Mantua has fallen from 61 per cent to 35 per cent.

In addition we might mention the surveys we have ourselves conducted in the region of Alexandria (where there are 110,532 people under obligation), which showed (1957) a 48.3 per cent participation in Easter communion;[107] and in the area of Rovigo (201,317 under obligation) which showed (1958) 73.9 per cent taking Easter communion.[108] Partial surveys we have conducted in the region of Padua showed a practice rate varying between 98.8 per cent and 50 per cent, while research carried out under our supervision shows a practice rate for the entire diocese (704,608 obligees) of 78.8 per cent.[109] In the diocese of Vieste and Manfredonia in 1957 the practice rate varied between 78.5 per cent and 30 per cent;[110] and in 1966 for the Gargano peninsula as a whole there was a mass attendance rate of 35.51 per cent. Although rather old, the results of a survey in the diocese of Volterra are very interesting. These show a mass attendance rate of 20.77 per cent in the city (10,314 obligees) and of 21.58 per cent in the diocese as a whole (109,604 obligees).[111]

Other local surveys have been conducted in Turin, Rome, Milan, Gallarate, Siena, Poggetti, Cesta, San Donato, and parts of Genoa, Treviso, Ascoli Piceno, etc.[112] The results of all these surveys point to the conclusion that religiosity in Italy follows the same trends as in other Catholic countries:[113] religious practice decreases over time,[114] decreases with the rise of population in the cities, and is lower among workers than among other social classes.

The collapse of popular religiosity, which accelerates the decline of the sacred in general, merits special attention.[115] One might ask what influence the decline of popular religiosity has had on the parallel decline of, so to speak, official religiosity. There is a vast area to be studied here, but it is certain that, in spite of certain aberrant forms of popular religiosity, the two forms of religion used to support one another, and in a number of cases they affected two different areas of the personality, and to different extents, and from different perspectives, they co-operated in maintaining the sense of the sacred, sometimes even cultivating and deepening it. But even though an analysis of popular religiosity might provide insights into the decay of the spontaneous substratum of the religious spirit, it may not take us very far.

The external manifestations of the religiosity of rural populations—processions, traditional rituals, superstitious practices, prayers, and legends—reflect the most genuine and least contaminated expression of the popular spirit. In them can be found the religious substratum onto which, in the West for example, Christianity was engrafted. The more one studies popular religious experience, however, the more it appears as an intimate and individual phenomenon which only superficially forms a part of the framework of shared habits. In every individual the mosaic of magical and superstitious practices, of lofty religious expressions, and of habit is differently put together, with a different scale of 'values', and with different elements having priority, according to differences in personality.

Of no less importance, especially within orthodox Catholicism, is the collapse of the so-called 'devotions', since these in turn represent the decay of the sense of the sacred.[116] Almost all of the 'devotions' of Catholicism are in a state of crisis. The typical figures of the saints are being abandoned by many of the faithful, and even the 'devotions' most closely connected with Christ, such as that of the Sacred Heart, Our Lady of Fatima, etc. are declining. In the construction and furnishing of new churches, a decreasing importance is given to 'devotions', perhaps in response to a change in the requirements of the faithful.

But is this crisis really an expression of the fundamental religious crisis? This is a difficult question: the reduction of the number and intensity of 'devotions' probably broadly corresponds to a parallel decrease in religiosity. 'Devotions' seem to focus the attention of the faithful and concentrate the surplus of religious feeling which tends to spread itself over a large number of objects. It is obvious that where the sense of the sacred is more intense, this process of multiple 'focalization' may be easier. This is a simple hypothesis, which seems more plausible if we consider the fact that these 'devotions' occur most often in settings which are, or at least seem to be, highly sacralized, or where the sense of the sacred is more dramatic.

Finally, mention must be made of the crisis in religious vocations. With the reduction in religious interest and the decline in the number of people who are involved, is associated the identity crisis among priests. All these factors, and many others, have contributed to the decline in religious vocations. This decline in the number of people who dedicate themselves full-time to religion (the phenomenon is important for the Catholic Church), suggests that, if this tendency is not reversed, there will sooner or later be a real collapse. The tendency is so pronounced that its effect is evident even over brief periods of time.

We need only look at the data available for six European countries over a five year period, although the crisis affects all the world's churches.[117] (The exceptions represented by Poland and Austria reflect particular situations.)

Secular priests ordained in several countries

	1965	1966	1967	1968	1969	1970
Germany			603	593	461	
The Netherlands*	363	339	278	173	108	
France	845	902	810	811	567	402
Belgium	266	202	163	149		116
Poland		671	765	769		
Austria	135	100	116	107		

*Total secular and religious.

In the 1970s this decline accelerated for the Catholic priesthood in England, as we have already noted was the case for the priesthood of the Church of England.

Thus, everywhere and in all departments, the dynamic of religious practice reveals a weakening of ecclesial religiosity and, within certain limits, of every type of religious belief, including the belief in God.

The brevity of the foregoing exposition (in relation to the vast size of the field considered), and the bareness of the figures (which we have not elaborated or critically revised) were intended to bring the reader face to face with the vastness of the phenomenon in the space of a few pages. Its significance might otherwise have been lost in a detailed analysis of its complex individual manifestations and in a multitude of distinctions. But a broad overview of religious practice, in Europe and elsewhere, reveals the similarity of the trend throughout the Christian world: the phenomenon goes beyond any particular and contingent interpretation.

Considering the data presented in the preceding pages, is our analysis of the crisis of religiosity inadequate?[118] Everything concurs in indicating (whether directly or indirectly and inductively) that religion undergoes a profound crisis in industrial society. Arguments to the contrary can be supported only by theories, by intellectual exercises which can find no comfort in the available data, which contradict such theories systematically. The evidence reviewed above might gain further significance by viewing it in a historical perspective, as relating both to more distant, and to recent, history and by associating with it a close analysis of indices which do not directly pertain to religious practice. Since such analysis presupposes some considerations to be developed in the following chapters, the reader must seek our conclusions on the subject in the first section of the last chapter.

3

Towards a Theory of Religious Crisis

1. IRRELIGIOSITY IN HISTORY: OUTLINES OF A SYNTHESIS

To determine how the religious crisis has developed, and just what factors have promoted it, we must take a historical perspective. In the centuries prior to our own, religiosity — at least externally, and with only marginal exceptions — was universal. The abandonment of religion was then no more than the passage from one religion to another, and not a shift from religion to atheism. Those who never engaged in any sort of religious practice were very few indeed, and locally could usually be picked out by name. Furthermore, such people were usually those whose social circumstances made it physically impossible for them to practise — people such as concubines, prostitutes, lepers, and others who were deliberately precluded from religious activity and sacred places.

To this near unanimity of practice there corresponded a fairly unanimous religiosity on the past of the individual: social life was shot through with religious significance. It is widely accepted that in the early stages of human history the structure of society was thoroughly pervaded by religious conceptions, and before we proceed with our analysis we must try to grasp the character of religious feeling in those periods. In the first place we must determine to what extent in primitive society the development of religious phenomena followed the evolutionary course of social structure, since if it turned out that the connection between social structure and religious structure was a recent development, the conception of religious change in more recent historical periods would certainly be affected. Secondly, we must formulate at least some working hypotheses concerning whether, in the solidly religious milieu of the past, there was any lack of depth in religiosity or any weak strands in the religious fabric. At the risk of boring the specialist we must restate points that are useful for the interpretation of the phenomenology of the sacred in the various phases of human history. [1]

(a) *The origins and proto-history of the higher cultures*

Taken as a whole, social and religious activities have always been inextricably integrated. The most important part of primitive social life was the observance of the rites and traditions of the group. Magical-religious concerns were an essential component of the life and mentality of the primitive. [2] Thus Spencer and Gillen observed of the life of the Australian aborigine, as reported by Tacchi Venturi:

> From the day of his initiation, his life is clearly divided into two parts. First of all there is that part which we might call 'ordinary life', which is common to all, men and women, and is connected with the search for food and with war dances. . . . Then there is that side of his existence which becomes increasingly important to him and is concerned with things of a sacred and mysterious nature. With the passage of the years he becomes more and more involved in these sacred practices, until almost all of his thoughts are concentrated on them. Ritual ceremonies, which seem to the white man to be irrelevant events, are for him very serious matters. They are all related to the memory of the great ancestors of the tribe. The native is firmly convinced that when his turn comes to die, the spiritual part of him will return to the ancient hearth where he will live in communion with his forebears. [3]

The primitive's consciousness of having a personality distinct from those of the other members of the group was either limited or entirely lacking. In this connection, Lévy-Bruhl observes that,

> For the man of even the most primitive societies, maintenance of his own being, the original and immediate expression of his need to live, includes safeguarding the existence of the social organism to which the individual belongs in the full sense of that term. He feels that his own being persists only if the social organism resists destruction. His own continuance is neither separable nor distinguishable (except from the biological point of view) from that of the social organism.

Thus one can understand how, for these 'primitives', death is an incident of only secondary importance (Driberg), a passing to another place, a change of residence. It would be tragic and frightening if the new conditions of existence should stop the dead man's continued belonging to his group. It would be something very different from isolation and solitude — it would be the terrifying threat of annihilation, the impossibility of maintaining one's own being, which is nothing if it ceases to belong to the social group.[4]

In this synthesis of individual and group, the magical-religious life became the centre of social life, the logical nexus that bound the individual almost organizally to the other members of the group. A corollary of this was that the mystical, in the broad sense of the term, was held in great esteem by primitives. Men who were thought to have had some supernatural experience were held to be sacred, and distinct from others. Often they formed a 'class', an organized professional group of specialists, in which may be seen the beginnings of a process of social differentiation.[5] Typical examples of the social life in simple and unified communities existed in societies such as the Arunta in Australia, the Vedda in southeast Asia, or the Bushmen in South Africa. In these groups, distinctive functions were fused: for instance, among the Arunta, the chief (alatunja) presided over activities of both a secular and a religious nature. Social life was unified in all its manifestations. This unity was, however, only the expression of the primitive's tendency to attribute sacred value to every act as well as to every fact, and it was also a consequence of the intrinsic simplicity of a life which, even in its practical aspects, did not require structural differentiations.

Unity was sustained by the sacred value attributed to human life, and this sacredness was accepted and recognized in all parts of the world. The analogies between different primitive groups are surprising, and there are many similarities between the primitive society of ancient Mesopotamia and the Indo-European tribes, the Greeks and the Romans, the Irish, Persians, or Brahmic Hindus.

Even in these first social structures we can already see the essential elements of differentiation between primitive and modern man as well as the slow development toward more secularized forms of life. Eliade remarks that

In fact, among the differences which separate the man of early cultures from modern man, one of the most important is the inability of the latter to live his organic life (especially where sex and nutrition are concerned) as a sacrament. Psychoanalysis and historical materialism claim that the best confirmation of their theses is to be found in the importance attached to sexuality and nutrition by peoples still in the early phases of their development. But psychoanalysis and historical materialism have failed to notice that for these people eroticism and nutrition have a value and a function which is completely different from their modern significance. For modern man they are only physiological acts, while for primitive man they are sacraments, ceremonies, means of communion with the force which represents Life itself. . . . This force and this life are only epiphanies of ultimate reality; for the primitive these elementary acts become a rite by means of which man approaches reality, enters a lofty realm, and is liberated from automatism (without content or significance), from change, from the 'profane', from nothingness.[6]

Thus the elements of the sacred penetrate the most intimate aspects of man and the most recondite aspects of social life. The expression *sociolatry*, which some authors have used, illustrates the difficulty of separating religious thought and feeling, expressions of the group, from the group itself. But even if we use this term, it would be foolhardy to maintain, as does Bouthoul, that among primitives the concepts of God, of imminent justice, and of creative providence are virtually non-existent, or that, in consequence, primitives embrace a more complicated ritualism in social life and a more conspicuous inclination toward magic as a replacement for what he considers to be authentic religious fervour.[7] Bouthoul over-generalizes, and makes questionable inferences from the alleged absence of a concept of God. Social and experimental psychology show us how difficult it is to trace a sequence of psychological reactions even in contemporary experience. It would be much more difficult to study sequences of reactions that have occurred in the past, and of which we see only the remote consequence or their distorted projection in some contemporary primitive society. Furthermore, the absence of a concept of God does not mean the absence of religion. It is conceivable that there is no logical gap between the spiritual vision of the primitive and that of more ad-vanced cultures; but that there is, expectably, merely evolution from one to the other.

Just as among primitives the life of the whole society was oriented toward the religious and the sacred, with religion as the centre of social life, so later on the material and the sacred aspects of suc-cessive civilizations were inseparably connected and intertwined. In the archaic periods of history, which we may distinguish from the preceding proto-history, that sociolatry that had characterized religious phenomenology persisted, even if in a lesser degree. The ancients continued to emphasize group worship: individual worship was regarded as useless. Religious life continued to be inseparable, if no longer from the tribe, then from the city. Alongside the great divinities of the, so to speak, international pantheon, local divinities continued to exist, such as many of the Etruscan gods, and minor Roman deities who presided over the various manifestations of social life. This more or less narrowly restricted localization of tribal, city, or national deities is to be found also in the East. Thus the gods of Assur, Phoenicia, and Babylon are local. They may belong to a city or at most to a nation, but they all have local origins.

Religiously structured social differentiation becomes more marked once there is a more refined division of labour.

Social classes become distinct according to the degree of control which they exercise over other classes or groups, and this too acquires significance in religious terms. The shaman represents the first example of social differentiation, and he presages the future development of a priestly class with its distinctive privileges. [8]

More recently, ancient Iranian society was structured on a class basis into three social strata, and in the Sassanid period into four: the priests, the warriors, the functionaries, and the populace. Imperial Chinese society was always subdivided into castes, [9] but its structure was less rigid than that of India, which is the most typical example of social organization based on caste privileges. The division of social strata may be rigid or flexible, according to the criteria of distinction and differentiation, but it is always more static when it is based on birth. It is always sanctioned and upheld by religious principles, although the degree to which religion is involved varies with the particular situations. As Thurnwald justly observes, even in many primitive societies the priestly element is often absolutely dominant.

But especially in some of the higher cultures it is the priests and not the warriors who constitute the first estate.

Among the many factors which give rise to class differentiation, one of the most fundamental is that of ethnic and racial distinctions which congeal and are codified through highly sacralized norms and taboos. These distinctions soon give rise to specific religious rules concerning the relationships between the classes, marriage, the structure of rights and privileges, and so on. The religious characteristics of the Polynesian hierarchy are well known: here situations of privilege and religious beliefs are strictly connected. This social religiosity both conforms with and codifies class distinctions. The progressive differentiation of classes on religious grounds begins much earlier than one would have expected. The Omaha Indians, for example, recognize distinctions which we would not hesitate to define as caste distinctions. A kind of caste structure of both a religious and civil nature was also present in long periods of Roman history. (The ancient sacred laws were the monopoly of the priestly classes until the famous *jus flavianum* became established.) Such structures were to be found also in Persia, Egypt, China, Japan, and Peru. They existed almost everywhere in ancient times, and to a certain extent also in the middle ages.[10] In all of these cases the superiority of the leading group is reflected in the religious structure which is differentiated along parallel lines. There are limiting cases in which only the nobles can hope for immortality, such as among certain Polynesian tribal groups, and in Peru where the *Children of the Sun* were obliged to participate in particular cult forms, and were bound by particular taboos.

These monopolies endure for long periods of time and often reappear in historical times wherever lay social life and religious social life overlap and become unified. These distinctions have not lacked opponents, of course, who justified their opposition no less on religious grounds. Such, for example, was the struggle of Cleisthenes in Athens which led to the reforms abolishing the privileges and cultural monopoly of the nobility.

(b) *Professional and cultural differentiations at the origins and in the proto-history of higher cultures*

Distinctions based on sex, work, age, and profession are also often articulated in religious terms. The tendency to form professional groups on the basis of a specifically religious connection has always been present. It may be seen in the primitive organizations of the Dahomey, which have been studied in great detail by Jean Herskovits; in ancient Egypt, where professional groups put themselves under the protection of a certain god (Thot and Sahmet for the doctors, Ptah for the artisans, etc.); and in the associations of ancient Rome, where the priestly groups exercised great influence (collegia sacerdotalia, sodalitates, collegia privata, collegia mercatorum, capitolinorum). In medieval Christianity, the corporations and the other associations enjoyed the patronage of saints. Nor should we forget some typical Germanic corporative associations such as the guilds (the term itself signifies a group which shares a common cult).[11] Also in Islam there were religiously based socio-professional distinctions: we might mention the Sufi-oriented medieval *futuwwa* and the Ghazi organizations (defenders of the faith). Thus, religious motivations have variously affected class systems, professional organizations, sexual life, and the physical and psychic development of the individual.

Religious orientation also responds to the general character of the culture of which the social group is the expression. The orientation of a hunting-based group, for example, is different from that of a group based on fishing or food gathering. Task assignments, duties and prayers are strictly related to the character of the prevalent activity. Thus, the cult of the Great Mother, illustrated a strict relationship between agriculture and the development of ritual ceremonies as well as of a priestly class.[12]

In effect, socio-cultural differentiation leads to an emphasis on particular ideas and rites which are linked to the characteristics of social life. In particular, professional, economic, military, and political groups foster the predominance of the cults of their preferred deities, while at the same time making such cults conform to their own activities and to their developing social life. The warlike characteristics of the Aztecs (which were perhaps in part acquired during the migrations in Mexico) give a ferocious character to their ritual and mythology: in Japan, Buddhism was modified by the military influence of the Samurai: in Europe the middle ages favoured the rise of religious, military, and chivalrous orders.

An analogous response to the requirement for change which arises from the intimate fusion of lay and religious social life is to be found among the intellectuals who tend to carry on a continuous critical re-elaboration of their religious concepts, and among the less cultured classes who also tend to transform their religiosity. Ancient Egypt offers a good example of this fusion and of the great influence exerted by the various components of the social structure on the phenomenology of religion and vice versa. All the resources of this culture are concentrated on the decoration of the tombs of their kings, of mausoleums, and especially of the temples. These latter, in turn, are the centre of a vigorous economic development. Having its foundations in the god-king, the afterlife, and an omnipotent priestly class, Egyptian civilization acquired an enormous stability. As long as Isis, Osiris, the Nile, and the related economic, social, and religious structure stood unaffected, Egypt also resisted decline. As Dawson remarks,

> It is indeed one of the most remarkable spectacles in history to see all the resources of a great culture and a powerful state organized, not for war and conquest, not for the enrichment of a dominant class, but simply to provide the sepulchre and to endow the chantries and tomb-temples of the dead Kings. And yet it was this very concentration on death and the after life that gave Egyptian civilization its amazing stability. The Sun and the Nile, Re and Osiris, the Pyramid and the Mummy, as long as these remained, it seemed that Egypt must stand fast, her life bound up in the unending round of prayer and ritual observance. All the great development of Egyptian art and learning grew up in the service of this central religious idea, and when, in the age of final decadence, foreign powers took possession of the sacred kingdom, Libyans and Persians, Greeks and Romans, all found it necessary to 'take the gifts of Horus', and to disguise their upstart im-perialism under the forms of the ancient solar theocracy, in order that the machinery of Egyptian civilization should continue to function.[13]

The Hebrew people, too, were able to maintain for thousands of years their ethnic, social, and economic identity, thanks to their monotheism and to the principles of their religion. The same is true of ancient Greece, founded as it was on the religion of the Olympian deities[14] which was the vehicle of a close feeling of community among the various cities.

We may thus conclude that social stratification, socio-professional distinctions, and the social fabric as a whole are intimately bound up with religion from at least two points of view: first of all, every social structure is 'also' a religious structure; and secondly, in view of this reciprocal interaction between lay and religious social life, religious transformations become also transformations in all other social phenomena. This is all the more true the further one goes back in time toward primitive cultures.

These observations are intended only as preliminary considerations on a theme which has already been well developed by students of the history of religion: they represent a frame of reference which will be useful in what follows.

(c) *The weakening of the bond between lay and religious sociality with the diffusion of Christianity*

Christianity represents a refinement of religiosity which in time leads to a readjustment in the mechanics of the relationship between profane and religious social life, a readjustment which, after many centuries, comes from some perspectives to favour the desacralization of society. Even during the Hellenistic period, a process of differentiation between religious and profane communities had begun. During this period specifically religious associations developed, and there was a partial disintegration of organizations which had a mixed profane and religious nature, and thus a predominantly public character. The extent to which this phenomenon developed in Christianity is not surprising if one considers, among other things, the influence of Judaism's prophetic and eschatological tradition. This tradition, together with the persistence of the concept of 'redemption', led to the rapid development of a theology of history, understood as social history, and of the Christian's place in it, as well as to the attribution of a new and profound significance to history itself. However, as we shall see, this new sense of history was, together with other factors, to lead to a desacralization of individual consciousness and of the entire society.

But there are a number of indications that close relationships between profane and religious life persisted even in those periods in which the world of the profane ceased to be identified with the religious world. One of the areas in which this occurred is the connection between religious phenomena and those heresies that were most directly concerned with the dynamics of social life.[15] In certain periods, almost all of the movements in which the need for radical social, political, and economic transformations found expression appeared in religious form. So it was in the early period with the Gnosis of Carpocrates and Epiphanes and the Donatist movements.[16]

Later on, there was a connection between the heresies of the Albigensians and the Cathari and rural and plebean populations, and this was also the case with events such as those involving Arnold of Brescia and John Ball. Among the more radical central European phenomena was the sect of the Brethren of the Free Spirit, which came to light in Paris in 1210, but which existed also in Alsace, Swabia, and other regions. This sect practised communism of goods and women, and justified free love. Peasants who aspired to the ownership of land were widely disposed to heresy in central Europe, revealing an interesting mixture of profane and religious sentiments.[17] The heresy of the Lollards in England had ramifications in Flanders and Brabant, and its advocates sought reform both in the church and in the laws of property. Among the thirteenth and fourteenth century heresies was the broad movement of the Spiritual Franciscans, and in particular that of Fra Dolcino who, together with Frate Umberto (a former blacksmith), preached poverty and social equality. After some successes, his followers were defeated in battle on Maundy Thursday, 1307. The Monforte heretics who arose in the diocese of Asti around the year 1000 taught chastity, abstention from meat, and communism of goods.[18] The principal representatives of these movements were almost always from the lower classes, as was Lituardo, described as *homo plebeius*, who preached against the payment of tithes. The majority of the Monforte heretics were runaway serfs and other indentured servants seeking greater liberty.

These demands for equality achieved their most critical expression during the peasant uprisings of the sixteenth century, particularly in Germany. Thomas Münzer was one of the more important leaders.[19] He saw the Kingdom of God as an organization of society in which there were no social differences of any sort, nor, as a consequence, any state authority which was independent of, or set over against, the members of society. Nor was there any private property. Any opposition to his programme, which was to establish equality and community of goods and labour, was to be overcome by force. A similar spirit was behind the teachings of Johannes Böheim (1471), who claimed to have had revelations from the mother of God, according to which there were to be no more monarchs of any kind, nor any ecclesiastical or lay authority. Everyone was to earn his living through work, and no one was to possess more than anyone else: taxes and tributes of all kinds were to be abolished, and pastures, water, and forests were to be held in common. Böheim's teachings were so well received by the peasants whose freedom was curtailed that he gathered daily audiences of up to 40,000. His words must have made a deep impression, since at one point he was able to mobilize 34,000 armed peasants, even though final success eluded him.

The social revolts of the peasants and the heresies that — although not always so obviously — are associated with them increased in number towards the end of the fifteenth century. A Dutch peasant insurrection occurred between 1491 and 1492, and the sacred league of Alsace (1493) was the origin of the famous *Bundschuh*, which became politically powerful between 1513 and 1515, at a time when almost simultaneous peasant insurrections were occurring in Switzerland, Hungary, and Slovenia. It is not established that all these revolts were conceived as religious heresies, but there was usually religious influence or an appeal to religious ideas for legitimation.

Among these insurrections, broadly parallel to those led by the *Bundschuh* and by *Arme Konrad* in Germany, a particularly important one was led by György Dozsa in Hungary. At the moment of his greatest success he proclaimed at Csánad the creation of the republic, the abolition of the nobility, general equality, and the sovereignty of the people. But he was finally overcome and was, apparently, roasted on a burning throne and then eaten by his followers, who could save their own lives only by undertaking this performance.

At almost the same time an insurrection occurred in Marca Vindica, Carinthia, and in part of Carnia and Styria. The German and Slovene peasants of the area raised the war flag of the 'Stara prava' (ancient rights), but the insurrection was repressed and ended in Carnia in the autumn of 1516. Between 1518 and 1523 there was a mushrooming of local insurrections that became more and more intense after the spring of 1524. The period saw the culmination, and the virtual extinction, of the great German peasant insurrections, which were violently suppressed. Among the final effects of these revolts was the attempt to set up an anabaptist kingdom in Holland in 1534 by a shoemaker, Johann of Wilhelmser.

What emerges from a consideration of these rebellions is that the most advanced and even Utopian social demands of this period found religious expression since religion was an inextricable element of social life. Any transformation of the social structure entailed appeal to religious ideals, both because men still retained a deep sense of the sacred, and because society itself was sacred both in its overall articulation and in its individual structures. Any conception of society automatically entailed a conception of the supernatural: society was conceivable only in religious terms, which defined, however inarticulately, its origins and meaning.

It was not until the eighteenth century that society became truly desacralized, so that lay and religious social life, although coexisting in single individuals, began to take different paths at the level of social organization. After the failure of the revolutionary initiatives of the sixteenth and seventeenth centuries, the peasant leagues went underground or disappeared, and the type of social consciousness on which they depended underwent gradual transformations. From them, as well as from the groups of revolutionary lower class in the cities who had often allied themselves with these leagues, there arose for a certain period a succession of more or less heretical movements and associations of a 'subversive' nature. These in turn gave birth to those proletarian leagues from which were to come some of the revolutionary and socialist groups of the French revolution as well as those ideologies that were in their turn to give birth to Marxism.[20] Communism, which between the eleventh and sixteenth centuries had had a markedly religious character, became desacralized in the eighteenth and nineteenth centuries with the desacralization of society, but was often indirectly derivative of the heresies and revolts of preceding centuries. The process of desacralization is exemplified in communist groups that had first a lay, and then a Marxist, character. The first forms of modern socialism are the expression of organized groups that have a clearly evangelical inspiration, such as the League of Equals. But this desacralization of communist demands is only one symptom of a complex and deep-seated process of desacralization of social life.

Thus, even after the advent of Christianity, social organization continued to find expression in largely religious forms. But desacralization was taking place, and this process later became more accentuated. The development before the Enlightenment, and the developments of that period, detached the masses from Christianity. This process began with the upper classes but spread to the bourgeoisie and down to the populace. The new ideas, which first appeared in an almost frivolous form among groups of courtiers, and in the form of ideological scepticism among philosophers, were latent for some time, but spread rapidly with the rise of industry and the appearance of the industrial proletariat.

Until now we have followed the path of history, seeking to gather here and there facts which allow us to attempt a logical systematization of the religious disintegration that was discussed at the beginning of this chapter. If what we have said so far is accurate, we may thus put forward an outline of the transformations of society with respect to its religious character.

(1) In the first phase, social history was, above all, religious history.

(2) In the second phase, a distinction can be made between social and religious history, although the two sets of phenomena remained closely related and intertwined.

(3) In the third phase, social phenomena tended to become desacralized, and social development occurred that was increasingly independent of religion.

The sacred shows, then, an almost constant tendency towards impoverishment. This general scheme is put forward as a tentative framework to facilitate discussion. We may ask if the sacred does indeed have this tendency toward impoverishment, and if so, what might be the cause. Once we have identified the cause, we may ask about the extent to which the process is irreversible.

2. THE DECLINE OF THE SACRED IN THE PRE-INDUSTRIAL PERIOD

(a) *Indices of the development of irreligion in the context of culture*

Our concern in the foregoing pages has not been to present a history
of the decline of religiosity, but rather to indicate certain broad
developmental trends. This framework suggests that religious
socialization has declined with increasing rapidity over centuries and
up to the contemporary period. The phenomenon of widespread
desacralization is a new one, however, and leads us to suspect the
existence of new causes, and it is our task to identify, catalogue, and
connect these causes. First we need to locate a *terminus a quo* of the
origin of the phenomenon, not by providing a history but by indicating points necessary for an understanding of the logic of the
phenomenon. Historians seem to agree that irreligion is a relatively
recent phenomenon, even though a certain dilution of religiosity is
evident in the past, particularly among the more cultured classes. To
discover the first symptoms we must go back several centuries, [21] even
though it is not altogether easy to determine the particular century.
The process certainly began long before a superficial study might
lead one to suppose.

There are those who assert with great confidence that as early as
the year 1000 there was a transition from one type of psychology to
another. For example, it was believed that the year 1000 would mark
the end of the world, and that once that year had passed, a new
phase of social life would begin: humanity appeared to turn towards
more profane interests. That 'new start' was affected, to an extent
that is difficult to determine with any degree of precision, by the
psychological shock of the uneventful passage of the millennium.
Glaber, who was alive during that year, says that when the year 1000
arrived, without bringing with it the expected event, 'it seemed as
though the world shook itself and cast off its hoary age, and clad
itself everywhere in a white robe of Churches'. [22]

Furthermore, in about the eleventh century, the deterioration
of social life, which was already appearing in the late empire, appears to have come to a halt. The castle, the monastery, the city,
where culture was emerging, show signs of the birth of a new life.
Between 1000 and 1100, sexual and sentimental elements began to
be given an official position in European society as 'values', and no

longer as items to be as thoroughly repressed and silenced as possible. In the eleventh century, erotic interest began to flower and to affect every aspect of life: the lover enjoyed the reputation of a superior person, and the call of love disturbed even the peace of the cloister. [23]

Naturally, the slow and uneven development of the growing significance of sex led to the emergence of a more human and physical conception of love. This is the first great challenge to Christian morals and customs, even though it was a muted challenge, coming, as it did, from people who still formally considered themselves religious and Christian. But this first step toward desacralization shows the faint first signs of a degree of theoretical self-consciousness. We see something of it in the dialogue of Aucassin:

> What would I do in Paradise? I'm not preparing myself to go there; I only want to possess Nicolette, my sweetest companion whom I love so tenderly. In Heaven one finds only the people I'm going to describe: those old priests, those old cripples, those wretches who day and night cough before the altars or in the crypts under the churches, those who go around with torn old cloaks and worn old clothes, those who are naked, bare-footed and in pain, those who die of hunger and thirst, of cold and poverty. These are the creatures who enter paradise, and with them I have nothing in common. But to hell instead go handsome nobles, bold knights fallen in tournaments and great wars, strong archers and faithful soldiers. I will go with them. There go also the courteous and beautiful ladies who have two or three friends in addition to their lord husbands. There go gold and silver, ermine and rich furs, harpists and minstrels, and all those who are happy on earth. I will go with them, so long as I can have Nicolette, my tender friend, at my side.

Few texts so felicitously synthesize the rising dualism between lay and religious social life which came in time to take on more and more explicit logical and ideological forms. But this incipient antithesis was to be found not only in erotic-sentimental form. After 1000 there was a growing interest in bodily forms, in art, in science, an interest which was no longer purely religious but included in its scope *also* profane things. This new interest eventuated in a first withdrawal, however minimal, of the religious world from the sphere of the profane. Although these first stirrings created a new equilibrium between the sacred and the profane and gave rise to a renewed religiosity, it was still the case that the earlier balance in favour of the sacred indicated greater spirituality, in both extension and depth, at least in culturally advanced circles.

This profanization showed itself in many aspects of social and cultural life: the decline of sacred drama which had formerly dominated the theatre, the rise of Provençal and Sicilian poetry, and the 'tournamente of love', which was obviously not a religious phenomenon, although they were permeated by a romantic-religious spirit. The songs of the troubadors were also signs of this first weakening of religiosity; although they were a cultural meteor, appearing about 1190 and already in decline by 1240. The barbaric unrest of the troubadors had only the barest hint of Christian sentiment. [24] Even philosophy began to detach itself from theology.

Toffanin [25] justly observes that when, around 1100, the Masters left the cloisters for the episcopal schools, [26] they found themselves among new scholars, and thus a different cultural world began to form with a different sense of religion. The twelfth century, with its growing number of educated laymen, felt the ever-increasing attraction of the future humanism; and with its own religiosity decreasing in the face of cultural secularization, it foreshadowed the Renaissance.

Culture, and thus the face of the world, was becoming desacralized. From the episcopal schools the scholars no longer retired to the peace of the cloister. They felt the attractions of profane life, and in turning toward another world they carried with them a more urgent perplexity about religious matters, which allied itself with profane knowledge as a competitor of theology. [27]

As reason, and civil and cultural life became desacralized, they also became liberated, on the intellectual level, from the hegemony of theology, and, on the pragmatic level, from that of religious values in general.

Around the year 1000 man had begun to have a greater interest in nature, and the 'direct' study of phenomena was on the increase. Experimentalism became more frequent: Roger Bacon, a scientist but also a Franciscan, studied experimental science. Albertus Magnus wrote a treatise on plants which is perhaps the best work of its kind in the whole of the medieval period. But religiosity was influenced also by the cultural reawakening. Technology and culture proceed in parallel and exert an influence on each other.

Averroistic (and later Aristotelian) rationalism reached Europe at the end of the great wave of religious wars which had covered the continent with blood, particularly in the preceding century. This rationalism was reinforced by the intellectual scepticism which these wars promoted among the cultured classes. [28]

But the desacralization of social life did not occur only through cultural, artistic, and philosophical developments. For example, new 'worldly' disciplines such as algebra, astronomy, navigation, and various sciences and techniques, appear almost simultaneously and become validated and consolidated with the development of the universities, beginning with Bologna, Padua, Salerno, Naples, Paris, Toulouse, and Montpellier.

Even the life of the populace was transformed. Formerly it had been shot through with more or less mythical components; the stars which aroused interest were those of astrology; numbers were bound up with the kabbalah. Every act and fact had at the same time both an earthly, and human, and a sacred significance. Beginning about the twelfth century, religious as well as magical ideas began to encounter competition. New problems and new ideas made themselves felt and led to a more intense concentration on nature. History began to leave the realm of the supernatural and the wondrous and attempted to deal with facts on a human level. Although it manifested itself only sporadically, and then primarily through the cultural aspects of social life, an incipient scepticism was present. How else are we to explain the naturalism of Montpellier and Salerno?

But all these socio-cultural and technico-scientific phenomena would have little significance, or at least a different significance, were it not for the fact that they developed in a context in which very important technico-economic transformations were also occurring. [29] Fire, domestic animals, the wheel, water transport, the sail, leather, bricks, glass—all represent decisive steps in technological progress, and had a substantial impact on socio-economic phenomena and on the characteristics of the various cultures and civilizations, as well as on religion.

This phenomenon repeated itself at the end of the High Middle Ages. The initial decline of religiosity in this period cannot be explained solely on the basis of ideas. The eleventh and twelfth centuries, besides being culturally momentous, witnesses the introduction of new techniques, which, as they diffused and multiplied, exercised a continuing and growing influence on society and on the individual. These same centuries also saw the beginning of an industrial transformation which, although of little import in its early phase, affected the religious spirit in a manner analogous to the similar phenomena of recent times.

Around the year 1000 several very important new techniques of production were introduced; for example the use of water power for the pumping of air and the consequent creation of the first blast-furnaces;[30] the production of paper and cloth on an industrial scale; and, shortly afterwards, the production of pig-iron which was already being produced in Germany by the end of the fourteenth century.[31] Nor must we forget the acceleration of transportation which occurred as a result of a number of new inventions.[32]

Although not always influenced by these major discoveries, even the work of artisans transformed individual psychology as it spread and multiplied. We cannot measure the extent of this influence, but, as Mumford says:

> Naturalism grew out of the daily occupations and the working life of the craftsman; in his struggle with obdurate materials, melting glass, hammering iron, hewing stone, heating copper, he learned to respect the nature of the materials and the objective conditions for successful operation. Prayer would work only if one added to its efficacy by intelligently manipulating the environment. That was the daily lesson of craftsmanship. Results might be fanciful; but the process of achieving them was matter-of-fact.[33]

These facts are the expression of a legal and industrial transformation which it is not our place to discuss here. More and more serfs fled to the urban centres where they could more easily obtain their freedom, and the cities began to grow. The first international fairs made their appearance, and merchants began to cross Europe more and more frequently, carrying with them ideas as well as goods. All over the continent vast areas were colonized, drained, and cultivated, largely due to the efforts of the monastic orders. Capital began to circulate more and more rapidly. All this led, among other things, to the rise of the first Italian capitalism, which was based on textiles and banking, and which could be defined, although some humanists might consider this heretical, as the cradle of the Renaissance and of Humanism.

In this burst of activity and traffic, in this flowing of money and thus of goods and services, in the freer development of the new techniques, the psychology of the times changed. Man turned his attention to the problems of the classics, of humanism, of the sciences, and a blow was dealt to religiosity and the life of the spirit, which became, even if at first only in small degree, less significant in people's affairs.[34] The process of deterioration took place at two levels. At the higher level, there was a lowering of religious content in the already existing disciplines, and the development of new disciplines. At the lower level, life was affected by new factors which, although they did not yet replace the religious factor, now stood alongside them. These two spheres, the higher and the lower, acted and reacted one on another, and gave rise to new transformations.

In such a complex process, it is not easy to indicate the relative significance of different factors. One banal item was the triumph of accounting. Between 1278 and 1340, double-entry book-keeping was already in use in the municipality of Genoa, and, in 1494, Pacioli published a treatise on this method in Venice. Mumfort observes that:

> Numbers thus came to exert an independent hold over the imagination: quantitative thinking and cash values displaced qualitative discrimination and aesthetic and moral values.[35]

The class of the 'clerk' was born, and within a few centuries their number became legion throughout the world. Can we imagine that this world, steeped as it was in *quantity*, could fail to displace that other, so very different, world of values?

Around the new industries and the new ideas emerged various corporate bodies and estates that made it possible for civil society to acquire its first consciousness of itself, although the state, in the modern sense of the term, was no more than a dream. Civil society was expanding vigorously through the emergence of small but vital groups that expressed new demands, particularly economic demands. The twelfth and thirteenth centuries saw the emergence of the main features of a money economy which progressively replaced the old agricultural and natural economy. Social life moved more and more from country to city, with a consequent shift in the locus of power, including intellectual and cultural power, from the agriculture-based monasteries to the new lay merchant classes. In this way, a strong social fabric was formed, which in time became the background against which many of the most open opponents of religion were to arise.

The opposing interests of religious and lay groups led initially to a period of hostility between the new society and the church, a struggle that undoubtedly accelerated the development of the lay spirit even in the intellectual world.[36] The twelfth century had already seen a certain number of ideological currents that were at the same time the roots and the products of the new spirit. These currents culminated in the *Defensor* of Marsilio of Padua, one of the most important figures embodying the new intellectual orientation. The conflicts between laymen and clergy, which had been relatively rare in the eleventh and twelfth centuries, became very common in the thirteenth. De Lagarde observes that:

> It is important to point out that in the history of eleventh and twelfth centuries there is no echo of so largely widespread conflicts, therefore (we get to the conclusion that) the development of the antinomy between the two authorities is a phenomenon peculiar to the eighteenth century.[37]

From this it appears that we might take the period around 1100 as the time when Christian religiosity began to decline. This is, of course, an issue for which the margins of uncertainty are wide and the available data vague, and the point can be made only tentatively.

There is already, in the first phase of technico-industrial development, an evident hostility of laymen towards religion, documented by a series of texts, of which *Defensor* is one. Even while the church was reaching the heights of its splendour, the germs of a profound decline were at work. After 1200, the efforts of the laity to control some part of social life as non-religious life, became more vigorous. De Lagarde observes:

> Laity, as we have pointed out, can originate only within a society where the distinction between clergy and laic; spiritual and physical; lay (laic) and clerical authority are clearly in decline. Isn't it something substantially different from the simple passionate expression of the effort of laics to regain the space denied by the Church? Or, isn't it better an age where the distinction between the two orders of Christian society has become a reality? This age is undoubtedly the eighteenth century.[38]

This is to say that the conditions for the social restructuring of the lay world were created as the first step toward the conquest of society. The assault, conscious or unconscious, on religiosity, took place at all levels, and even the ideas of the most Christian of writers were rather more secular than those of the predecessors. Slow as they were, there were evident changes in the church and its thinkers. Thus, with Aquinas, in spite of the strict logic of his arguments, the church made concessions which at an earlier time it would have vigorously rejected. As Mumford observes, the time for rejections was over, and a period of dangerous concessions was beginning. Religiosity and the sense of the sacred which had continuously advanced in society for at least seven centuries now underwent their first serious defeat. At one time it might have seemed that civil life was little by little becoming so imbued with religiosity that the European West would have soon resembled the old Brahamic and Buddhist worlds in the extent to which it was permeated by religion. Instead, almost imperceptibly, the tide began to ebb, and the course of history to change. This development was, however, very slow, and contemporaries had difficulty in perceiving it.

In broad perspective, we see that the world of the thirteenth century is less religious than that of the eleventh, the world of the Renaissance than that of the thirteenth, [39] and even the Renaissance is deeply religious in comparison with the rationalistic spirit of the seventeenth, and even more of the eighteenth, [40] century.

In this regard, Whitehead observes that 'Each revival touches a lower peak than its predecessor, and each period of slackness a lower depth.'[41] To give only one example: the Counter-reformation was a little thing compared to the Franciscan renaissance, as was the Enlightenment when compared to the Renaissance.

Over the centuries the decline was sometimes more explicitly religious; at others, moral. Thus, for example, the reduced sense of the sacred during the Renaissance was matched by a still looser sexual morality in the Baroque period. In the meantime, technology itself directly accelerated the impoverishment of mores, although not as yet, the impoverishment of the sacred: in 1564, Falloppio produced the first safe contraceptive, the cloth condom. This prevented contagion of the terrible 'French disease' which was spreading at that time. Ironically, it saved the more experienced libertines, not those who naïvely and occasionally exposed themselves to contagion.

Quite apart from this, various discoveries in the fourteenth, fifteenth, and sixteenth centuries caused profound changes in the style of reasoning that men were beginning to employ. Thus, in 1543, Vesalio founded anatomy with the publication of his *De Humani Corporis Fabrica* at Basle.[42] The circulation of the blood was discovered and explained by Realdo Colombo, Andrea Cisalpino, Michele Servedor, and William Harvey. These discoveries and others led to a more 'materialistic' attitude towards the human body, and even affected the attitudes of the man in the street, and led to the increasing naturalization of medicine, which had for centuries developed in close association with religion, and which had what, in many cases, might be called a sacred character.[43]

Humanism was originally nourished by the first symptoms of irreligion, which humanism itself, in turn, favoured. Toffanin observes:

> If the irreligiosity of the Renaissance depends on the rebirth of paganism, then paganism and irreligiosity very soon become one and the same thing, a single beautiful and horrible monster which throws itself more and more impetuously down the broad streets of the fifteenth century towards its natural end, Enlightenment and modern laicism.[44]

This is basically our thesis, which Toffanin later elaborates by asserting that the irreligiosity of Humanism was limited, being more pervasive than the irreligiosity of earlier periods, but not subscribing to the much more aggressive secularity of following centuries.

Yet, in the writings of de Vinci, Bacon, and others, the outlook of the new world of the machine was already implicit. There was a desire to break the net of symbolism that seemed to keep man at a distance from the real nature of things. The growing interest in technology and physical science led Western man ever further away from the problems of the human spirit and a religious sense of the meaning of life. Instead of man, the machine began to take its place as the measure of all things.[45] If this is Toffanin's thesis, then we find ourselves in full agreement.[46] The new irreligious ideas were not so much the product of individuals, as of the social structures that were developing, within which a new type of intellectual was encouraged. From the proliferation of scholars and technicians, with their new attitudes, there finally emerged a Descartes. He, in spite of his formal orthodoxy, was the new type of lay and irreligious thinker. Whereas one may view humanism as having religious roots when compared with the currents of thought that followed, the impact of a more mechanistic and technological style of thinking was in itself anti-humanist, and it made itself increasingly felt over the centuries, finally giving birth to what must be regarded as lay philosophies.

Technology first influenced those who lived in direct contact with new techniques, but steadily its effects increased, offering new logical and epistomological values which later thinkers elaborated and employed, and which made their own contribution to the process of desacralization. Descartes, with his scientific positivism and his technicism,[47] was but one among the destroyers of classical-medieval-Renaissance thought.[48] Many physical scientists tended to identify the quantitative with the real, and the qualitative with the unreal. Kepler, for example, wrote:

> Just as the eye is made to perceive colour, so the mind of man is made to understand, not all manner of things, but quantity. It perceives any given thing more clearly the closer that thing is, in origin, to pure quantity, but the farther a thing is removed from quantity, the more there is in it of obscurity and error.

Naturally, the problem of the adaptation of the world of ideas to increasing technico-scientific development was *explicitly* posed only *after* these ideas began to exert their influence on human thought. Veit observes that:

> there was thus posed from the beginning the question as to whether it was possible to find a place for technology in a conception of the world.[49] But this question had only an unconscious and indirect influence on . . . the spiritual currents of the first half of the century. Then the only thing of which everyone was aware was the unease engendered by the fact that the foundations of the world had changed, while the bases of the spiritual view of that world remained the same. The thinkers of the age of enlightenment did not yet feel this tragic dissonance. For them the external world was still at peace and offered to reason a reliable and attainable picture or 'conception'. They were not aware that they themselves, in exalting reason, were providing the foundations for a new power which was destined to empty and destroy that peaceful and knowable world.

Only later were the logical and epistemological connections between the distinct spheres of ideas and technology recognized. But even in this period:

> Eighteenth century Deism was but the ghost or shadow of Christianity, a mental abstraction from the reality of a historical religion, which possessed no independent life of its own. It retained certain fundamental Christian conceptions — the belief in a beneficent Creator, the idea of an overruling Providence which ordered all things for the best, and the chief precepts of the Christian moral law, but all these were desupernaturalized and fitted into the utilitarian rational scheme of contemporary philosophy.[50]

Although we have not yet arrived at nineteenth century materialism, nuclei that may well be termed anti-Christian were already forming in urban areas. The strongest were evident in Holland, a meeting point for diverse ideational and cultural worlds. Under the pretext of carrying on the struggle against Catholicism, a series of anti-deist and anti-Christian publications appeared there, and from there the currents of irreligiosity spread to England, especially to the universities and to intellectual circles.[51] With the Enlightenment, these ideas spread rapidly, and we are at the eve of modern era.

Thus, it becomes obvious that although the foregoing remarks do not provide either a full account, much less a full explanation, of the decline of religiosity, none the less, they indicate that the decline is not a recent phenomenon. It is to be related to a long process of diverse changes in society, and it has its own logic: and this remains to be clarified.

(b) *Quantitative indices of the development of irreligiosity and their relationship to social change*

Although in the long run, the ideas with which we have been concerned were to change the face of society as a whole, initially they profoundly affected only small groups of individuals, cultural circles, which then had their own slow and limited effect on the surrounding social environment. The masses were barely touched by the new concepts, by the new scientific and philosophical horizons, even by technology and the flowering of commerce: these phenomena had their real effect on only limited strata of society.

The economy remained basically agricultural. Incipient secularity began in the urban area, which developed only slowly, and which did not at first depend primarily on commerce or technology. The ideas that were the expression of a way of life of the educated classes and, to a certain extent, of the rising bourgeoisie, had little resonance among the masses of the rural or urban proletariat, who still lived in the spirit, if not of the eleventh century, at least of the Renaissance. Yet, the first symptoms of urbanization and technical development were increasingly accompanied by attitudes and dispositions that in turn were to be the vehicles, if not of a 'rational' irreligiosity, at least of a *de facto* irreligiosity, which is significant because it affected in particular certain social groups.

Just as we have tried to outline the general process of transformation by drawing attention to some macro-sociological characteristics of the development of fundamental ideas, so, in the same way, we shall try to locate the early symptoms of mass desacralization by appealing to various particular facts, even if we do this more to exemplify than to analyze a social process.[52]

The new ideas, arising in a context which had seen the formation of technical-scientific theories, of philosophies based on them, and of new logical concepts, became simplified and vulgarized, and then began to circulate among the masses. Their receptivity may be related to parallel changes in the conditions of life and to a series of factors which, taken together, had a desacralizing impact.

In the first place, as had happened in other times, new and more permissive mores begin to appear, and in the second, there was an unprecedentedly rapid process of urbanization. In the third place, urbanization was accompanied by a more technical organization of social life, and this appears to be one of the main vehicles for the diffusion and acceptability of new ideas. *Finally*, at this point urbanization and industrialization gradually created a myriad of new roles, professions, and work settings which have a negative impact on religiosity.

Of these phenomena, the increasing permissiveness of mores, is typical not only of this time and must have occurred frequently in previous centuries, both in the history of Christianity and in the history of other religions. As Le Bras[53] has explained, even in the so-called 'age of faith', the religiosity of the Catholic world was far from being uniformly shared. In the apparently immutable structure of Catholicism there were cracks and gaps which, although superficial, foretold the coming crises. In later years, the desacralizing factors would exercise their strongest influence in the geographical areas, the milieux, and the classes which had been made more receptive by previous crises, particularly moral crises, which, although contained and limited, had not been completely surmounted.[54]

It was not by accident that the first great wave of revolutionary anti-clericalism and irreligiosity spread out from Paris, a great metropolis and perhaps the most densely industrialized of all continental cities. Furthermore, Jansenism and the Reformation, overthrowing traditional beliefs, had instilled doubt among the masses whose faith was now further weakened by changes in the social structure. Little wonder that these masses were shaken by the French Revolution without offering any marked opposition to it.

On the other hand, in the mid-eighteenth century when rationalism and scientism had already begun to have a profound effect among the nobility and the bourgeoisie, particularly in the cities, the level of conformity was still very high in the countryside in France as well as in the rest of the Catholic world.

The number of those not engaging in religious practice was growing, and it became quite high in an increasing number of urban centres. But new causes of this phenomenon were emerging even though the parallel between the new technico-scientific world and the growth of irreligiosity was not yet apparent. Those hostile or indifferent to religion are always recruited from the same categories[55]—from the innkeepers, artisans, merchants, nobility, and wealthy bourgeois. The relationship between these individualistic and primarily urban professions and irreligiosity is more evident than before. This happens, at least in part, because with growing urbanization there was a corresponding increase in the membership of these professions. The growth of the cities and the improvement of the standard of living led to an increase in the number of those not practising religion in the number of places which were unfavourable to religious practice. The tavern, the anti-church *par excellence*, as Le Bras calls it, was to be found everywhere: and there talk was free and ideas circulated rapidly. At the same time the development of transport and commerce increased the number of boatmen and carriers; the greater frequency of mobilization and of 'total' warfare swelled the ranks of soldiers; and the company of merchants, artisans, bureaucrats, and doctors continued to grow and become more and more imbued with a new consciousness and new ideas.[56]

Factors which had previously favoured desacralization increased in importance and were now joined by new ones. The numbers of the sceptical, the malcontent, the 'lukewarm', and the eternally protesting, continued to grow as a result of this progressive differentiation of social life and mores. The first symptoms of the nineteenth century industrial revolution began to exercise their influence on the previously simple and primitive economic and social organization. These phenomena, which had already done some damage to religious practice and religiosity, were further intensified with the progress of urbanization that accompanied the industrial revolution from its beginnings.

(c) *The progress of irreligiosity in moral and religious life*

In the two preceding sections we have established some relationships and located some indices which, taken by themselves, might be thought insufficient confirmation of the hypothesis concerning the progress of irreligiosity, and to this we now add further documentation which will give greater cogency to the argument that we have pursued.

For the centuries with which we are concerned, we have collected data about religious practice, popular religiosity (albeit not as extensively as might be wished), religious vocations, and illegitimate births. By itself, no one of these indices is of much significance. For instance, many factors affected the high number of religious vocations in the medieval period and in the modern age, and many of these factors were not themselves religious. It is, however, rather significant that all of these indices consistently point to the same conclusions. If, as we have seen, the data concerning the evolution of culture and the development of religious practice within professions point in a certain direction, and if these conclusions are supported by a parallel development in religious vocations (a decline); in religious practice (a decline); in popular religiosity (a decline); and in the illegitimate birth-rate (rising)—then the proposed hypotheses become more credible.

Until the year 1000, we may take it that there was a continuing increase of religiosity in Western Europe, and although its further spread was less rapid, the appeal of the supernatural maintained its intensity in the immediately succeeding centuries. Religiosity is not, however, the same as religious practice, nor is it the same as Christianity. Especially in the High Middle Ages, the very great sense of the sacred must have been a conglomerate of Christianity, paganism, and superstition, although our evidence, to which we shall refer later, is not very satisfactory on this issue.

With Toussaert, Le Bras, and Brezzi,[57] we must reject the equation, Middle Ages = Christianity. It is more difficult to reject the equation Middle Ages = Religiosity, unless we wish to substitute for it the less exclusive, Middle Ages = Religiosity + popular religiosity, plus magic, plus superstition, occultism, but in any case, plus experience of the sacred. And in fact, Toussaert's studies, or those cited by him, confirm this opinion.[58]

Thus, if some evidence suggests a decline in religious practice between the twelfth and the fourteenth centuries, this does not signify a parallel decline in religiosity. It is difficult to establish precisely the state of religion in this period, although we have some information. However—and this is the first interesting datum—as Mollat[59] suggests, it is evident that unbelief was an impossibility.

What of religious practice? Were the seeds of unbelief and scepticism hidden in the folds of superstition and occult practices, or were the latter only particular aspects of religiosity, expressions of the circumstances in which the religiosity of the time developed? What of the rather unworthy conduct of the clergy and their absenteeism: were there not much evidence to the contrary, these phenomena might suggest that religiosity was beginning to ebb throughout society.[60] I would not deny the importance of this religiosity *do ut des*, which was based both on popular attachment to relics, rites, ceremonies, animism, superstition, and to the concrete in general, and on a deep religious ignorance. This was merely a different form of religiosity, perhaps not very sophisticated, and yet it was a profound religiosity. The conclusions to be drawn from an analysis of the available documents, and from Mollat's synthesis, seem to be unequivocal.[61]

Baptism was a universal and deeply revered practice. This is evident from the fact that the diocesan councils did not feel it necessary to encourage its practice. There are recorded cases of parents who, seeking a priest to baptize a child, exposed themselves to great personal risk from storms or from enemy soldiers, rather than leave a child unbaptized.[62] The situation was no different with respect to confirmation, matrimony, and death. Death without sacraments was particularly abhorred and feared. In the case of excommunication:

> The body was then thrown in the garbage heap, outside the cemetery, in any pit as the remains of an animal. The refusal to burial in consecrated ground was so feared that everybody did one's utmost to avoid it, since it still represented one of the few feared consequences of excommunication.[63]

These practices were often linked with magic and superstition, as for instance, as was very common in France, the vessel used for giving Extreme Unction was burned once used, *propter maleficia.* But these practices did not, by virtue of this connection, lose their sacred character.

Attendance at mass was, in most parts of Europe, fairly universal. Attendance at divine service, which was traditional in Christianity from the time of the apostles and the Habraic Sabbath, became an explicit precept with Aquinas and the canon of the Lateran Council of 1215 (reaffirmed in the Corpus Juris Canonici of Clement V in 1305). There were occasional instances of failure to attend, although these varied from area to area; total failure to attend mass on the part of a single individual, however, was in most parts of Europe absolutely exceptional. The Grenoble register of episcopal visits, for example, refers to the unique case of an individual who had not attended mass for nine years.[64] Yet, in the synodal statutes, calls for attendance at mass are frequent and there are insistent complaints about lack of attendance. Sometimes one finds the formula 'rari missam audiunt', but it is usually in a context of complaints which make one doubt its significance, all the more so in that where precise information is available it shows that failure to attend mass is always sporadic.

Toussaert's excellent work on Flanders, in spite of being oriented toward different conclusions, can only confirm the high degree to which medieval consciousness was imbued with sacredness (and, from a certain standpoint, with Christianity). In spite of the pessimism that is evident at various points, Toussaert concludes by observing that he is dealing with an era of Christianity, since, in contrast with the modern world, there is no desire to build anything outside of the church or against the church. [Which is not perhaps entirely true.] Only the church is thought to be still capable of providing a solution for all of the antinomies of life. [65]

But he adds: 'It is, however, a somewhat disconcerting age, if we consider the general picture of it, so close to paganism.' But in the last analysis, religiosity is very deep.

Pity, faith, moral sense practically develop by tradition, while we find no trace of a thorough and substantial education. No doubt that, in the Middle Ages, the psychological effects of this lack of round education were important. In fact, the logical counter-party to the extreme emotionality in which receptivity, primitivity, and total lack of abstraction were mingled together, was instability and the religious sentiment was based upon the spasmodic unevenness of impression and sensation, as for instance, the water of a brook which is not restrained by any natural or artificial weir. In such a way we can explain the unevenness in the religious observance and all paradoxes (. . .). [66]

And again:

This is the reason why we are led to think that the same conception of believer and non-believer can be applied to men having entirely different characteristics, according to the different ages. The medieval Flemish, for instance, who is a Christian and a believer, does not know any form of scepticism and any rebellion; in fact he could not choose to be a Christian, he was dipped in the water of baptism since his birth and therefore automatically lives in an environment legally and openly Christian. [67]

And thus, Toussaert concludes:

the 'pagan' medieval Fleming pays his tithe grudgingly. He accepts the principle of the cultural and sacramental obligations prescribed by the Church; he submits to its laws. But he lacks moral conviction and faith.

The society is shot through with sacrality, with religiosity, but not necessarily with a consciously Roman Catholic religiosity. Religious

practice was apparently almost universal, but this is not the most
fundamental index of what is, in fact, a still more intense religiosity,
for evidence of which we must turn to several indirect indices.

Even Mollat, speaking especially of France, emphasizes that

> On the whole, the practice of religion seems to be marked by the
> characteristic that is common to every aspect of the social life of
> that age: it is spasmodic.[68]

Spasmodic and yet universal. To give another example: at the
beginning of the fifteenth century in the diocese of Narbonne, with
the exception of two villages where there were 'some' who did not
practise, religious practice was everywhere the norm.[69]

Into this consistent picture, Toussaert inserts a dissonance by
suggesting that those failing to attend mass amounted to about 10
per cent in Flanders. The percentage may have risen to this level in
some areas, but it must have been exceptional, if not in Flanders
then throughout Christendom as a whole. Furthermore, collateral
manifestations of religiosity confirm the high degree to which society
of that time was suffused with religious conceptions, (even though
this could, without contradiction, be accompanied by a certain
moral decline).

There are many minor indices of prevailing religious consciousness. Thus, it was generally the case that a judge, before attending a trial that might end with a death sentence, must go to
confession. There was the frequent obligation to go to confession at
the moment of entering a hospital and before receiving any treat-
ment. There were many, very long and passionately followed
processions. In the forests there were hermits not unlike oriental holy
men, who were, for example in France, very numerous. There were
thousands of other 'sacred' practices which touched on every aspect
of existence.[70] Popular religiosity, imbued with superstition, was
extremely solid and was to be found everywhere.

Perhaps, as Mollat maintains[71] on the basis of Toussaert's already
mentioned study, those who practised frequently really amounted to
10 per cent; regularly, 40 per cent; irregularly, 40 per cent; and
never, 10 per cent. In spite of this we may still affirm that grass-roots
religiosity was intense and that the percentage of those outside the
church was almost nil. The cases of refusal to believe in the religious
values taught by the church are extremely rare, amounting to no

more than very small groups in any given region.[72] The situation in the thirteenth and fourteenth centuries, and at the beginning of the fifteenth, before the Reformation was to change the way of being a Christian, was one of solid church religion associated with intense popular religiosity focusing especially on the seasonal acts of Christian life, but also on mass, confession, and communion. There were, however, indications of weakening, especially in the cultural sphere and in social life, with the incipient development of laicism, and the declining fear of excommunication which had, at one time, been a very effective tool of religious control.[73]

The situation in the sixteenth century was not so very much changed. The indices concerning both official and popular religiosity, if we include semi-religious manifestations, still indicate a solid sense of the sacred, even though certain cultural trans- formations were then beginning.[74] One index of change was the proportion of illegitimate births, which had apparently been relatively high at the end of the fifteenth century, even though the parish registers throughout Europe do not reveal a really significant number. Contemporary witnesses indicated a high number of illegitimate births,[75] but they gave no figures, or figures that are not easily interpreted. Hofler has said that 'the age of bastards' really began 'am Schlusse des Mittelalters'. The correlation between the spread of illegitimate births and the religious crisis becomes clearer as we examine conditions in the centuries that followed.

The association of an increase in illegitimate births and social conditions becomes clearer from the fifteenth century onwards. Ottolenghi gives us a picture of the situation in Siena,[76] where the relationship between social conditions and the illegitimate birth-rate is evident. Later, toward the end of the sixteenth century, when Italian social life was in a stagnant phase, there was a decrease in the rates. Pavia, which was economically static, maintained a stable illegitimacy rate, and on this Aleati remarks:

> Without taking into account the sometimes rather large oscillations in the illegitimate birth-rate that are indicated by the ten-yearly indices, one can detect a reduction in the incidence of illegitimate over total births in the last sixty years of the seven- teenth century in comparison with the whole of the previous period. Although in the last forty years of the sixteenth century

there is an average of one illegitimate birth in thirty, and in the first forty years of the seventeenth century this figure rises to one in twenty-eight, from 1640 to the end of the century one can see a very definite fall in the illegitimate birth-rate to an average of one illegitimate out of fifty-three births. This is in contrast to other urban centres which generally show an increase in the phenomenon during the sixteenth, seventeenth and eighteenth centuries. But without making dangerous inferences concerning a possible parallel between the general decay of the seventeenth century Pavian environment and the greater austerity of mores, it is certain that factors of a strictly local nature, which we are unable to identify precisely, lie at the bottom of this phenomenon.[77]

As economic industrial development occurred, so illegitimacy increased, while other negative indices of socio-religious development also reached sizeable levels. See the figures for Pavia.

Average illegitimate births in various parishes from 1561 to 1700

Period	Illegitimates per thousand births	Period	Illegitimates per thousand births
1561–1570	20.3	1641–1650	30.0
1571–1580	38.4	1651–1660	19.4
1581–1590	29.9	1661–1670	20.2
1591–1600	37.1	1671–1680	17.0
		1681–1690	23.6
		1691–1700	15.8
16th century avg.	33.0	17th century avg.	26.0
1601–1610	32.2		
1611–1620	32.3		
1621–1630	41.0		
1631–1640	34.0		
		avg. for the entire period	27.4

Changes in the percentage of illegitimate births in Bologna between the fifteenth and the nineteenth centuries are also significant.[78]

Illegitimate births per 100 baptized for periods of varying duration in Bologna

15th century	5.0	1771–1780	5.3
16th century	5.5	1781–1790	5.3
17th century	5.5	1791–1800	6.1
		1801–1810	10.2
1703–1725	5.4	1811–1820	11.5
1729–1740	4.6	1821–1830	9.5
1741–1750	4.2	1831–1840	8.9
1751–1760	4.0	1841–1850	9.3
1761–1770	4.5	1851–1860	9.7

The percentage increases, indeed practically doubles, with the arrival of the French.

The trend continued in association with economic advance (although with periods of stagnation and crisis). In Germany, for example, the percentage of illegitimates rapidly reached very high levels: Mols gives significant data for three German cities.[79] There was a rapid rise from a rate of one illegitimate in about 100 births to a rate of about one in five — twenty times higher! (See p. 119.)

Thus, here as elsewhere, the number of illegitimate births increased considerably, especially during the eighteenth century. Although the figures may be regarded as somewhat imprecise, and although a considerable margin of error is involved in comparing them over such long periods, this margin of error does not change the substance of the discussion.

Mols is also the source of some information regarding some less important German and Belgian cities which confirms the preceding considerations.[80]

Number of births for each illegitimate birth

Weiden		Frankfurt am Main		Leipzig	
1552–1560	87				
1561–1570	104				
1571–1580	183				
1581–1590	322				
1591–1600	180				
1601–1610	103				
1611–1620	50				
1621–1630	93				
1631–1640	210	1635–1639	113		
1641–1650	162	1640–1649	126		
1651–1660	363	1650–1659	112		
1661–1670	91	1660–1669	107		
1671–1680	68	1670–1679	98		
1681–1690	131	1680–1689	78		
1691–1700	68	1690–1699	83	1696–1700	33
1701–1710	57	1700–1709	87	1701–1710	18
1711–1720	49	1710–1719	83	1711–1720	12
1721–1730	65	1720–1729	43	1721–1730	8
1731–1740	67	1730–1739	22	1731–1740	7
1741–1750	28	1740–1749	24	1741–1750	7
1751–1760	28	1750–1759	21	1751–1760	7
1761–1770	24	1760–1769	18	1761–1770	7
1771–1780	18	1770–1779	15	1771–1780	6
1781–1790	21	1780–1789	10	1781–1790	5
1791–1800	12	1790–1799	10	1791–1800	5

Number of legitimate births for each illegitimate birth

Bad Tölz (Bavaria)		Schwäbisch Hall (Württemberg)		Engelberg (Obwalden)	
1576–1667	23	1601–1650	166	1610–1649	45
		1651–1700	123		
1668–1767	17	1701–1750	40	1700–1749	168
1768–1867	7	1751–1800	25	1750–1789	164

Number of legitimate births for each illegitimate birth (cont.)

Ath (Hainaut)		Theux (Liège)	
1601	91	1700–1719	143
1741–1750	37	1720–1739	45
1844–1846	8	1740–1759	29
		1760–1777	27

Only Engelberg provides an exception to the general pattern.

The general tendency was for an increase, especially in the seventeenth and eighteenth centuries, in acceleration of a trend beginning in previous centuries. At the end of the eighteenth century, percentages of illegitimate births between 5 per cent and 10 per cent were fairly frequent. This situation also arose in the individual parishes and cities which have been specifically and accurately studied by various authors such as Dalabade (reported by Galabert),[81] Willemsen,[82] and Helin.[83] Nor was the pattern different in Europeanized overseas countries such as Canada.[84] As Canada gradually assumed a modern social structure, the percentage of illegitimate births increased as follows:

Illegitimate births per 1,000 live births in Canada

1701–1710	2.04	1761–1770	5.57	1821–1830	7.18
1711–1720	2.58	1771–1780	7.20	1831–1840	7.41
1721–1730	7.69	1781–1790	6.05	1841–1850	8.07
1731–1740	9.69	1791–1800	4.80	1851–1860	10.88
1741–1750	11.71	18.01–5.50	5.50	1861–1870	17.15
1751–1760	12.21	1811–1820	6.23		

(Today's rate is about 30 per 1,000).

There is another indirect index that may be of some importance and which may be considered in relation to the increase in the illegitimacy rate, beginning in about 1600. This is the rapid increase in the number of children abandoned in the great cities, some of whom no doubt came from the countryside or from small towns. Lallemand,[85] who studied this question, did not go into the causes for the increase in the number of abandoned children, but he regarded it as largely due to a high incidence in illegitimacy. Since, at that time, society rejected the illegitimate, both morally and socially, they were abandoned. (Later, the percentage of abandoned children declined, in association with the decline in illegitimacy rates—all of which was the result of complex factors including, in recent times, contraceptive techniques. Society appears to have relaxed its attitudes and partially to have accepted illegitimates, and then, at a later time, to have introduced techniques for eliminating them.)

Abandoned children became a recognized social problem in cities such as Paris and London. Mols gives statistics for Paris that show a remarkable increase. The number of admissions to the hostels for abandoned children were as follows:

1640–1649	305	1690–1699	2,115	1740–1749	3,291
1650–1659	360	1700–1709	1,786	1750–1759	4,457
1660–1669	453	1710–1719	1,739	1760–1769	5,611
1670–1679	688	1720–1729	2,063	1770–1779	6,703
1680–1689	1,027	1730–1739	2,671	1780–1789	5,713

In 1772, foundlings represented 40 per cent of the baptized in Paris: one can only speculate on the percentage of these abandoned, mainly illegitimate children, the rejects of society, that took part in the assault on the Bastille in 1789. Analysis of the French Revolution from that perspective might explain something of the animus and the behaviour of the Parisian *banlieue*, and perhaps of the basic motivations underlying certain aspects of the revolution. The abandoned illegitimates were, of course, often brought to Paris from the countryside more or less secretly, although the proportion, which we may take to be high, remains uncertain. Yet, the percentage of illegitimates was growing all over France, as Mols tells us. At Aix the average rose from 107 per thousand in 1722–67 to 249 per thousand in 1768–78. Their number increased sixfold in Pau between the period 1769–73, and the period 1784–88, and so on.[86]

Nor was the situation different elsewhere. In Madrid in 1786, the percentage was already 16, and in Amsterdam between 1726 and 1770, the number of abandoned illegitimates varied between a minimum of 7 and a maximum of 31, and between 1771 and 1784 they increased in number from 41 to 257; between 1785 and 1805 they increased again, with a maximum of 488 in 1800. By 1817 the number had increased yet further. Thereafter there was a rapid decrease, between 1818 and 1850 from 666 to 14. The zero level was reached during the twentieth century.[87]

The behaviour of the Milenese population was no different.[88] The following are the figures per thousand for Milan:

Children abandoned per 1,000 children born in Milan

1660–1669 405.7	1700–1709 531.7	1750–1759 683.9
1670–1679 371.5	1710–1719 510.4	1760–1769 679.9
1680–1689 359.0	1720–1729 442.2	1770–1779 681.2
1690–1699 531.5	1730–1739 614.7	1780–1789 959.4
	1740–1749 712.5	1790–1799 1499.4

(Thus there were more children abandoned in Milan than were born there: this is explained by the fact that children were brought to the city from the countryside and abandoned there.)

As we have noted already, the increase in the number of illegitimates in Italy occurred later than in the rest of central and northern Europe, but so did the industrial revolution, which we may take to be the over-riding social circumstance conditioning this increase. Research in Italy shows that there were basically two substantial increases, one at the end of the eighteenth century (at the time of the French and Austrian invasion during the Napoleonic wars) and the second during the nineteenth century, at the time of the war of independence. Bandettini's research[89] on the Tuscan population indicates a constant increase in the number of illegitimates that was clearly connected with political and juridical phenomena (the unification of Italy and the introduction of civil marriage). The Tuscan situation mirrored the situation throughout Italy, as the studies of Benini[90] and Raseri[91] show. Only in this period did Italy attain the level of economic, social, political, and cultural development reached by other continental countries at least fifty years before: and the moral (and religious) crisis follows with precise punctuality. Bandettini[92] gives figures for specific areas of Tuscany. (see p. 123.)

The province of Lucca, where percentages were particularly low,

Illegitimates per 100 births in various districts of Tuscany 1863–66

District	1863	1864	1865	1866
Province of Arezzo	4.88	4.68	4.62	5.77
Province of Florence (excluding Rocca S. Casciano, Pistoia e S. Miniato)	8.27	8.97	8.80	9.22
Province of Livorno	5.64	6.82	6.48	6.35
Province of Lucca and district of Garfagnana	1.82	1.93	1.57	2.47
Province of Massa Carrara (excluding the district of Garfagnana)	3.51	2.81	3.34	3.37
Province of Pisa and district of S. Miniato	3.13	3.26	3.18	3.85
District of Pistoia	5.04	4.67	5.37	5.45

is still today the region of Tuscany where overall religious practice is the highest (except, for obvious reasons, the coastal area). It seems likely that there is a relationship between the illegitimate birth-rate and religious practice.

Let us conclude our remarks on Italy by citing our own research on Lion (near Padua) for which we have collected data both on illegitimate births and on children born less than eight months from the date of marriage, for whom illegitimate conception is thus probable.[93] The following results (in percentages) were obtained:

Illegitimate and irregular births in Lion

Year	Irregular births for all marriages	Irregular births for all births	Illegitimate births for all births
1740–1750	?	?	0
1817–1821	0	0	0
1851–1855	3.44	0.67	0
1906–1910	29.44	4.40	0.39
1931–1935	43.10	8.99	2.53
1938–1942	31.14	8.63	1.81
1950–1955	31.95	16.40	4.25

In conclusion, during these centuries the percentage of illegitimates continues to grow, in spite of brief periods of stability and long periods of decrease. This shows *at least* a progressive relaxation of morals, which seems to coincide with a process of religious decline.

Other indices of religiosity suggest the character of this process. Thus, although we do not have as continuous information for the rate of religious vocations as we have for illegitimate births, we are able to compare the percentages in particular periods. In the fifteenth, sixteenth, seventeenth, and eighteenth centuries, the number of priests was particularly high. Including both secular and religious clergy, their number oscillated between one priest for every ten people, as against the 300, 1,000, or even 10,000 inhabitants per priest in various parts of contemporary Christendom.

The percentage of priests, monks, and nuns was continuously high in Rome between the fourteenth and seventeenth centuries.[94]

	1313–39	1591	1592	1595	1603
priests	785	—	1,221	1,776	1,241
monks	451	1,605	1,489	2,001	1,819
nuns	470	2,080	1,641	2,339	2,693
TOTAL	1,706	3,685	4,351	6,116	5,753
total population	—	—	99,627	93,671	104,878
ecclesiastics in %	—	—	4.4	6.5	5.5
members of religious orders in %			3.1	4.6	4.3

For Bologna, where the situation was the same, we have the following data, for members of religious orders only.[95]

	1570	1581	1591	1600	1617	1645
monks	1,112	1,165	1,123	1,091	983	1,208
nuns	2,198	2,255	2,430	2,461	2,631	2,429
TOTAL	3,310	3,420	3,553	3,552	3,614	3,637
total population	61,742	70,661	64,673	64,844	67,871	58,565
% in religious orders	5.3	4.8	5.5	5.7	5.2	6.2

The situation was not very different in the other cities and regions of Italy. Members of religious orders accounted for 4.2 per cent of the population of Brescia (1600), for 3 per cent at Bergamo (1583), for 3.3 per cent at Vicenza (1585), 7.5 per cent at Treviso (1639). In

Verona during the same period, 4 per cent were members of the secular clergy.

In Siena the members of religious orders accounted for 9.3 per cent of the population in 1657 to 10.9 per cent in 1670. In Pisa they were 6.2 per cent (1662); in Pistoia 8.9 per cent (1672) and during the same year 11.2 per cent in Prato.

In Naples 2.2 per cent of the population were members of religious orders in 1596; 2.5 per cent in 1599; and 1.9 per cent in 1606. In Ferrara in 1604, 6.2 per cent were monks and nuns; in Perugia in 1588, 8.4 per cent; in Modena in 1620, 5 per cent; in Piacenza in 1618, about 5 per cent, in 1758 about 9 per cent; in Lodi in 1608, 4.2 per cent.

In many areas the situation does not change throughout the seventeenth century, as the figures concerning Tuscany show:

	1622	1642	1663	1672
monks	916	1,027	893	1,069
nuns	4,001	3,733	3,912	2,888
TOTAL	4,917	4,760	4,805	3,957
population	66,056	69,465	66,249	69,783
% monks and nuns	7.4	6.9	7.2	5.6

The following are data from Catania for 1639 and 1675:

	1639	1675
priests	132	—
unordained clergy	229	—
monks and nuns	—	905
TOTAL	361	905
population	14,602	16,421
ecclesiastics %	2.5	—
monks and nuns %	—	5.5

In a previously cited work, Beloch sums up the situation for a number of Italian cities giving the percentage of the total population who were monks and nuns between the sixteenth and the seventeenth centuries. (See page 126.)

Prato	1672	11.2	Bologna	1645	6.2
Siena	1670	10.9	,,	1600	5.7
,,	1657	9.3	,,	1591	5.5
Pistoia	1672	8.9	Catania	1675	5.5
Perugia	1588	8.4	Bologna	1570	5.4
Treviso	1639	7.5	,,	1617	5.2
Florence	1622	7.4	Modena	1620	5.0
,,	1663	7.2	Bologna	1581	4.8
,,	1642	6.9	Rome	1595	4.6
Pisa	1622	6.2	,,	1603	4.3
Ferrara	1601	6.2	Brescia	1600 c.	4.2
Piacenza	1618	4.0	Venice	1593	2.5
Vicenza	1585	3.3	Lodi	1605	2.4
Rome	1592	3.1	Naples	1596	2.3
Bergamo	1583	3.0	Venice	1563	2.0
Naples	1509	2.5	Naples	1606	1.9
Venice	1586	2.5	Venice	1552	1.8

The highest percentages are in central Italy, the lowest at Venice and Naples. But the situation had already changed in the eighteenth century.

Beloch reports in his summary a total percentage for Italy of 1.8 per cent, although this refers to secular clergy (including those who were not yet ordained) and regular clergy (male and female) including the 'lay sisters'.

	priests	monks	nuns	TOTAL	%	population
Kingdom of Sicily (1737)	22,430	13,179	11,397	47,006	3.6	1,307,270
Kingdom of Naples (1804)	35,627	17,928	15,490	69,045	1.4	4,984,639
Sardinia (1751)	2,055	2,000	—	4,055	1.1	369,861
Grand Duchy of Tuscany (1758)	12,007	5,501	9,400	26,908	2.0	924,625
Republic of Venice (1766)	22,307	7,770	10,790	41,075	1.8	2,334,972
Duchy of Mantua (1786)	950	415	400	1,765	1.1	156,528
Duchy of Modena (1767)	7,013	1,797	—	8,810	3.2	275,646

	priests	monks	nuns	TOTAL	%	population	
Duchy of Parma (1758)	3,412	965	819	5,196	2.5	200,425	
Duchy of Milan (1774)	9,967	4,815	6,555	21,337	1.9	1,110,152	
Piedmont (1734)	8,621	—	—	—	0.6 }	1,496,390 }	1,625,576
					1.3		(average)
Piedmont (1750–55)	) —	6,860	5,212	12,072	0.7)	1,774,763 }	
City of Rome (1760)	2,865	3,836	1,797	8,498	5.4	157,085	
				245,767	1.8	13,446,734	

As Beloch tells us, the statistics are largely incomplete for many of these states, excluding, among other things, data for entire regions,[96] but within these limitations it is indicative enough for our own purposes.

In Tuscany, in 1745 the situation was as follows:

dioceses and prelacies	regular and secular clergy		dioceses and prelacies	regular and secular clergy	
	absolute number	per 100 laymen		absolute number	per 100 laymen
Florence	7,577	3.68	Bologna	74	1.32
Fiesole	1,480	2.24	Lucca	298	2.96
Pistoia & Prato	2,238	2.86	Sarzana	1,213	3.61
			Brugnate	166	1.01
S. Miniato	1,008	2.24	Imola	13	2.02
Colle	292	2.51	Faenza	403	1.19
Borgo S. Sepolero	599	4.69	Forli	83	1.29
			Bertinoro	122	2.63
Pisa	1,831	2.57	Sarsina	32	1.21
Siena	2,064	5.99	Montefeltro	4	2
Soana	314	2.63	Citta di Castello	2	0.80
Massa	136	2.76			
Grosseto	177	3.09	Citta della	56	2.66

dioceses and prelacies	regular and secular clergy		dioceses and prelacies	regular and secular clergy	
	absolute number	per 100 laymen		absolute number	per 100 laymen
Chiusi	569	4.26	Pieve		
Arezzo	2,600	2.93	Acquapendente	18	3.49
Cortona	620	4.42	Arcipr. di	59	3.86
Pienza	361	2.31	Sestino		
Montalcino	182	2.72	Abb. di	108	3
Montepulciano	363	5.54	Bagno		
Volterra	1,205	3.23	Abb. di S.	219	2.21
Pescia	1,023	3.53	Ellero		
			Abb. delle 3 font.	16	1.89
			Granduchy as a whole	27,486	3.253

But as Parenti rightly remarks:

> the variability in the relationship between the clergy and the lay
> population is considerable, since these local units are
> heterogeneous from our point of view. In the first place, there are
> parts of the dioceses and prelacies which do not include the
> population of the city centre, which is the seat of the bishop and
> has a strong attraction for the clergy of the diocese. We can get
> some ideas of the intensity of this attraction if we look at Siena,
> Prato, Pistoia, and Pisa. In these four cities, the clergy accounted
> for 13.63 per cent, 12.23 per cent, 10.98 per cent, and 8.51 per
> cent respectively, of the population of the town. If we compare
> these percentages with those for the dioceses as a whole, we see
> that the percentages of clergy in the centres where the bishop held
> his see was about four times what it was in the diocesan con-
> stituencies as a whole.

For our purposes, this geographical distribution is not very
significant, but the figures taken as a whole have some use for a
global valuation.[97]

These statistical data are indirectly confirmed by those available
for the eighteenth century, and for the Papal States.

	priests	monks	nuns	total	%	population
Bologna (1708)	1,656	1,724	1,757	5,137	2.3	222,511
Ravenna (1701)	—	423	368	—	[1.7]	44,637
Cesena (1656)	—	—	—	588	2.6	22,640
Gubbio (1708)	515	201	467	1,183	4.5	24,866
Perugia (1708)	—		1,606	—	[3.5]	48,700
Todi (1708)	—		416	—	[1.9]	23,208
Città di Castello (1708)	—		614	—	[2.1]	29,235
Ripatransone (1708) —		144		—	[1.4]	10,729

Over all, according to Beloch, the percentage of the Italian population constituting priests and religious of both sexes in the middle of the eighteenth century was about 1.9 per cent. It remained at this level until the French Revolution, or perhaps until the French invasion of Italy. Beloch concludes that when we analyse the figures for the various periods and when (we might add) we consider that they refer sometimes to regions, sometimes to states, and sometimes to cities, then we may equally conclude that the percentage of people in the religious profession was more or less stable until about the last half of the eighteenth century. After that, there was a decline that expressed, among other things, a change in mores, which eventually led to a crisis in religious vocations. Between the fourteenth and eighteenth centuries, religious vocations reached percentages that were very high when compared to those of contemporary times.[98] Yet, we must not forget that these percentages reflect the real situation only within certain limits. On the one hand, in many cases, and for a long time, the monasteries were not able to accept all of the aspirants. Thus, at the convent of Santa Chiara in Assisi, in 1492, the bishop, Marcello Crescenzi, had to choose two new nuns from fourteen aspirants. On the other hand, we must recall the conditions under which individuals became members of religious orders. To have a daughter who was a nun was an honour and an advantage. Some children were received into convents at seven years of age, although they could not become nuns until later (at the age of sixteen at Santa Chiara). Clearly, at seven they made no spiritual choice.[99]

Following a few warning signs, the percentage of religious vocations decreased rapidly almost everywhere at the time of the French Revolution.[100] This can be seen in data about Bologna.[101]

Year	Ecclesiastics per 100 inhabitants	Year	Ecclesiastics per 100 inhabitants
1570	5.4	1729	5.2
1573	5.2	1741	5.5
1581	4.8	1759	5.6
1587	4.9	1761	5.7
1588	4.4	1764	5.7
1591	5.5	1768	6.2
1595	6.1	1771	6.1
1597	5.6	1774	6.5
1600	5.6	1777	6.2
1606	5.6	1784	5.8
1617	5.3	1791	5.3
1624	5.8	1799	0.8
1631	7.4	1822	1.0
1645	6.5	1843	1.3
1708	6.4	1844	1.3
1718	5.5	1845	1.4

These data alone indicate the way in which the decline took place:
in many areas of Italy, the percentage of those who attend church
today is much lower than the percentage who wore the habit not only
in the Renaissance but even as late as the eighteenth century.

Taken together, the crisis in religious vocations and the increase in
illegitimacy have a clear significance. The percentage of illegitimates
was very high from the fourteenth to the eighteenth centuries. Then,
it began to decline, not because of the force of Christian morality,
but simply because men 'become more skilled in their evil ways'.
Then began the crisis of religious vocations which, apparently, has
not yet reached its culmination. Finally, there is the crisis in religious
practice, particularly between the eighteenth and the nineteenth
centuries, accompanied by the wide diffusion of unbelief[102] and the
collapse of popular religiosity. Nor is there any lack of further
symptoms[103] of this decline in sensibility to the sacred, although they
cannot be discussed here.[104]

The percentage of those who did not practise in the eighteenth
century was not yet very high and the geography of the progress of
irreligion began to become clear only towards the end of the century.

The available information indicates the universality of religious practice before that time. For example, the figures for Rome during the seventeenth and eighteenth centuries confirm the general trend: the total number of those who have not taken communion was extremely low. [105]

	1602	1652	1702	1760
those eligible	80,082	90,959	106,740	119,509
others	19,230	28,088	31,828	37,576
total	99,312	119,047	138,568	157,085
correct total	same	118,047	same	same
communicants	79,758	88,899	106,592	
non-communicants	324	87	148	
	80,082	88,986	106,740	

Burgalassi, who has a wide knowledge of the progress of religious practice in Tuscany, seems by and large to concur with our hypothesis concerning a delayed decline in religious practice. He remarks that:

practice and the frequency of communion have undergone a change from the times in which all who attended Sunday mass took communion (the apostolic period) to the crisis of the barbarian invasions and the successive religious reconquest of these barbarians. We shall thus see that although taking communion had again become common practice around the year 1000, it was later affected by growing abstension, limited at first but becoming more widespread. In a Tuscan diocese in 1468 one frequently finds 'multi non confitentur nec communicant' or 'non omnes communicant', (N. Caturegli, *Popoli e parroci della diocesi di Pisa nel secolo XV*, 'Orientamenti sociali', XV, May 1959, n. 5, pp. 173–8), although there are still parishes where everyone confesses and takes communion. Someone does not take communion because 'the Easter season is short' (it was in fact six days). Of some it is said that 'iam pluribus annis non faciunt'.

The decrease in the number of communicants becomes rather serious in Renaissance Florence and in Jansenist Tuscany, but they slowly returned to their normal figures towards the end of the eighteenth century. Also in the nineteenth century, when political vicissitudes did not leave the church and religious practice unaffected, we find the figures oscillating. And even in the twentieth century between 1903 and 1907, we find many places where those who usually observe Easter at once stop doing so when confronted with a particular phenomenon (such as the foundation of red leagues, socialist proselitizing, strikes, etc.). As we have noted elsewhere, in the parish of Basati this development occurs most markedly in 1905. [106]

With a few strokes, Burgalassi thus depicts a development which, in some of its aspects, was repeated almost everywhere. On the other hand, the diffusion of authentic irreligion or the true profession of atheism was generally slow in Italy and in parts of France, occurring to quite a different rhythm. [107] This is confirmed by Barengo's information on the Venetian Republic, where, although fairly restricted, the activities of the Supreme Tribunal were significant in this connection. Berengo observes that:

the first signs of unbelief, being of what one might call a learned origin, appear in the Masonic world where the fraternal spirit was often tinged with deism. Figures like Count Vimercati Sanseverini of Crema, who died in Parma in 1785 refusing the sacraments and declaring himself faithful to the laws of the sect and to the cult of a Supreme Being, cannot have been unknown among the nobility of the Venetian mainland. The very tone of these secret societies, in the growing prevalence of the Enlightenment climate and of a culture that was based on the eighteenth century French writers, led to the formation of heterodox attitudes. . . . Some indications of irreligiosity were to be found in previous decades. Here is a porter belonging to the craft of cheesemakers who asserts that 'he doesn't believe in what he doesn't see and that the Holy Fathers are men like us', and who makes fun of Paradise 'showing that he doesn't believe in it'. And here is another man of the people who affirms 'that things happen by chance and that priests do everything for money'. Here is someone who defines as 'whimsical' 'the explanation given of the Scriptures by priests and interpreters'. These are indications that Catholic orthodoxy is being rejected or completely revised in the name of reason. [108]

And again 'From these stirrings of unbelief, the development toward revolutionary atheism seems direct and clear.'[109]

None the less, the religiosity in the Venetian provinces was still solid during this period. Berengo himself observes that:

> true atheism is rare and is to be found mostly only among the learned. Whoever studies the few trials conducted by the Holy Office in the last two decades of the eighteenth century and the vast documentation of the state Inquisitors will soon become aware of a not insignificant fact: the charge of Jacobinism is usually made by an informer or by the Venetian representative who uses his own spies and is, in short, of official and police origin. The unbeliever, on the other hand, is always charged as such by a citizen, and sometimes by three or four together. In the trials, then, while in the first case there is often a witness who doesn't know, who doesn't remember or who had heard exactly the opposite and attempts to reduce the charge, in the second case the accused is surrounded by a halo of diffidence and antipathy, and it is very rare that someone comes to his defence.[110]

If this is true for Venice, it is also true for other parts of Europe. In the diocese of Padua, between 1744 and 1753, we find 0.09 per cent of the people of the entire diocese, as against 0.43 per cent in the city, refusing to go to confession. Two centuries later, in 1960, in some country parishes, 50 per cent of the population did not go to confession.[111] The religious decline in practice, which began in the fourteenth or fifteenth centuries, became most marked between the end of the eighteenth and the mid-twentieth centuries. From the increase in illegitimacy, we see a subsequent decline in religious vocations, followed by decline in the rate of religious practice, and with this a fall in church membership.[112]

3. IRRELIGIOSITY TODAY: URBAN, SOCIAL, AND INDUSTRIAL DEVELOPMENT AS CAUSES OF THE CRISIS

Our documentation of the development of irreligiosity in the period before the industrial revolution has as yet done no more than provide general indications of the causes of the decline of religion, to which we must now turn. It is noticeably the urban centres that first gave rise to sizeable irreligious groups. Subsequently urban mores were diffused throughout the countryside, and the causes of urban religious decline made themselves felt in rural environments. [113]

Contending that urbanization did not in itself have such an effect on religiosity, some authors have observed that even in the past there were migrations of the kind that have given rise to modern urban structures and to high levels of geographic mobility. This thesis is arguable: yet, although there were large migrations in the past, it is evident that they were prevalently rural phenomena, or were connected with the development of crafts and urban services, and had very different characteristics from modern industrial migrations. Apart from the formation of the great Greek and Roman cities, and perhaps excluding the cities of Phoenicia, Carthagiania, and Egypt, sizeable urban migrations did not occur in Europe before the eighteenth century. The highest incidence of rapid urbanization occurred between 1750 and 1970, [114] and these were the two centuries which saw the highest rise of irreligion. Before this time few large urban conglomerates existed. Paris, with its perhaps 200,000 in the fourteenth century, [115] was an exception, while the major Italian cities had populations of about 30,000 (and in that period Italy was not only the cultural, but also to a considerable extent, the economic centre of Europe). Explosive urban development occurred only in the eighteenth century, [116] when the primarily commercial and artisan urban expansion of previous centuries was transformed in scale by industrialization.

Since the really pronounced symptoms of desacralization occurred in this period, the industrial revolution might all too easily be regarded as the cause of desacralization. Yet, it must be clear that there are both persisting causes of this process, and new reinforcing causes. Le Bras justly remarks that there have always been those who were disposed to be irreligious, sceptical, and apathetic. [117] There have always been professions that recruit rebels against every form of religion, or at least of organized religion, even if not to the extent that this has been the case since the beginning of the eighteenth century. Serious disturbances in ecclesiastical organizations and serious immorality have always occurred, although they are quickly overcome. Thus, at the beginning of the eighteenth century, the economy of European society still bore the marks of the Thirty Years War: but although destruction and poverty were widespread, a return to religion appears to have been very rapid. The Seven Years War, perhaps more terrible at the moral and economic level, did not leave behind the serious religious after-effects that became the normal and usually irreparable results of later wars. But if these effects of war became worse, so too, the effects of urban life became more profound, as the cities came to protect — almost jealously — the irreligiosity that they had been slowly acquiring. Thus, in inter-personal differences in dispositions, in the proclivities of some professional groups, in ecclesial disturbances, and in wars, there are causes to reinforce the irreligiosity of the city, which is their most receptive locale.

The new conditions or urban and industrial life clearly intensified the process of desacralization, until by the nineteenth century it had become a conspicuous aspect of social reality. The nucleus from which desacralization radiated was predominantly urban, and the countryside followed the city as ideas and life-style percolated from urban to rural areas, a process which, slow till the French Revolution, then acquired speed and intensity. By the end of the nineteenth century, country dwellers had begun to imitate city life, and the differences between town and country diminished, in some respects virtually to disappear in the twentieth century, even in the religious sphere. Centres, once classified as agricultural, become urban even though their population does not increase: none the less, their structural characteristics, the habits of life of the people, the attitudes that prevail, become town-like.

Both Boulard and Remy[118] regard variations in religious practice as conditioned by the expansion of urban conglomerates, by their size, and by the influence of the suburban and peripheral population. They point out that urban practice is connected with practice in the surrounding rural areas, and that the countryside often has a lower rate of practice than the neighbouring cities: and this is particularly the case when the rates of practice are relatively low. This fact, however, does not contradict the thesis propounded here, but rather shows that in the countryside phenomena such as social control have a stronger influence. Nor need we be surprised that it is the smaller cities that have a very low practice rate, if again we consider the phenomenon of social control. That there is unity between city and surrounding countryside does not contradict the contention that the city is the area in which the crisis in religious practice first appears. If this is not clear at the level of more refined statistical analysis, it becomes apparent when one analyses the historical genesis of the phenomenon, and considers that the communication of religious innovation moves from the city into the countryside, even though particular phenomena may return from countryside to city. Typical in this respect is the case of Marxism which was developed in the cities in the context of an urban life style and urban problems, but in a later revolutionary phase, especially in underdeveloped countries, was re-launched toward the city by the peasant masses who assimilated it.

In summary, let us make the following observations: (1) *Historically*, it is clear that the phenomenon of irreligiosity proceeds from the city to the countryside. (2) *Currently*, particularly in the countries where irreligiosity is more advanced, differences between countryside and city are scarcely noticeable. (3) *Culturally*, the distribution of religious practice over large geographical areas shows the extent to which it is bound up with regional cultures. (4) *Macroscopically*, the crisis of religious practice is a product of the development of an urban life style (a phenomenon which clearly now affects the countryside as much as the city) and of industrial civilization, although it is often, and for the reasons we have indicated, a crisis that is stronger in the countryside.

The process of desacralization affects all the institutions of society, formal and informal, in association with urbanization and industrialization.[119] Thus, the family, which for centuries was an eminently conservative agency with respect to the sacred, has undergone a profound transformation.[120] From being a closed nucleus it became an 'open' group, and, unlike the patriarchal family, no longer maintains itself unchanged from generation to generation — nor does it maintain and defend common traditions. For centuries before the modern age, the family, as the focal centre of social life, kept the individual immune from external influence to a large extent. Today, the structure of the nucleus formed by the parents and the young children has become molecular and inter-family relations are to a large extent being replaced by external social relations. The accelerating changes in the family favour change in the religious environment, not least in the changing attitudes to sexuality.

Political processes also bear on the problem of desacralization: the class struggle, the protest of 'frustrated' and exploited social groups against those who hold power, power struggles between religious and non-religious movements, have all been channels for the dissemination of irreligious attitudes, both because of the overt appeal that is made to irreligious values, and because class action strengthens these values by arousing the resentment of 'frustrated' classes towards dominant groups which have so often appealed to religious values in defence of their own positions.[121]

We refer to the family and to politics purely by way of illustrating the ramifications of the desacralization process in other areas of life. Nor can we ignore the connections with, for instance, hedonism, critical acumen, political consciousness, the tendency to public contentiousness, insensitivity or sentimentality, among other un-quantifiable qualities that characterize society at particular points of time. The emergence of new professions and the texture of social relationships, are no less to the point, but in this case we can perhaps relate religion to class, age, occupation, and other quantitative values.[122] Yet, these various items do not clarify the dynamics of the desacralization process, and in seeking some general principles, we must be aware of the consequences that these changes have produced in the rhythm of life.

A commonplace, but one that is by no means unimportant, is the time distribution of everyday life. There is less time for meditation, for religiosity, for those intimate concerns that belong to the periods of rest. New patterns of work and leisure have left less room for religious life. The very organization of the modern day has become a hindrance to religiosity, squeezing out religious experience.[123] The cinema, the press, the radio, by focussing on profane concerns mount a constant psychological attack on the personality. The effect, little as it may be intended, is to make religious concerns appear unduly remote. The sensual and the material are favoured by this development. In the technicized anonymity of the city, the individual finds himself rootless, and this, too, may be seen as promoting the spread of eroticism.[124]

Chelini, in his work, *La ville et l'Église*, lists some factors that have affected, and in part still affect, desacralization, such as housing conditions, work, the acquisitive mentality, the increased tendency for women to do paid work, commerce, popular dancing, the club, the bar, means of transport, and the automobile.[125] These are all phenomena that have all in turn spread to the countryside, of course. [126] Today there is no village not easily accessible from the city, and no rural area where the technology and the mores of the city have not become established. The areas of low religious practice, often the area surrounding the cities, thus grow larger. Through these concurring and extending developments, the psychology of modern man appears to have become deeply rationalized: men now live in circumstances in which they are permanently served by machines, the influence of which is profound and intimate. The human individual is, willy-nilly, affected by the unified technical environment that completely surrounds him — an environment so different from the natural environment of earlier times. [127]

The significant impact of this development is recent. Until the early seventeenth century, technology was still primitive, and man was still directly exposed to the elements. The horse was still the most rapid means of transport, and man was still in contact with the natural components of the universe — earth, water, fire. [128] Religion was naturally affected by this state of knowledge and technology. It is a commonplace of the sociology of religion to point to the connection between religious phenomena and technical and scientific development. Thus Yinger observes that 'the more primitive the technology and the more precarious and uncertain the results from one's efforts to obtain food and other goods, the more religion is used to bolster man's efforts.' [129] He sees a functional connection both in individual cases and in general. [130] As man has become the master of his environment, the function of labour has changed, and with it there have occurred changes in human psychology that have affected man's religious sense of things. But although human labour has changed over the centuries, they have never changed with the rapidity and profundity of recent times. Modern technology, the creation of a technologically determined environment, have produced a result that is in some respects entirely new. If we examine periods of history in which profound changes occurred, we may, by comparison with our own times, discern the determining importance of scientific-technological components.

Thus, many phenomena familiar in our new technico-industrial society, including spiritual phenomena, were also to be found in a society such as Rome, where transformations in some ways similar to contemporary changes took place, but the technological-scientific aspect was of course by no means so evident. Even where there were developments such as the growth of a large labour force, a proletariat, and where new ideas were easily received and taken up, those ideas in themselves came from centres where the nature of industrial change had been most powerfully affected by technico-scientific change. Indeed, there appears to be a certain analogy between the desacralizing psychological consequences of changes in the work environment and the economy on the one hand, and those occurring in the technological-scientific sphere, on the other. This appears to be the reason for the rapid penetration of ideas that result from technological, scientific, and industrial development into other spheres of society in which a large proletariat exists — even if it is a proletariat that is essentially agricultural in its character. Only in this way are we able to explain the low rates of practice and the lack of religiosity in economically and culturally depressed areas such as large parts of Spain, Portugal, and southern Italy.

A distinction may be made *in the first phase* of the religious crisis as it occurs among agricultural workers on the one hand, and in-dustrial workers on the other. Broadly speaking, among industrial workers, the technological-scientific attitude and the mores of the new society are absorbed through what might be said in the main to be direct experience. Among agricultural workers, in contrast, the contact with industrial civilization is in large part mediated through vehicles such as trades unions, schools, and political movements that answer the immediate requirements of the agricultural worker and his world by introducing ideas from the technological society, and the mental attitudes that prevail there.

Sometimes, ideas born in industrial society penetrate agricultural areas before technology itself arrives to produce its own direct psychological effect, but this does not mean the new technological mentality, once it has been acquired and its ideological orientations understood, cannot be equally stable and deep-rooted.

One principal objection to the foregoing argument is that desacralization derives from contingent factors, such as the disorganization of the clergy, and from other dislocations that, it might be said, the churches could themselves easily remedy. Thus, it is argued, that if the spread of unbelief is 'mediated' by propaganda, then counter-propaganda might be used to halt this advancing desacralization. Certainly, this consideration cannot be altogether dismissed, but lack of counter-propaganda cannot be regarded as a determining cause of desacralization. The weaknesses of the clergy have always existed, but there has not always been a crisis of religion. As Desqueyrat remarks:

> . . . if the English churches are deserted, this cannot be due to the fact that in France Catholic baptisms and funerals are performed according to graded categories of ceremony, or to the fact that the Third Republic has been anti-clerical. . . . If the Chinese become materialists, it is not because French Catholics are, or are thought to be, idiots and criminals, or because French schooling is secular, free, and compulsory. [131]

Clearly, more profound causes are at work that quite transcend the local and episodic that are sometimes invoked by way of explanation of particular cases. The policies of the churches, the extent of religious propaganda, the education of children — are all at best only local factors in process of decline, but they do not make decisive difference, although they may, if the general circumstances of social evolution permit, contribute to the process. The central facts undoubtedly include the development of science and technology.

Of the character of technology, we may agree with Simondon, when he writes:

> . . . by reducing the object to nothing but its dimensions, technology does not recognize in it any internal or symbolic meaning, or any significance beyond its purely functional utility . . . the object is sufficient in itself, and is not the carrier of intentions. For this reason, one might say that 'technology desacralizes the world' to the extent that it progressively imprisons man in nothing but objects, without allowing him to catch a glimpse of a higher reality. [132]

The importance of a study of the essential differences between the pre-technical and the technical worlds with respect to the transformation of religiosity is obvious. Studies of this kind have been undertaken by many specialists, but none has yet produced a comprehensive theory that might serve as a basis for further research. The effect of technological transformations is always greater than superficial analysis initially reveals. This is particularly the case when an invention is used by a large number of people — a banal example is contraceptive devices. In the long run this leads to a transformation in the behaviour of women, not merely sexually (the aspects first seized upon) but because eventually they find themselves with more leisure, and so occupy themselves with issues that previously, when bearing and rearing children, they had no time for. Thus result changes in political, social, and cultural life, in income distribution, relations between social classes, and so on. Thus, apart from the influence in its own area of rational application, a technical device exerts influence over a wide area of secondary effects. To encompass all this, an interdisciplinary approach is clearly essential, and only with such an approach will the implications for religion be made fully apparent. The analysis to be followed here has two phases, one primarily empirical, and the other more abstract and theoretical, rooted as far as possible in social psychology.

4. INDIVIDUAL BEHAVIOUR AS A LOGICO-COGNITIVE CATEGORY: ITS SIGNIFICANCE IN THE CONTEXT OF INDUSTRIAL SOCIETY

We may distinguish three levels of analysis of religious behaviour: that typical of social groups or agglomerates (i.e. religion in urban contexts); that typical of individuals specified in terms of their position within social groups (i.e. the religious behaviour of the worker, the clerk, etc.); and the behaviour of the individual as an expression of his psychology. The principal key to the solution of the problems of religious dynamics in modern society lies in research conducted at the third level. We accept the position of Landheer in regarding the individual as historically and logically prior to the group, and even though personality changes are influenced by changes in the group, we take the individual as the fundamental unit.[133]

To relate religiosity to its urban and rural setting, as we have done in foregoing pages, does not explain adequately the development of religiosity. What are offered are purely contingent factors, variable in time, and in need of repeated verification, or broad correlations in themselves without causal significance. This approach may help to clarify the significance of individual changes that affect or condition religious practice, but it does not expose its full significance nor indicate its more remote origins. For this we are obliged to seek in the individual's psychology: only there shall we find the relation between changes in society and those in attitudes toward religion and in the sense of the sacred. Only after touching on the level at which the individual meets the social is it possible to refer back to the social itself in a widened perspective.

Starting with the individual as a group member, viewed from a religious point of view, we must consider that

> the individual possesses an aptitude to select among his diverse experiences, in such a way as to arrange into a coherent whole, capable of being judged as such, the ego, objects, and others. Sets of symbols and consciousness of self are encompassed as elements in a system of ego-objects-others relations, that is a social system. [134]

In this we may recognize the connection that exists between given socio-structural conditions and given religious attitudes, which in themselves might be considered as flowing purely from an individual's will. The ego-objects-others triad leads to concepts of role and attitude. [135] The position of the individual as group member may thus be referred to the role he occupies, without, however, ignoring the fact that, as he performs his functions, each individual makes selections and forms judgments.

As we have remarked in a previously cited work, 'each social relationship, in that it refers to given others and to given objects, constitutes a mutual adaptation and at the same time a combination of the individuals it involves.' [136] Furthermore, 'such a combination can maintain itself and function toward the preservation and the evolution of the social relationships in question, only on condition that each individual in the combination should be aware of the meanings of his own gesture and of how he stands within the network of relations of which the gesture is a part'; [137] and, one may add, on condition that his attitude should be correspondingly oriented. Thus the individual must become conscious of his own gesture or attitude, and grasp the *meaning* it assumes with respect to himself and others.

Quite often, even in the absence of any theoretical rejection of religion, individuals cease practising religion, praying, and holding religious attitudes. Their new modes of behaviour and new attitudes, often adopted within contexts characterized by high urbanization, immorality, technology, or a combination of these, involve precisely the selective activity previously indicated. Naturally such selections may be made *a priori* or *a posteriori*, wholesale or piecemeal; often the new roles and attitudes are adopted without surrendering tenets with which they are in conflict, thus frequently engendering psychological tensions.

At any rate, an individual who takes up roles and attitudes generated by industrial, urban, and technologized society, is by the same token involved with people, ideas, and objects that differ profoundly from those that he has previously known, particularly on the religious plane.

But if shared impulses engender shared reactions, if the exercise of selection favours shared judgments and attitudes, if, in sum, a modern, urbanized, and technologized society possesses distinctive sets of roles, then clearly such a situation places the individual under pressures that continuously and coherently modify his personality. The utility of this concept for the purpose of grasping the psychological features of individuals who live the new roles is apparent. Apparent, in fact, up to a point, since one must allow for the considerable diversity (in space and over time) of the roles and correspondingly of the attitudes.

This diversity, however, is not so great as to make it impossible to formulate general logical categories of the kind we need. For all their variety and complexity, all roles connected with the desacralization of society share some characteristics. Thanks to these it is possible, on the one hand, to view those roles in a unified perspective, and on the other, to specify their impact on the individual's psychology within which the dynamics of desacralization develop.

For all the variation in personality features and in the attitudes connected with them, the new roles which have emerged in such great numbers over the last two centuries display a surprising continuity and consistency. The changes in personalities, habits, and ideas that we have previously discussed amount, in face, to changes in the general psychology of society. Given (a) that such changes have taken place; (b) that they have given expression to new roles and attitudes, and finally (c) that by involving ideas, attitudes, and roles, they have amounted to psychological changes — it then behoves us to think beyond the duality of socio-economic context (roles) and ideological and cultural setting (group ideas), and to think instead of a three-fold set: roles (with attendant attitudes); ideas; and overall human psychology.[138]

To sum up: in the first phase of our study, having acknowledged the existence of a desacralization process, we have established a (as it were) mechanical connection between certain facts and that process. In a second phase we have indicated that the connection involves roles and attitudes engendered by the new structure of society. With reference to these we have then indicated a further connection significant for our theme between the individual and ideas. To close, the chain of our argument we must now deal briefly with the individual and his psychology.

In order to do so we must sketch, on the one hand, the evolution of the individual's psychological orientation over the period in question, and, on the other hand, the evolution of the new roles. We shall then find it possible to put forward a logical model for the interpretation of the process of desacralization and secularization.

5. TRENDS IN PSYCHOLOGICAL ORIENTATION AS A GENERAL PHENOMENON: ITS BEARING ON THE CRISIS OF RELIGION

The transformation of man's cognitive and psychological make-up has of course been a long process, which we do not need to follow through in detail. The themes presented in the following pages, are partly a re-statement of well-established findings in social science as they bear on our concerns, [139] but very few of these transformations in psychology, in which even the nuances are sometimes of importance, have been examined in relation to contemporary religion in the way in which we propose to review them.

Friedmann has used the following categories in his attempt to deal with changes in contemporary psychology: [140] (a) changes in the rhythm of life; (b) changes in the conception of time; (c) changes in sensitivity and perception; (d) changes in mentality. The philosophy behind this classification presupposes that man both adapts to the environment in which he lives, and has the power to act upon it; has a receptive, communicative, and active system similar in some respects to that of animals; and a symbolic and ritual capacity that permits him to communicate. He communicates through a language based on common-sense, feelings, scientific understanding, artistic sense, and so on. When we speak of an evolution that affects the senses of rhythm and time, sensitivity and perception, we are dividing the homogeneous flow of experience, of knowledge, and of human communication into working logical categories. Our classification is not Friedmann's but it is broadly similar, comprising three sections (a) rhythm, space, and time; (b) sensitivity and perception; and (c) cognitive attitudes.

(a) Rhythm, space, and time

All concepts, ideas, and theories must have a location in space and time. Harvey Cox has remarked that, 'As a new religious vision may modify the sense of time and space, so may a new sense of time and space modify the religious vision.' Thus an evolution in the representation and perception of space and time is one integral component of the total evolution of human experience. There is a transition from the almost biological representation by the primitives and their cultures all the way to the most modern scientific theories. But, at least in part, such a transformation reflects changes in man's experience of space and time; and a profound change in the rhythm of life itself is connected with that transformation. A pre-technical society possesses a natural rhythm, derived from the seasons, day, night, the weather, animal life, and the human body, sensitivity, and perception; (d) changes in mentality.

This four-fold classification may be open to objection, but they are useful as working categories. The philosophy behind this classification presupposes the validity of the idea that man both adapts to the environment in which he lives and can act upon it, possesses a receptive and a communicative and active system that is partly shared with animals; and a symbolic (and ritual) system that allows him to communicate. He communicates through a language based on common sense, a language of feelings, a scientific language, an artistic language, etc. When we speak of an evolution that affects the senses of rhythm and time, sensitivity and perception, we are dividing the homogeneous flow of experience, of knowledge, and of human communication into working logical categories.

Friedmann's classification is not followed here; we have constructed one that is broadly similar and man's work is itself intimately related to all of these rhythms. As Mauss remarks, [141] man is a unified whole, and so there is a close connection between the rhythms of physical and intellectual activity, even if that connection is sometimes obscure. In former times, mind and body were controlled by such rhythms in both rural and urban environments, albeit in differing measure. There was a different sense of time and space, and the absence of a sense of urgency, and the pattern of slow, deliberate movement were merely an external translation of these rhythms in the flow of daily life.[142] Contemporary man, in contrast, exposed to the tensions induced by technology that is used in both work and leisure, and dominated by the effect of calculated speed, follows, willy-nilly, a quite different rhythm, and one that allows few pauses, little introspection, or profound religious reflection.[143]

(b) Sensitivity and perception

Friedmann emphasizes the greater depths of feelings of men in former centuries, before the machine had gone so far to sterilizing human relations. Human contacts were freer and closer as a consequence of the more relaxed rhythms of life. He asks:

> How could . . . relationships in space and time be the same as today's among men whose span of experience did not go beyond the range of a horse or, more often, of their own feet or those of their oxen? . . . even expressions of sensitivity depend on the total human environment.[144]

Leaving these considerations aside, we should not forget that mental and psychic activity are modified by physical factors: changes in diet and metabolism, the use of alcohol, noise, tranquillizers—all have their effects. However marginally, these and other factors have affected the psyche over the course of history. Changes in consciousness are affected in all of us by a wide variety of minor gratifications, frustrations, and deprivations in everyday experience, and it seems reasonable to attribute analogous and more far-reaching influence to the changes in the rhythm and contexts of human life over long time periods.[145] The emotions appear to have been much stronger among pre-technological men, but as human relations have been increasingly mediated by machines, impersonal tools and roles, so the effect has been to rationalize men's orientations and attitudes.[146] Whereas once, emotional energy was directed towards a very few phenomena such as sex, religion, and food, in contemporary society, the proliferation of objects, information, roles, and distinctive social structures, disperses attention and, simultaneously, disperses emotional and sentimental energy. The emotions become sterilized as a more distinctly machine-like and rational model is put forward as the standard towards which all relationships and orientations should conform. Phenomena that were once regarded as natural and human, and which elicited a response as such, are increasingly seen in rational mater-of-fact terms: and religion is among these things.

(c) *Cognitive attitudes*

According to Eliade, the cognitive orientation encompasses the whole person: man, in a sense, thinks with his whole being. Language, art, myth, science, history, experience, human relations, are differentiated aspects of one fundamental expressive system. Beneath the forms and manifestations of such a system there lies a fundamental unity, rooted in man himself who synthesizes all of this and at the same time constitutes a standard of judgment and of existence. Given this interaction among the various aspects of knowledge, their development has involved an evolution in man's total *Weltanschauung*, with respect to language, the judgment of reality, and so with respect also to religion. The locus of all this, which we emphasize by way of example, is in logic, the language *par excellence*. The evolution of logic conditions changes in other cognitive areas. Even ordinary language, which is conditioned by logic, assimilates terms that have a religious, or a rationalizing, significance. Terms having a religious significance are no longer being added to the language; their number and range diminishes with respect to the total; they lose their expressive force. This occurs since logical classifications are dictated by needs and requirements that vary, as Cassirer has pointed out, and with variations in the conditions of social and cultural life. When life and psychology change, language also changes. In the presence of this trend toward rationalization, changes in language are both a produce and a stimulus.

For centuries, scientific language, in the modern sense of the term, was practically non-existent: human knowledge was encompassed in vague concepts of omnipotent, mysterious nature. Creative nature appeared to have infinite power.[147] Or as Russell has put it:

> Alongside the first timidly advancing scientific terms and concepts
> there are to be found on an equal footing, also terms and concepts
> having a superstitious character: philosophers pass indifferently
> from logic and metaphysics to the cabbala. Thought, in short, is
> permeated with irrationality.[148]

In a word, language and the unfolding of argument did not develop,
as today, at the level of logic and rationality: the processes of
cognition were themselves different, embracing non-cognitive
elements. The rational and critical components found in modern
thought was not so evident, since these have been nurtured in
science, technology, and in a style of social life that has itself become
in considerable measure rationalized.

The progressive elimination of pre-logical thought (pre-logical,
that is, from the viewpoint of modern logic), such as magical
phenomena, superstitious beliefs, had occurred in the last two
hundred years. As these have been purged, so at the same time, logic
has been enriched with concepts flowing from recent scientific and
technological development. Once this stage was reached, the
standards of judgment of nearly all men were substantially modified,
and so a negative interpretation of religious phenomena readily
suggested itself. It seems probable that most men found themselves
without appropriate standards by which to judge religious
phenomena, once these terms of discourse were rendered obsolete by
the development of modern, scientific logic.[149] What this has
amounted to is of course a continuous regression of religiosity in the
face of science, following the unsuccessful attempts by the agents of
religion to encompass science. The result has not been to absorb
religious elements into scientific culture, so much as to produce a
secularization of the sacred.[150]

6. CONCRETE CONSEQUENCES: PRODUCTIVE CENTRES
AS LOCI OF DESACRALIZATION

The foregoing considerations indicate the circumstances conducive
to a crisis of religion, although they account only partially for its
progressive acceleration. Although new ideas are asserted through
the scientific and technological mentality, their penetration of social
life is accelerated only when productive processes undergo a decisive
change. Technological development takes place on (at least) two

levels: (a) in the context of productive technology *per se*; and (b) in the context of the organization of production, as technical development occurs increasingly within the industrial firm, the typical product of modern society. The firm has become one of the major nuclei for the diffusion of new customs oriented toward the conquest of matter and the achievement of well-being. It reveals itself as an instrument of economic struggle and economic power, and as such, even though it is not specifically anti-religious, it is bound to produce irreligiosity or to favour its development.

The transition between one and another phase in productive organization does not take place overnight: on the contrary it is 'slow' even at the purely technical level, since obviously there is not an abrupt transition from manual to machine production. Machines tend to replace men in the transformation phase of the productive process, but this is a gradual replacement.

> For a long period of centuries, individual human movements and activities are facilitated by the employment of more and more perfected working tools. But these instruments do not separate man from the object of his labour. On the contrary, they do nothing more than make his activity easier and more pleasant. This is the case with the hammer, the file, the saw, etc.
>
> At a later stage there is a greater distance from the object of work. The tools become more complex, until at a certain point they become machines proper.
>
> The problem of *when* this happens is almost insoluble, and at any rate inconsequential. First of all it would require a clarification of what is meant by machines. One might produce an infinite number of definitions, including the hand of man among machines, or, at the other extreme, reserving this term for the most complicated automatized instruments.
>
> Thus, leaving aside the problem of definition, we can generically affirm that the hand of man is separated more and more from the object of his work due to the interposition of a growing number of instruments and intermediate operations which the hand itself does not perform. [151]

At this point machinism begins to have a significant effect on human psychology.

The problem of machinism is discussed in our book, *Automazione e nuova classe* and here we do no more than mention some of the essential points. The religious importance of these transformations is apparent both with respect to the contact of man and machine and in a wider context. We have only to think back in time a little in order to realize that:

> The technical changes, which we have briefly mentioned, had momentous consequences.
>
> We state nothing new when we observe, first of all, that industries became more mobile since they were no longer tied to the forests or flowing water as sources of energy. The majority of them became concentrated around the larger cities, in areas of consumption or of sources of machines and raw materials, and near the main routes of communication.
>
> For these reasons, urbanization led to the formation of a number of centres which we may well call industrial.
>
> Migrations which put greater and greater masses of people in contact with new techniques and customs progressively destroyed the old urban and rural structures. As people began to move, either permanently or seasonally or as commuters, from the countryside to the city, the old personalities and the old psychologies were demolished by the growing world of technology.
>
> In the city — the crucible of the new rural and urban proletariat and of the old urban proletariat, which was still partially organized into guilds — the new proletarian class, a distinctive product of the industrial revolution and of technology, was being formed. The unfavourable economic conditions of the wage workers accelerated the formation of the particular characteristics of the proletariat and its typical position with respect to society and the dominant classes. [152]

The proletariat now began to adopt new anti-religious and irreligious attitudes as an aspect of its struggle with the dominant classes, and yet within those dominant classes, the influence of the new socio-industrial context was already leading to the development of secular attitudes.

If the workers groups had their attention directed away from religion by the political and other organizations in which they gathered, it is also true that the organizational structures of the working class were themselves a consequence of its experience of ideological elements of practical needs, and of the factors that conditioned the formation of these new structures. In practice there was, and is, a certain unity between these structures and the individual psychological experience which such organizational and ideological structures sought to interpret and to which they responded.

The individual experiences connected with industrialization lead to the spontaneous formation of new groups. These gradually identify shared demands and problems, and elaborate a kind of group morality. This in turn leads to the formation of ideologies and associations, whether legally recognized or otherwise. Since they reflect shared experience, such ideologies have common characteristics in spite of sometimes considerable divergencies. [153]

The worker, and in general the man who lives within the productive system, is easily disposed to form or to participate in atheistic or areligious organizations. But it is also true that this happens because his personality is affected by the fact of his being in industrial society and in the new world of firms and production. Individual firms — the nuclei for expansion of the world of production and of machines — become the centre of a kind of gravitational field and of a complex network of psychological relationships, sustained by science, by the machine, by technology, and by the new conditions of life, all of which have a desacralizing effect.

The penetration of technology into all sectors of social life, with the world of production operating as intermediary, makes a deep impact on human psychology. It advances steadily, following the lines of least resistance and penetrating into every setting.

Alongside and together with machines, there enters human life a series of new technologies having a social character ranging from those more closely connected with the productive process to others that are more directly related to the human and social aspects of existence. Even the most intimate nucleus of social life, the family, is affected by technology. Technology has a profound effect on leisure, as is shown by recent research on the psychology of the automobile, the cinema, television, and radio . . . *the human person is affected by a unified technological environment* which completely surrounds him. Such an environment must be viewed and studied as a unified whole. [154]

The organizations that function as channels for irreligiosity (such as firms, productive units, organizations built up for self-defence by those who live in the firms, political organizations which express the world of production, and so on) progressively conquer even the levers of power.

To them belong the financial resources and the political apparatus, whether capitalists or workers are concerned. Ramified and complex pressure groups arise which contrast with and oppose those that previously existed, and that were generally more religiously oriented.

The new pressure groups, which are the expressions of a prevalently irreligious world, are themselves equally irreligious. However unconsciously, they favour, sustain, and stimulate the process of expansion of irreligiosity, of the new vision of the world, and of the new customs in the surrounding society (which itself is not yet properly speaking industrialized and thus not yet permeated with this spirit).

The significance and the meaning of the transformations in the rhythm of life, in sensitivity and perception, and in logic, the development of which we have traced, can be understood only in the light of a synthetic view of the development of the technological-industrial world. Without such a view one could not understand the rapid diffusion among the masses of a cognitive and ideological complex which intrinsically could have appealed to only a relatively small number of individuals, and the advance of which have been relatively slow (although faster than of old) if it had been sustained only by the factors we have previously considered.

The new roles and attitudes, as well as the new media of communication produced by industrial society, introduce a new socio-cognitive world or play a decisive part in its diffusion.

7. INDIVIDUAL PSYCHOLOGY AND CHANGES IN COGNITIVE PROCESSES

In sum, at the basis of religious transformations there lie profound transformations in the rhythm of life, in sensitivity and perception,

in logic and in the cognitive attitude of man, all of which in turn are
supported by the more recent dynamics of industrial society taken as
a whole.

There is a close relationship between the

> behaviour of the single individual, the group of which he is a part,
> and the meaning of the behaviour. But the interaction is such that
> it is impossible for us to establish chronological priorities and
> causal relationships. On the one hand we have the individual who
> judges and assumes attitudes, on the other hand individual items
> or patterns of behaviour as bases of judgment. [155]

Naturally, in religious matters, the *judgment* accompanies the
individual's experience of the sacred. Thus we must consider the
attitude taken by the individual vis-à-vis religious practice and all the
other activities which are in some way connected with the experience
of the sacred but which in their turn are influenced also by the
context within which the attitude is 'situated'. A further reason for
behaviour to operate as one basis for judgment is that, within the
religious experience where there is such a close co-ordination between
experience of the sacred and religious behaviour, there is generally
no behaviour without experience or experience without behaviour.
The experience becomes concrete in behaviour and, in fact, in
religious practice. Thus, for example, I may experience a given
sacrality, but I achieve this through meditation, by *practising*
meditation. However, unless I already have a certain experience of
the sacred, nothing leads me to practise that particular meditation,
or indeed any meditation at all.

Naturally (and this holds quite generally and not only on the
religious level), human behaviour, as we have already indicated,
acquires significance when it is inserted in a cultural setting which
conditions it and which, in a certain sense, limits it to a certain
determinate range of possibilities. This is true although culture itself
includes the

> *totality* of physical and mental reactions as well as of the activities
> which characterize the behaviour of the individuals constituting a
> social group in their relations with the natural environment, with
> other groups, with members of the same group, and finally, in
> their reciprocal relationships. [156]

As Barbano remarks, this definition eclectically juxtaposes man and the cultural products of social life; and the solution of the problems that concern us may well revolve around this pair of terms. Cultural processes place the individual into learning situations and compel him to adjust and revise both cognitive processes and attitudes and behaviour.

Thus, the configurations of different cultures determine distinctive individual attitudes vis-à-vis religious phenomenon and vice-versa. The human person is a 'field' the structure of which synthesizes that of man and that of the context. The individual becomes concrete within the context from which to a large extent he draws the cultural equipment that he makes his own.[157]

Quite generally, then, within the formation of the personality one can see the confluence of basic *individual* factors (those Leonardi calls constitutional) and of social factors, connected with the culture. Finally one must take into account occasional elements which 'often decide the individual's socio-cognitive position.'[158]

At this point it appears obvious that to focus upon the transformations in religiosity, one needs to analyse the individual's psychological transformations in connection with the environment and the culture, as well as the three-way effects these factors exercise upon one another.

Thus we must refer back to the individual's socio-cognitive and psychological processes: considerable interpretive errors may be made if the focus is entirely on the cultural dimension of the process to the neglect of its precultural aspect.[159] The development of the human psyche and the absorption of new themes that come forward in the environment do not occur without differences among individuals. What takes place is a varying form of psychological stratification, where, however, upper 'strata' do not wholly replace the lower ones. In fact, there is reciprocal harmonization between the strata, as is convincingly shown by the role that memory plays. There is no behaviour without memory, and the latter entails some extent of harmony (apparent harmony, at any rate) between the phases of knowledge and of experience. The data conveyed by memory help us to construct schemata of behaviour, systems of reference, on the basis of which we evaluate the changing situations with which we are confronted.

Naturally, this holds true also within religion. Successive experiences of a religious nature are oriented by schemata of reference and by previous tenets having both an 'individual' psychological nature and a cultural nature. The crisis of religiosity takes place at the two levels (psychological and cultural) and is conditioned by both.

It is of course true that the cognitive process, even concerning religious matters, unfolds within the human psyche as it reacts to certain stimuli and themes. But this reaction takes place within a context which in turn is largely shaped by previously acquired and shared 'patterns of thought'. The individual's psycho-physical characteristics, and the nature of the fresh data that he receives lead generally to re-adjustment in those patterns. Only very slowly and almost imperceptibly does this process, through which new information is assimilated into a previously acquired frame of reference, alter the frame of reference itself.

Such a process can be detected at work, albeit to a varying extent and with varying results, at all points in human action. Even as an individual carries out a given act, consciously or unconsciously he adduces motivation for it, and as he does so he *knows* that act.

Even when man seems merely to register 'impulses', in fact they operate as his 'motives', no matter how he evaluates them.[160] I 'register' a reluctance to go to church, and, however subconsciously, I perceive a feeling of tedium which makes me unwilling to attend. I may not be in a position to formulate a motive, but I am half conscious of the impulse that keeps me away from church. Only later may such an impulse be acknowledged as such:[161] at this point, that is, the individual within whom a sequence of impulses has made itself felt acquires consciousness of them.

For example: up to a point it is purely the demands made upon him by the machines to which he must attend that 'limit' a worker in his religious life. But then, as his setting becomes more and more dominated by machines, he may become aware that there is a connection between a technologized setting and irreligiosity. Here emerges, however embryonically, a connection between sign and meaning. Irreligious behaviour, which has previously been a 'continuous and confused psychic experience',[162] now shows its meaning in that it appears connected with that expression of a technologized and desacralized world—the machine. The machine now appears as a medium through which the meaning of the irreligious behaviour may be grasped, while the latter in turn stands for a new vision of life.

At first we have a series of discrete steps from individual significances to individual values, leading to the formation in the psyche of a complex of meanings each connected to impulses, to the registering of such impulses, and to their acknowledgment. Within this complex, now crowded with the products of environmental, technological, and scientific factors, one may already note that religious themes have lost some of their previous high priority, although this has happened purely as a matter of fact, unselfconsciously.

In such a situation perceptions and attendant values still constitute a fairly chaotic complex, where individual judgments and values may well contrast with one another, and to which data flow at random without a prearranged order. In spite of this, we are dealing with a significant situation: new values already exist or are being formed, however uncoordinated with standards of judgment; the areligious data which keep flowing in may well lack a pre-arranged place within the culture, but for that very reason are bound to affect it in the long run. In particular, the new data generated by technology over the centuries slowly deposit into the culture their own desacralizing rationality, their distinctive language. This happens because the individual meanings cannot yield values, cannot find an orderly and logical place within the cultural context, cannot lend themselves to judgment and to further elaboration, unless a language operates as a medium for their communication and for judgments to be made about them.[163] As we have seen, this has happened in the case of technology: it has generated a language of its own, one which eliminated pre-logical, and thus also religious, concepts from cognitive processes.

But once a language (broadly understood) has emerged, the cognitive process attains a social dimension. 'Significances' are no longer entertained on a discrete basis, but become terms of reference in a process involving a plurality of subjects, who employ language and communication as instruments for processing reality in the same way that light flows through a prism. Thus as the prism changes (that is, as language and the media of communication change) so does the image of reality which each man possesses. Thus also desacralization previously an individual phenomenon, becomes a group phenomenon and becomes radicalized.

In turn this reality, to the details of which language and communication have already imparted some degree of coherence, becomes the object of the last phase of knowledge, the process of abstraction. Through this process, knowledge, which in the phase of perception had been purely individual and had then become social through communication, becomes impersonal: it begins to construct those very wide categories that characterize philosophy and the sciences.

Since this abstractive phase presupposes the previous one of linguistically mediated communication, even its products, when studied in depth, reveal the traces of its social background. For this reason students are often misled into identifying the ideas of certain thinkers with the ideological positions held at the folk level during the times when those thinkers operated.

In fact, also the man-in-the-street carries out some abstract mental operations: but he does so mainly through intuition, not through rigorous reasoning (although he may feel that he is operating rigorously through deduction and induction).

Intuition operates in a psychological rather than a logical frame of reference: the individual intuits some connection between his own view of things and external reality, and then fits an *image* of that reality into his own system, which to some extent becomes modified. Thus understood, intuition is not very different from reflection: it leads man to grasp, within a disorderly flow of 'images', one apparently coherent complex of connected things, which is then fitted into his own frame of reference.

Clearly it is at this level, where intuition and abstraction intermingle, that the ideologies of wider or smaller social groups emerge and become diffused. Such ideologies, when they respond to new psychological demands, to new social roles, attitudes and languages, prove capable of reacting back (and sometimes violently so) upon the very society from which they emerge. Sometimes through a kind of boomerang effect they speed toward a tragically rapid conclusion processes of change which had previously advanced more slowly. This may be said to have happened with respect to Marxism and religion: having been brought forth by irreligious or anti-religious groups, first in philosophical, then in ideological terms, it has thus begun to operate as a medium for the diffusion of atheism among masses which had some degree of disposition towards it.

The Marxist thinkers have operated through *abstraction* upon the anti-religious or areligious results of previous *intuitive-abstract* mental operations. Their abstractions, in turn, have been diffused among the masses and generated among them new areligious or anti-religious intuitive abstractions, or at any rate have facilitated their development.

Naturally, even at the stage of abstraction there is continuity in the themes that are being raised, and which human knowledge always encounters as it finds new behavioural and linguistic expressions. In novel ways abstractions still raise the problems of the sacred and of ethical obligation. The themes of *sacred or hierophanic* thinking, which as we have seen, express the experience of the sacred, come forth continually: so do the themes of *ethical* thinking, in which behaviour is regarded from the standpoint of 'ought'; and so do those of logical thinking, now at the level of abstraction.[164] The hierophanic, the ethical, the logical phases interact intensely, even though one gets progressively nearer the target of building an abstract logic more and more in keeping with technological-scientific thinking.

The phase of abstraction itself, furthermore, continuously recapitulates previous phases, as changes take place in perception, in language, in external (material and social) life, abstractions also change. They change because knowledge advances through analogies established between the various objects of knowledge and through the relations that are posited between abstract cognitive thinking and other facts, acts, and objects.[165]

The cognitive process ought to be grasped as a *totality*, involving as we have said, the phases of impulse, perception, registration, communication, and abstraction. In the context of communication, particular importance attaches to behaviour which generates new objects of knowledge for the actor and for those who see in such behaviour a sign or symbol of cognitive attitudes. In sum, the cognitive process is the elaborate and complex result of the components we have mentioned and the phases (impulse, registering, etc.), that we have considered. Within each phase the individual, both as he lives his experience and as he finds a location for such experience, pieces together the components of his total personality. Once the abstractive phase has been attained, it becomes perhaps possible to indicate more clearly whether and to what extent such personality is religious or irreligious. Naturally the abstractive process which (sometimes) fixates the features of religiosity or irreligiosity, may achieve higher or lower levels of elaboration: it may amount simply to the reception of a few, simple ideological elements (so simple that they may not seem even to involve abstraction).

The weakest aspect of the argument so far lies possibly in its admission of the existence of a *qualitative* difference between the object of religion (the experience of the sacred) and the other phenomena described above. On this basis a connection between the experience of the sacred and the other experiences reviewed above seems difficult to establish.

The factors we have emphasized variously affect religiosity. Sometimes they seem part of it, since some impulses, perception abstractions, may be considered religious; however some authors would hold that, when viewed all together, these factors do not actually converge toward the central point of the experience of the sacred.

The experience of the sacred, which stands at the centre of religiosity,[166] apparently has characteristics wholly peculiar to itself. The facts, the phenomena, the perceptions, the abstractions to which we have been referring relate only to the periphery of the religious phenomenon. They affect it only to the extent that they make the experience of it more or less easy. In the case at hand, all these impulses, perceptions, cognitive attitudes, changes in logic, new abstractions, etc., negatively affect the experience of the sacred: they impoverish it, they make it less frequent, they hinder it in manifold ways, and on the whole they diminish the sacrality of human society.[167]

8. THE ADVANCE OF IRRELIGIOSITY AND ITS LOGIC

Human psychological phenomena are so complex that they do not readily lend themselves to a simplified schematization of the type set out in the foregoing pages, but perhaps it is now possible to bring into focus the logic of the process of desacralization in contemporary society.

Over the last few centuries, social life has presented to the individual new impulses and stimuli, both on the objective plane (new 'facts') and on the subjective ('activities' which over time have become signs and symbols). Among the growing multitude of such facts and activities (which ultimately determine social attitudes), those connected with the new patterns of existence, with technology, urbanization, etc., have become more frequent. Viewed from a religious perspective these must be considered negative phenomena (and we have seen wherein lies their negative character).

Their impact on religiosity has become more marked once the significance of these impulses has been *perceived*, since such perception has been accompanied, or followed, by its own translation into communicative behaviour. Individuals, affected by a multiplicity of religiously negative impulses, have acknowledged and communicated their meaning: hence the relationship *sign-meaning-communication* within the religious context.

In an early phase, such a relationship is only occasionally enacted Some negative impulses, once perceived, from time to time engender isolated manifestations of irreligiosity in given individuals, who then perceive phenomena without attaching religious significance to them. This tendency is then distributed over time and space, and makes an impact on subsequent perceptions. Thus a myriad of religiously negative meaningful experiences become involved in the progress of desacralization, since each tends to engender others of a similar kind. In turn, these interpretations fuse with earlier ones and engender new ones at all levels, thanks to the facilitating effect of the social conditions previously described. Although this replication of meaningful experiences takes place chaotically, without co-ordination, at length it brings forth cultural expressions of irreligiosity that are clear and unmistakable.

In concrete terms, the phenomenon follows the lines of development suggested by Pellizzi with reference to social phenomena in general. 'Elementary significances' engender a culture 'through the medium of a general structure or of an intellectually self-conscious mode of behaviour, which in turn obeys 'laws of its own'. This corresponds to the above phase of 'communication' or 'language'. Within language the first and dominant element is not a 'relationship' but meaningful behaviour, which the individual refers in the first place to himself and then to third parties.

In this phase, as we have remarked, society changes most deeply in the direction of desacralization. Here the transformation of logic which we have previously mentioned takes place, and it does so in connection with new interpretations.

These changes engender others, these latter unfold most completely in the final abstractive, or intuitive-abstractive, phase where irreligious ideas and doctrines multiply.

The individual enters society with his own psychological background and with particular tendencies and dispositions that allow him to interact positively with the social environment. He may possess a preconstituted tendency toward religion or its contrary, but his position on religious matters changes over time, as his relations with his fellow men, with objects, and with the environment (broadly understood) unfold. Within industrial society such relations bring about a decay in religiosity [168] from a certain moment in history onwards, [169] and arising from the factors discussed above.

Thus the process of desacralization (a) is not connected, as some students maintain, only with contingent phenomena, but is rather the result of a radical transition in the development of human society; (b) is rooted in distinctive features of human psychology and of man's cognitive processes.

Thus the sense of the sacred decays for many profound reasons, engendering irreligiosity to an extent previously unknown in human history. [170]

4

The End of the Sacred?

J. Milton Miles

Whenever the Presbyterian bell
Was rung by itself, I knew it as the Presbyterian bell.
But when its sound was mingled
With the sound of the Methodist, the Christian,
The Baptist and the Congregational
I could no longer distinguish it,
Nor any one from the others, or either of them.
And as many voices called to me in life
Marvel not that I could not tell
The true from the false.
Nor even, at last, the voice that I should have known.

Edgar Lee Masters (Spoon River Anthology)

1. HYPOTHESES TOWARDS A CONCLUSION: ARGUMENT FOR AND
AGAINST THE SURVIVAL OF RELIGION

(a) *The emerging relationship between economic and cultural
stratification and religiosity*

Until now our discussion has had two main bases: sociographic
analysis and arguments concerning the analysis of psycho-social
mechanisms of the crisis, i.e. the relationship between the external
factors that provoke the crisis and the human individual, especially
with respect to the problem of knowledge. Our final conclusions can
be reached only after a critical reassessment of these two fundamental groups of factors. To this end, we shall
(i) attempt to consider religious practice and field research from a
different point of view, albeit always within the limits of empirical
analysis;

(ii) examine what has so far appeared as a basic incompatibility between religiously-based reasoning and 'experiencing', for instance, in the scientific world. Is the incompatibility intrinsic and irremediable, or is it historical and, for that reason, contingent?

Turning to the first problem: may we interpret the data differently? Among the variables that affect the decay of the sacred and the development of atheism there are some the significance of which changes over time. Until recent times the development of industrial civilization has everywhere shown certain common features. In the first place, it has taken place in the presence of considerable imbalances between technico-industrial development and the level of education. In the second place, it has carried to a high level of development that secondary sector of society (industry) that is initially the most hospitable to irreligiosity and atheism. In the third place, industrial society has developed in the presence of strong internal politico-social tensions between social groups and classes, and this has certainly favoured the disintegration of many groups, including religious groups.

With the development of industrial society, the educational explosion, particularly at the university level, and the rapid rise in per capita income in many industrial countries, the variables involved have changed considerably, as has the significance of previously operative variables. It is not surprising that with the advent of industrial society the less cultured classes have been most rapidly affected by irreligiosity and atheism. These classes, among them at least a part of the working class, have often attained only a relatively low level of cultural maturity. Hence their understandable inability to withstand the psychological, social, and cultural stimuli of contemporary society. For example, in the industrial city, nature is now thought of as an object of science, and it requires a high level of maturity to discover that nature is capable of being interpreted in quite different ways and of being of quite different significance.

It is also difficult to view society, a human product, as the expression of a creating God. Beyond this, only a high level of culture and self-control allow an individual to resist becoming standardized, socialized, and moulded by a society which almost naturally desacralizes man. Educational level (along with the quality and quantity of culture) and income are, as we have said, among the variables which have undergone considerable changes.

The consequences of these changes have been remarkable, especially from the beginning of the sixties and during the last decade. But in these two periods the religious consequences seem to be different.

Let us look at the first period. For the sake of simplicity we refer again to the indices of religious practice, but analogous phenomena clearly exist also at the deeper levels of religiosity, as is indicated by certain more sophisticated studies. We may look at the relationship between educational level and income on the one hand, and church attendance on the other.

A 1954 Gallup Poll shows the following rate of weekly church attendance for different educational levels in the United States:

College	51%
High School	47%
Grade School	43%

To have any significance, the analysis of these figures would need to be more detailed and, first of all, it would need to be clear whether there were any relationships between particular income levels, particular social conditions, and the type of society in which the social groups were to be found.

In fact, as has been clearly shown by Pin in his study of Lyons in the fifties (the results of which have been amply confirmed by others), in the fifties there was a connection between religious practice and educational level as well as between religious practice and socio-economic level. With the improvement of economic conditions practice increased, as it also increased with higher cultural levels. Some have maintained that the bourgeoisie had become Christian again.[1] This is a complex phenomenon that involves also family relations, class relations, and the phenomena of urbanization, but, within this context, socio-economic and educational conditions were fundamental variables. Pin shows the rates of family religious practice on page 165.[2]

The same can be said for individual religious practice.[3]

The situation is no different among the young. In classes where socio-economic and educational conditions are better, young people receive greater care.[4]

Social classes and Sunday religious practice in Lyons

(Sunday family practice in %, according to the professional category of the head of the family)

	Fully practising	Partly practising	Non-practising
workers	9.1	12.4	78.5
shopkeepers, artisans	14.9	1.5	83.6
white collar	16.7	10.2	73.1
managers and executives	34.2	19.7	46.1
wholesalers and contractors	21.6	29.7	48.7
free professions	50	19.4	30.6

Religious practice of young people between 7 and 21 years of age in %, according to the socio-professional category of the head of the family in Lyons

Workers	30
Shopkeepers	—
White Collar	54
Managers and executives	71
Contractors	53
Free professions	86

The same scale of religious practice, i.e. practice increasing with higher social conditions, is to be found with respect to educational level. Pin's table represents a clear example.[5]

Sunday religious practice in % according to educational level in Lyons

	Adult men	Their wives
did not finish primary school	9.9	14
stopped school at 15 with diploma	13.8	21.1
higher primary studies with diploma	21.7	34.8
technical studies with at least a diploma	30	37.5
schooling until age 16–20 without diploma	32.8	52
secondary schooling with diploma	50	50
higher studies (university degree, etc.)	57	88

Pin's theses have been confirmed also for more recent periods for instance by Kelly's research in relation to socio-economic conditions in the United States:

Religious practice in %, determined on the basis of replies given by the informants in a diocesan survey

	Easter Communion	Sunday Mass	monthly Communion
free professions, businessmen	80	81	85
white collar, shopkeepers	80.5	79.5	41.5
domestic servants	77	75.5	40.5
agricultural, fishing, and forestry workers	71.5	71.5	35.5
skilled workers	74	73.5	33
specialized workers	72.5	75.5	39
unskilled labourers	67	64	29.5

and also in relation to educational level.[6]

Religious practice in % as reported by the interviewees during a diocesan census

		Primary schooling incomplete		Primary schooling complete		Secondary schooling incomplete		Secondary schooling complete		University	
		Public	Catholic	Public	Catholic	Public	Catholic	Public	Catholic	Public	Catholic
Easter Communion	M	56	60	56	66	62	70	68	81	69	84
	F	58.5	71	65	78	67.5	83.5	79.5	84.5	79	86
Sunday Mass	M	61	58	55.5	71.5	66.5	78	74	85	76	85
	F	64	72.5	67	81	69	86.6	77	87	83	88.5
Monthly Communion	M	28.5	24	25.5	38	29.5	37	33	49.5	30.5	50.5
	F	32	44.5	35.5	48	34.5	50	37	50	46.5	58

The situation is much more complex in communist countries, of course, because of the difficulties introduced by a number of concomitant and distorting factors. Surveys carried out among Warsaw students, for example, seem to show a lower level of religiosity among

those who come from the intelligentsia, but there is a certain
political selection involved in determining who qualifies as the intelligentsia, and this results in a prevalence of Marxist-oriented
individuals and thus in a lower percentage of religious practitioners.[7] The conclusion seems to be that, while 69.3 per cent of
those having rural origins practise regularly, among those of working
class origin the rate is 63.4 per cent, and among the intelligentsia,
54.4 per cent. Similar conclusions are suggested by other surveys.
The survey of Warsaw young people also concludes that religiosity
decreases with increasing level of education.[8] But anti-religious
propaganda, the tendency of communists and militant atheists to
concentrate in the leadership cadres, other factors such as the intense
anti-religious propaganda in schools, the official atheism of elites (as
a consequence of which atheism became necessary for cultural acceptance), all complicate the issue and make well-authenticated
results from scientific inquiry difficult to obtain. The statistics
themselves are not easy to evaluate: what is one to make of figures for
the Jugoslav census of 1953, which give 18.4 per cent as the proportion of atheists in the population aged between nought and six years?[9]

Results from various surveys support Pin's conclusions. Not to
burden the argument, we refer only to data available for Germany
(since those for France are very well known) on the relation between
social conditions and religious practice.[10]

Social situation	Marl	Dortmund (a)	Essen (b)	Trier	Mannheim (c)	Munich
professionals	58	39	41	43	10	10
public servants and managerial	49	49	51	50	49	33
white collar	49	53	43	44	35	33
artisans and wage workers	31					
workers	15	16	18	19	24	16

(a) average of 18 parishes
(b) average of 12 parishes
(c) principal parishes

The implications of these data do not differ much from those to be
drawn from Pin's studies. But even these data must not lead us to
hasty conclusions. In spite of these figures, Isambert, for example,

suggests that: 'The personal interest in religious matters does not appear to be significantly connected to one's professional or study level, however it is a little higher among average incomes.' Moreover, 'among those who have attained a high level of instruction, those who give a religious education to their children are less numerous, but at the question: "Do you often — or very often — discuss religious topics?" the percentage is rising as the level of instruction increases.' Similar considerations are made by Lenski and reported by Isambert.[12]

It is an objective and uncontroversial fact that rising educational and cultural levels, together with better economic conditions (albeit within certain limits) favour religion, at least in Western society and at least until the beginning of the 1960s. There are, of course, problems in expressing the precise relationship between education, social, and economic conditions, and religion. The effect of specific variables — educational level; economic circumstances; family culture — are not always easily isolated, but the resolution of these issues is not necessary for our purposes. We can recognize that in some circumstances the working classes may find difficulty in identifying with religious organizations within which they are placed in a condition of distinct cultural inferiority. Beyond this, it can be readily conceded that when such a situation occurs, the working classes may reject the church as an institutionalized expression of a society in which the workers experience a sense of rejection or inferiority.

We must also recognize that particular variables may operate in different ways at different times. Thus, until a few decades ago, high educational level and material well-being appeared to be associated with a measure of religious disaffection, which was sometimes considerable. Later, the pattern appears to have changed, and disaffection became more strongly marked among socially and educationally under-privileged groups who were not very fully integrated in society.[13] Pin has given expression to this problem with respect to the social life of the proletariat.[14]

> The only characteristic which appears to be common to all categories of non-observants (workers, merchants and artisans, line personnel, low white collars, etc.) is the low level of education statistically sided by a less autonomous personality.[15]

Given the trends in average educational attainment, and changes in social stratification, it was possible, until not so long ago, to suppose that the general situation might become more favourable toward religion. There were three broad reasons for this assumption. First, especially in the nineteenth century, the crisis of religion was mainly connected with the transition from a peasant to an industrial society: the crisis resulted from a clash between the psychological characteristics and attitudes of the individual, as an expression of the preceding phase of civilization, and the new developments engendered by the industrial revolution. This clash of often radically antithetical value systems found ready expression in the crisis of the sacred. But in a fairly short time many of these characteristics of peasant society were being obliterated in most advanced countries: men were increasingly assimilating scientific and technological perspectives from early childhood. They no longer occurred as sudden discoveries, provoking religious crisis later in the life cycle. The clash of values was reduced, but the new scientific values were not in themselves hospitable to expressions of religiosity.

Second, as we have noted, at least in Western countries, the religious crisis involved groups with relatively low educational levels: thus it was supposed that as educational levels rose, the massive breakdown of religion, or at least of its external and institutional expression, would be avoided. Yet the assumption that by raising average educational levels to the point at which high levels of religious practice have been normal, would reduce the severity of the crisis of belief, has become more questionable. [16]

Third, the proletariat, the class least disposed to religious practice, was always a large proportion of the total population: but social change was leading towards a diminution in the relative size of the proletariat, both urban and rural. [17] Changes in the structure of the work force of advanced nations, following the pattern that developed in the United States between 1900 and 1970, appeared to augur well for religion: there were larger percentages of people moving into classes in which the breakdown of religious practice had been least pronounced. But assumptions about the permanence of class position and religious dispositions have proved unfounded.

There has been a marked abandonment of belief in God among more educated groups. Studies carried out in the United States show that the percentage of those who believe in God has declined from 79 per cent in 1948 to 58 per cent in 1968. [18] The IFOP survey of 1968 gave the percentage of French adults who believe in God as 73 per cent. Among young people between fifteen and twenty-three years of age, 65 per cent were believers, and 11 per cent were uncertain. *Pro Mundi Vita* reported that in France non-believers accounted for 13 per cent in 1958, 17 per cent in 1968, and 24 per cent in 1970. As usual, the figures are contradictory, but there seems to be a single underlying tendency. Perhaps more significant — non-believers become more frequent as educational level increases, beginning with secondary schooling[19] but especially among the university educated.[20]

The *mass* drift toward agnosticism is a fairly new phenomenon, often very recent indeed, at least in Western countries. Decreasing belief in God among the university educated is equally new. But this situation and these data should be viewed with caution: many of those who give a negative answer to the blunt question 'Do you believe in God?', would respond differently to a question posed in a more critical and sophisticated way. The phenomenon may be connected with the spread of irreligiosity, but it may also indicate a more critical religious attitude, particularly at the extra-ecclesial level. Surveys conducted in the 1950s and early sixties, permitted some to be optimistic about the future of religion, but those of the late 1960s and seventies undermined these expectations, at least with respect to institutionalized religion. The situation appears increasingly volatile, however, and from these evidences no definitive conclusions are to be drawn. Thus, we turn to other aspects of the matter, those directly or indirectly connected with the problem of knowledge.

(b) *The relationship between religious and irreligious knowledge*

Science may be said to be one of the essential sources of the culture and the logic of irreligion: from many points of view, it appears to expel from social life both religious conduct and its justifications as non-logical. That this should be so appears almost as an *ex post facto* justification and confirmation of Pareto's thesis which distinguishes between logical (scientific and rational) and non-logical (irrational and religious) conduct. However, the opposition between religious discourse (and experience) and irreligious, especially scientific discourse (and experience) may not be as radical as it appears, at

least as far as our own themes are concerned. In emphasizing the
progressive differentiation of these two types of knowledge, we have
ignored some aspects of these two cognitive levels, and the channels
in which each type of knowledge develops. There are important
points of connection between religious and non-religious (particularly scientific) cognition. Although it is common to concede that
there is a 'break of ontological level', or at least a psychological leap,
between sacred and religious knowledge on the one hand, and non-
religious knowledge on the other, yet from another perspective man's
Weltanschauung appears to possess a certain coherence and unity.

The paradox is resolved by the fact that the experience of the
sacred becomes part of social reality through the media of myth,
ritual, and symbol. They form part of the communicative language
from which human social experience is woven.[21] They impart to the
sacred some aspects of its rationality. Their significance is evident,
since at no point in history has one of these ways of knowing, the
religious and the logico-rational had anything like a monopoly.
Neither

> one has overcome the other, in such a way as either to subsume it
> within itself or exclude it from the course of events, thus ter-
> minating the alternative. On the other hand, it cannot be denied
> that at various times, now one and now the other has been
> dominant, forcing the other into an inferior position.[22]

The thought of the Greek poets, undoubtedly intrinsically religious, was by no means deprived of logical qualities. Pre-socratic
naturalism arose in opposition to this religiosity, but even it was not
entirely lacking in mythical and ethical value. Analogous examples
could be found throughout the history of human thought. Thus, in
general it is an oversimplification to suggest that myth has belonged
exclusively to religious thought, and *logos* to philosophical or
scientific thought. Cognitive experience must be studied within a
wide social and cultural context, and the mythical, logical, and
ethical elements of which is is composed must all be duly considered.
We must inquire into the dynamic relations between myth and other
aspects of human life, since we believe that, at bottom, a symbolic
and mythical substratum underlies all logical thinking, and that, on
the other hand, not even mythical thinking is devoid of a kind of
deep logicality.

Clarification is to be sought by examining the way in which man knows and interprets the reality that surrounds him, and the role of myth and logic in this process. This task is easier today, since many students have abandoned 'the old passion for analysis . . . where one aimed at isolating mythical, logical, and ethical forms in their splendid, yet fictional, purity.'[23] It is now more obvious than it was to some in the past that religion is not merely 'myth' and 'ethics', but has also an implicit and at times explicit logic, while it is also clear that not even abstract theoretical and quantitative systems of knowledge exist without myth.[24]

One may even maintain that knowledge of a situation may be attained in a more diverse and richer way through myths embodied in symbols, which appear as alternative (and to a large extent psychological) interpretations of a single reality: a series of interpretations that are all, in a certain sense, simultaneously true. Images and symbols permeate the psychic life even of modern man: desacralized as it is, it is shot through with myths, with 'decayed hierophanies'. The human psyche is an immense collection of images, of symbols, of myths, and even of prejudices and fossilized ideas, often the legacies of an infantile religiosity, secularized and degraded.

As Eliade observes, even in the most simple 'plus terre à terre' consciousness, the free flow of images and symbols comes to the surface of consciousness when we are weary, when we are walking down the street; every distraction or digression unleashes a complex of myths, symbols, and traditional rituals. But it is precisely on this psychological symbolic stratum, the fabric of memory, learning, reflection, and association, that knowledge of reality rests.

Even within this world of myths, symbols, and decayed images, continues Eliade, the actualization of a symbol, of a myth, and its incorporation into a cognitive context, is not a purely mechanical fact. The symbol or myth is incorporated into a psychological context which is favourable to it, and not into another; it sustains one line of discourse, and not another; it finds a place within one trend in the development of society, rather than in another. Thus it is an instrument of knowledge which responds to specific requirements of the person; it forms a part of his frame of reference no less — perhaps more — than the most abstract knowledge. Otherwise how could we explain the almost universal diffusion of certain rituals, myths, and symbols? Evidently they respond to a 'situation' (one might say a psychological situation) that is essential to the human spirit, and not merely contingent. Religious, and especially sacred, myths are a response to every man's need to have an image of the world and to be at its centre. (A clear demonstration of the validity of this concept is furnished by the mushrooming of the so-called symbolism of the centre in the history of religions.)

There is the same difference between logical and mythical discourse as there is between direct and allegorical discourse, that is, between argument by analogy and argument by identity. But is there a real difference between these two types of discourse? Do we not always speak by similarity and difference? That is, in fact, by analogy?[25] This 'mythical allegory', this symbolization, of religious discourse and knowledge — are they so different from the allegorical nature of non-religious discourse and knowledge?

The preceding considerations lead us to recognize the analogical character of every cognitive logic: but the symbolic character of knowledge is a further witness to its analogical structure. As we have seen, behaviour as a bio-psychological totality in relation to an environment, is the foundation of knowledge. Behaviour, in turn, must be grounded on communication: without communication there is no relationship with the environment. Among the essential instruments of communication, and thus of knowledge (as communication with oneself or with others), are to be found the significant gesture and the significant symbol: that is, knowledge is essentially symbolic. The symbolic value of both religious and secular myth is obvious, as is the place occupied by mythological knowledge in the general scheme of knowledge.[26] Furthermore, a single mythological representation does not always function identically:[27] every symbol takes on a different significance depending upon the subject who uses and re-interprets it in accordance with his own personality.[28] But although myth and symbol are 'logical' vehicles of communication, there is another (sometimes indispensable) technical or, so to speak, auxiliary instrument of communication: this is ritual, be it religious or otherwise.

The preceding considerations demonstrate the cognitive importance of ritual. The complex character of knowledge, in which act and attitude are so deeply involved, shows that it is associated with a ritual, variable or uniform, simple or complex, essential or marginal — but always present. Thus one should not underestimate the general significance of ritual. As Pellizzi observes

> if properly religious ritual (liturgy) represents the most solemn and established form of basic significant behaviour, we must remember that this type of behaviour appears in the most diverse circumstances, at every level of conscious life . . . we expect to find it more salient and vivid in the childhood and youth of both human cultures and individuals.[29]

That is, ritual is associated with all basic significant behaviour. It is a 'general' instrument, always connected with the mythical and analogical character of knowledge.[30]

It may or may not be religious according to whether it is associated with a myth that is or is not sacred, a myth which will, in turn, express either religious or irreligious perception or knowledge.[31] But whether it is sacred or secular it is always connected with meanings and thus with mediated or immediate, but always analogical, knowledge which is revived and repeated through shared ritual ceremonies. These ceremonies may be perceived as such (as happens primarily with religious rituals) or not so perceived (the case especially with secular rituals). In both cases the ritual is present, and it occasions the repetition of previously assimilated knowledge or, analogically, leads to the development of new knowledge on the basis of knowledge already shared by a plurality of individuals.

Thus there must be a 'community', either in knowledge or in the analogical base from which knowledge emerges.[32] From this it follows that myth is or can be significant in every context, and it is thus possible for experience to be 'communicated' from the secular and irreligious level to the sacred and religious level, although this may not happen directly but by means of symbol, ritual, and myth instead, through those routes we have previously discussed.

In what sense is this argument valid? Let us explain by means of an example. Let us suppose that we are present at the celebration of the 'Long March' in Peking, and that the essential part of the ritual consists in paying homage to the flags of that time. We will have at least two categories of ritual, mythical, and symbolic significance, and thus two categories of knowledge deriving from these rituals, myths, etc. For the veterans of the Long March there will be the ritual repetition of a lived experience, and thus the flag will probably symbolize sacrifice, sadness, pain, pride, a series of already mythicized facts. For these veterans, the myth of the Long March will become the fundamental symbol through which communism finds expression.

The young will have feelings of admiration, of esteem, etc. Their perceptions and knowledge will not be identical with those of the veterans, *but by means of analogy*, by establishing a relationship between their own world and the mythicized world of the Long March, they will have a symbolic perception of communism, analogous to but different from that of the veterans, although attained through the same ritual. For both groups the ritual and the myth will maintain their significance as an initiation which on this occasion assumes a 'mediating' significance very similar to that taken on by the sacred myth when it 'mediates' the experience of the sacred in space and time.[33] Thus there is diversity only in the basic experience, secular and irreligious in one case, sacred and/or religious in another. Within the mythical-ritual structure of knowledge, the logical break between the two worlds is in part only apparent: the logico-cognitive universe is basically shared and intercommunicative.

Now notice that the ritual component, which is so basic to the analogy between the two cognitive processes, is not limited to those cases of non-religious knowledge that have a strong emotive charge. In this connection Pellizzi gives an example that is worth repeating:

> Meeting X by chance, and listening to him, I have practically no specific predispositions toward the encounter. If, in spite of this, I understand his speech and his actions, one must conclude that X and I have in common an enormous range of potential 'rituals'; that then and there he can select a certain series of rituals and enact it, and that I will follow the meaning of each ritual sign he produces; and that, furthermore, I will probably grasp also the significance of the totality of these signs.[34]

Thus the logical and pragmatic fissure between the two spheres of knowledge is to a great extent only an apparent one.[35]

In short, there is a continuity between the two aspects, a continuous shading of one into the other, with a difference only in the way in which the cognitive components are put together, with respect to both their structure and their quantitative ratio. At any rate, the intercommunicability between the two worlds is functional. If there were no communication between the two spheres of knowledge, it would be difficult to interpret one in the light of data supplied by the other, and it would be impossible to give any semblance of unity to human logico-cognitive categories.

Naturally, this shading into one another, this concurrence, is to be found only when the immediacy of knowledge is transferred to the level of awareness and the perceived datum is integrated into one's conception of the world, of communication, etc. But different from this, there remains that immediate first-hand knowledge, which Otto considers an *a priori* category of the human spirit, and on which we have felt it to be neither necessary nor possible to form a definitive judgment.

Unfortunately, we cannot here attempt to untangle the intricate question of the more or less relative and contingent validity of every religious and sacred, or scientific (or simply secular) discourse. In any case, we cannot agree with those authors who deny validity to 'mythical-sacred' discourse, assuming it to be erroneous when compared with scientific discourse which is 'certainly exact'. Non-religious knowledge of reality is equally doubtful and uncertain, even when, as in the case of myth, there is a deeply rooted presumption of its veracity on the part of those who live the experience.

Let us give a trivial example. We know and we see man, but we do not perceive the exact physiognomy of the figure 'man'. We perceive and know only a series of events to which we give an approximate interpretation, and this interpretation, as such, is open to discon-firmation or modification by the progress of the sciences. The solid matter which appears to us as 'human flesh' is not what it appears to be; the real colour of the hair is something different from what we see; science gives ever new meanings to the term 'colour', and so on. In short, what we know are 'events': we interpret them inexactly, never dreaming of the existence of other much more real 'events' that comprise them. Thus in the case of flesh we have a clearly inexact knowledge of its real composition and of the real meaning of the term.

In conclusion, the sacred and religious experience is not distinguished from the profane experience by its erroneousness, but by the series of reasons and characteristics that we have listed, and above all by its *tendency* to lead to an ontological plane that is different from the plane of existence of every hierophanic manifestation.

This *wholly other*, this break of ontological level, has led some to see in the religious world and in mythical-sacred and ritual-sacred knowledge, a clear and irreducible antithesis to the rest of social reality, a communication gap between the two worlds. And once the fruitfulness of the cognitive and scientific world is accepted, this lack of communication is taken as grounds for denying validity to the mythical-ritual-sacred cognitive component.

However, as we have seen, sacred and religious experience is channelled through myth, symbol, and ritual—fundamental instruments for the communication of knowledge. But they are not instruments for sacred and hierophanic knowledge alone; and this is why myths, symbols, and rituals, whether sacred or not, become instruments and vehicles of communication between the two cognitive spheres. From these considerations we may conclude that it is possible to embrace the two worlds within a single logical discourse and to identify, within a basic logico-cognitive unity, a tight and orderly network of relations at all levels in the society within which these two components, the sacred-hierophanic and the profane, participate in each other.[36]

(c) *An historicist hypothesis concerning the religious crisis*

The theories that give an unfavourable prognosis concerning the future of religion on the basis of data relative to religious practice and other indirect indices of religiosity depend on certain implicit or explicit historicist presuppositions. To test their validity these assumptions must be made explicit. In the light of our discussion of myth, symbol, and ritual, we must inquire whether the undoubted decline of the sacred is a historical social trend leading towards its eventual disappearance altogether.

We have already seen that to regard the sacred as an *a priori* category yields unfruitful results. Since we do not know the most intimate nature of the sacred, we must focus our attention on its immediate external expressions, and these we may either identify with the sacred, or, if the sacred is seen as an *a priori* category, they may be regarded as deriving from it. In either case, it is these expressions that we need to consider in their contact with the new technical-industrial order. Clearly interpretations of the significance of the sacred in the process of social change in industrial society, differ in accordance with whether the sacred is seen as an *a priori* category or as a purely psychological component. De Martino, who advances criticisms of Otto,[37] may be taken as typical of those who believe that the future of religiosity may be predicted without the insights of the human sciences. With respect to the thesis that the sacred must be seen as an *a priori* category, he writes:

> Even when the experience of sacred otherness (which is qualitatively different from profane otherness) has been described, and when the *tremendum* and the *fascinans* have been characterized as the internal polarity of this peculiar otherness, the problem remains whether what is experienced within man's consciousness as the irrational component of the sacred should not be seen by the scientist as capable of being further analysed, over and beyond its configuration within the living religious consciousness. It is possible that if we approach the irrational component of the sacred with particular analytical methods, that component may reveal its own coherence and rationality to the scientist in such a way that the sacred as a whole will appear in a new light.[38]

Thus we cannot, as De Martino rightly indicates, view the sacred simply as an *a priori* category. Even the psychologically based concept of the *wholly other* discloses the sacred as at least potentially embodying a rationality which, as an *a priori* category, it would *perhaps* lack.

The considerations developed in the preceding chapter also point away from the interpretation of the sacred as an *a priori* category. Within the physical, psychic, and logical context the connection of the sacred with other aspects of the human person suggest a different orientation.

But De Martino goes beyond this: he suggests that the sacred can be inserted within a wider category, thus clarifying its significance within the dynamics of history. To this end he tends to reduce the category of the sacred to ritual and myth, and sees it as an expression of mythical archetypes of primordial events which have occurred once and for all in *illo tempore*.[39] We, too, have turned to the dynamics of history and the history of religion for answers to our questions about the sacred, but we have come to believe that only if we frame the problem with reference to the total society and continuously refer back to the 'individual psychological context is it possible to explain why, as society and the external world change, the individual's attitude to religion and the sense of the sacred also change.'[40]

The *mirum*, the *fascinans*, the *misterium*, etc., cannot but participate in the transformation of the total emotional and cultural setting of the individual and must necessarily be influenced by components introduced by the age of technology.[41] New logical categories, the rationalization of language, the proliferation and often predominance of technico-scientific terms, concepts, and perceptions that accompany the development of industrial society: all these things bring about basic changes in the individual's frame of reference, since they constitute his every cognitive and communicative orientation. As a consequence, since knowledge preserves its analogical and partially mythological character, the position of myth within the totality of knowledge is diminished at the same time as the mythical-sacred component is impoverished. There are, thus, complex relationships between the process of social change and changes in the sense of the sacred, and it is not always clear that they have fully taken into account by those who view the recent process of desacralization as irreversible.

Basically two types of argument are used to support the view that the phenomenon is irreversible. The first is of a logical nature: the religious phenomenon as such is seen as anti-historical and thus in contrast with the historicity of modern thought. As the contrast becomes more evident it more clearly reveals the intrinsic contradictions of religious phenomenology and ideology. In the long run this leads to the inevitable end of religion, at least to the extent that the sense of history and the cultural constellations typical of Western civilization prevail in the world. The second argument is sociological, or nearly so: if society in its development demolishes the sacred and the religious[42] and if the process of rationalization of society is irreversible, then the end of religion is inevitable.

The major exponents of the first argument, accept the concept of the sacred as *wholly other*. But they accept it more on the logical-rational level than as an aspect of human psychology, which is our own understanding of it. But they do recognize in the experience of the sacred a break with the previous ontological level.

However, sometimes in opposition to Otto's concept of the sacred as an *a priori* category, it is maintained — by De Martino, for example — that, in following Otto and others of similar opinions,

> one unjustifiably gives up the more properly scientific task of reproducing in thought the immediate experience of the numinous, the ambivalent polarity of the *wholly other*, which is lived again and again in the religiously committed consciousness. Now this serious step could be justified only if it were impossible, by means of analysis, to go beyond the irrationality of the *numinous*, and only if there were no way of understanding how and why the cultural life of humanity gives rise to the experience of the wholly ambivalent. It would be justified, that is to say, if it were impossible to resolve the immediate datum of the ambivalent *wholly other* into two components: to see it, on the one hand, as the result of unconscious motivations, and on the other as the product of consciousness in its groping towards rational values. Otto understood very well that religious consciousness reaches for such values; but he failed to ask himself whether also the irrational nucleus of the sacred did not possess its own 'reasons', a question that might have occurred to him had he taken unconscious motivations into account. [43]

In some of its aspects De Martino's thesis is similar to ours: we have already said that there is no justification for Otto's attempt to reduce the experience of the sacred to a simple *a priori* category. But De Martino goes further: using certain psychoanalytic arguments, [44] he interprets the mythical-ritual fact (as a sacred phenomenon) as an instrument for reliving the reality of primordial times.

This is, in part, the thesis of Malinowski, of Preuss, of Lichtenstein, etc.; [45] it is Eliade's thesis in *Le Mythe de l'éternel retour* and in his treatise on the history of religion. Eliade would say that myth and ritual allow man to get outside of time: in many cases and for many mythologies temporal existence seems to be ontological non-existence, unreal, a total vacuum. In Hindu mythology, for example, the historical world (and the civilizations built by the labour of thousands and thousands of generations) 'is illusory because, on the level of cosmic rhythms, the historical world of human history endures for barely an instant'. [46]

According to De Martino, the myth of eternal recurrence and its ritual repetition (the profound significance of which cannot be

ignored) have been essential components of the human attitude, s.
through with religiosity, until the rise of modern civilization. The
ritual re-enactment of primordial myths defends the human
psychology from the precariousness of being in a world that manifests
itself in historical development: thus is it protected from history. This
protection takes place first of all through the rejection of history itself
and then through the re-interpretation of history in Christianity.[47]
By placing Christ at the centre of history, the Christian liturgical
year interprets, transforms, and in a sense deforms history, pro-
jecting its significance and its value beyond itself into divinity.[48]

But De Martino also sees Christian symbolism as representing

> the coming to awareness of the historicity of the human condition
> and the acceptance, on the eschatological level, of irreversible time
> as against the eternal recurrence of the religions of the ancient
> and primitive world.[49]

In spite of this greater sense of history, for De Martino the
mythical-ritual component of Christianity still resolves itself into a
partial 'de-historicization of development'. But in the West,
Christian mythical ritual symbolism has performed the cultural
function of mediating the sense of history.

According to De Martino, however, it is just this embryonic sense
of history, typical of Christianity, that has allowed the Western world
energetically to push forward the process of desacralization,

> although the process of the liberation of the profane from the
> sacred is already in evidence in the ancient world, the progress of
> the increasing autonomy of the human with respect to the divine
> took on an accelerated rhythm in Christian civilization, especially
> since the Reformation and the Renaissance. Today we have
> discovered the mythico-ritual 'origins' of the theatre, of the
> figurative arts, of literature, of the dance, and of music; the
> connection between myth, theology, metaphysics, and philo-
> sophy; the transition from the sacrality of the social group and
> from theocratic ideologies to the problems of modern demo-
> cracy; the liberation of technology and the production of
> economic goods from the 'numinous' context in which they so long
> developed and found protection. But this discovery amounts to
> nothing more than our becoming aware of a process which has

advanced, primarily in Western civilization, with its more or less explicitly Christian 'sense of history'.[50]

It is a brilliant thesis, but the reader who has followed our discussion, especially in the third chapter, will be aware of a certain tendency to schematize a complex phenomenon. This tendency is revealed only by means of an analysis conducted with the aid of the human sciences.

There are innumerable inter-related and overlapping factors that have accelerated the process of distinguishing the human from the divine, so accelerating the desacralization of society. *One* of them is the sense of history, but at best it is only one of the more important factors which, furthermore, has exercised its influence mainly among the cultured classes, whereas we know that the phenomenon of desacralization, particularly in recent times, is a wave which pushes from below.

We thus hesitate to follow De Martino when he maintains that

the Christian mythico-ritual symbol conveys the value of human history. But as it does this, on the one hand Christianity becomes distinct from other religions and acquires its distinctive pedagogic function in the cultural history of the West; and on the other hand, it necessarily occasions a religious agony; in fact, it constitutes the beginning of the death of *all* mythical-ritual symbols and of all numinous horizons—at any rate as long as the memory of Western civilization remains significant in the history of humanity.[51]

This interpretation of the phenomenon should be tested through sociological and social-psychological research. However, even if one were to accept the argument that there is no place for an intrinsically anachronistic religion in a society endowed with a sense of history, it remains difficult to see how such an argument could gain a hold on the masses, which increasingly lose the sense of the sacred. Certainly, such an argument could never attain the degree of evidence, the simplicity, and clarity, which alone would make it easily understandable by individuals of average culture and intelligence.

The process of desacralization, which De Martino accounts for so neatly, regards the sacred as coming to its end. But, as we have seen, the phenomenon is much more complex and involves a multiciplicity of causes and auxiliary causes, of negative and positive factors, in the complicated flow of the history of society; and this makes it impossible for us to reach securely founded generalizations.

Furthermore, we must bear in mind that myth and ritual, which are a focus of attention for De Martino and others who propose analogous theses emphasizing the anti-historicity of the sacred, are a *posterius*, a later phase with respect to the experience of the sacred. They constitute vehicles for the communication, and instruments for the repetition of the experience, but we cannot identify them with the experience itself in its totality. Suppose we grant that the mythical-ritual world is anachronistic. We might then impute this feature to the very essence of the sacred experience. *But* it might also result *ex post facto* from the interpretation of that experience, rather than being built into it.

It is true that we find in man the desire to do away with profane time in favour of sacred time in order to live eternally and in eternity. But this tendency need not arise directly and exclusively from the experience of the *wholly other* felt at the psychological level and within the sacred experience. Rather it might arise from a conjunction of that feeling with a wish to make utilitarian use, in temporal terms, of the radical discontinuity which the sacred experience reveals.

This is only an hypothesis, but it is certainly clear that the sacred experience in itself cannot be definitively characterized either as anti-historical or as historically rooted.

But within the mythico-ritual context, the individual draws from the sacred and religious experience conclusions that seem to be in contrast with modern civilization. If there is such a contrast, however, for the reasons put forward above, it cannot be considered so momentous that it will with certainty bring about an ultimate disintegration of the sacred.

We maintain this thesis also because we find it difficult to recognize within the sacred the radical anti-historicism attributed to it by certain students. We also find it difficult to accept the wholly historicist interpretation of modern culture when it is put forward in complete contrast to that anti-history *par excellence* which is represented by the sacred and religious world. In clarifying and emphasizing this point we do not intend to deny the value of any historicist philosophy. We only doubt the possibility of finding the cause of the rise of anti-religious attitudes and ideas among the masses in the contrast of these ideas with certain historicist positions which have come into prominence.

A few considerations on these radical interpretations will serve to sustain our doubts. In the first place, let us remark with Eliade that:

> every myth, in announcing an event which has taken place *illo tempore*, represents a pattern for actions and situations that will repeat this event in the future. Thus, instead of anti-history we might speak of 'exemplary history', that is, of a history that has been re-evaluated and rendered significant and luminous with respect to the simple and trivial chronicle which it previously was, a history which has been liberated from the greyness of the featureless instant.

Myth means not so much a flight from history as a flight from profane reality. Myths, Eliade observes again,

> by virtue of the fact that they announce what happens *illo tempore*, are themselves an exemplary history that may repeat itself (periodically or otherwise) and that finds its significance and its value in this repetition itself.

Furthermore, it would be difficult to maintain that other fundamental sacred interpretations of reality are totally antihistorical. Samkhya Yoga itself, which is characterized by De Martino as 'the anti-historicist form of spiritual life par excellence', recognizes the world as basically real, although it is the product of human ignorance. It is true that

> in the moment in which the spirits (purushas) recover their liberty and their perfect harmony, in that very moment the cosmic forms, the totality of creation, will be reabsorbed into the primordial substance (arakrti). [52]

But it is also true that this is a complete vision of history which, in fact, is neither less coherent nor less complete, for example, than the traditional vision of Marxist historicism. The latter propounds the definitive and ideal perfectability of human society, which, no less than in the Samkhya Yoga, expresses itself in the annihilation of the currently existing society. This is a form of historicism that eventuates in antihistory. In fact, at some point, no matter how deep, every form of historicism is based on anti-history.

Historicism may aspire to an ideal and final society and reality which as such are anti-historical (Marxism), or it may assume the infinite perfectability of human society; or it may amount to a simple acceptance of the possibility of locating any phenomenon within the dialectical scheme of history as it is framed by human logic, today and tomorrow.

For example, for yoga the slavery of the soul resides in the fact that it is bound up with the cosmos, and thus with history and society. For the Marxist it resides in the fact that it is bound up with a contingent society instead of moving, by means of Marxist 'liberating techniques', towards an ideal society, the 'perfect' classless society. It might be objected that Marxism sees in development a 'dialectic' of historical facts and their logical co-ordination, but is there a dialectic that is greater than, for example, that of Karma?

To accept De Martino's thesis would shift us to an evaluative, philosophical plane, would require us to give a definite judgment on religious 'values', and would entail our becoming involved in a philosophical controversy thereby rendering our argument untenable from a scientific point of view. It is sufficient to emphasize that accepting his thesis would involve our taking a position and making a judgment on history as a whole, something which is rejected, for example, by Mircea Eliade, although he argues from the same historico-religious grounds. In this connection Eliade observes:

For, although contemporary thought prides itself upon having rediscovered the concrete man, it is no less true that its analyses refer mainly to the condition of modern Western man, so that it is biased by its lack of universality, by a kind of 'provincialism' tending, in the end, to monotony and sterility. (Cf. *Images and Symbols, op. cit*, p. 118.)

A discourse such as De Martino's could perhaps be carried on on the basis of only one conception of history, but what then of the many other conceptions of history including *sacred* interpretations?

And then, even if we accept the concept according to which the religious ritual-myth is a repetition of an archetypical fact which occurred *illo tempore*, why must we see in this 'anti-history *par excellence*'? As Eliade observes, the archetypes are history to the extent that they are phenomena, facts that happened *illo tempore*, but which none the less happened, and thus form the basis of an historical chronology.[53] We must not forget that the attempts of oriental liberation techniques to nullify or overcome the human condition amount to an attempt to create a new man, a man-god. Here lies the creative value of the sacred interpretation of history, a creative value which is no different from that of traditional historicism.[54]

At any rate, the sciences of man show us that schematizations, however fertile methodologically, cannot be exact and cannot have universal validity, even though they may be valid within certain limits. In its dynamic aspect, reality is the result of the concurrence of an innumerable series of elements, and every attempt to force its development into a unitary and definitive schema has systematically resulted in failure.

In fact, what happens is that we define as anti-historical those phenomena which give to history a sense that is 'different' from the one we usually give to it. We classify 'certain' interpretive myths as anti-historical because we consider them invalid, while at the same time we are convinced of the validity of our own myths. This is not very different from the situation in which the 'logical' knowledge of our own times is contrasted with that of the primitives, which, in view of its sacred character, is held to be prelogical.[55] As has been shown, primitive knowledge was not prelogical, but, since it was based on different beliefs and notions, whether true or false, it led to different results.

Similarly, in interpreting historical development, modern logic leads to different conclusions to the extent that it starts from a different series of beliefs: but there is no reason why this should lead us to reject other conceptions of history which may or may not be erroneous, but which—to the extent that they are total interpretations of historical development—are in no way 'anti-historical'. (This remark applies to the sociological, social-psychological, and historical-religious levels, naturally, rather than to the philosophical, where very different considerations become relevant.)

(d) *Extra-ecclesial religiosity, the privatization and secularization of religion in the context of the* wholly other

De Martino's arguments and the historicist position are now somewhat dated. In the new reality of post-industrial society, the foregoing discussion of the fundamental unity of religious and non-religious, ecclesial and extra-ecclesial, knowledge assumes considerable importance. This unity requires that our own argument confront the problem of a new religiosity that is no longer connected with the traditional matrix,[56] a spontaneous and privatized religion that some see as indicating that there is in fact no crisis of the sacred and the religious. They argue that what is taking place is not a crisis or a termination, but only a concealment.[57]

The new image of God which is taking shape, the new forms of morality, the space now available for a non-Christian religiosity — these are all well able to develop within the technopolis to which Cox[58] refers. Both historicist theses based on historical analysis, and theses connected with the sociology and theology of secularization — the former opposing and the others favouring religion, or a new religion, or Christianity without religion, and so on — operate with assumptions that transcend empirical verification.

But posing these last problems, and particularly those of extra-ecclesial religion and secularization in empirically meaningful terms entails questions about the relationships obtaining between the experience of the *wholly other* (that is, the dimensions, psychologically lived by the individual, of the experience once characterized as religious) and these more or less new theoretical models. More precisely, if there is an area of extra-ecclesial religiosity, how is it to be understood, and what are its boundaries? To what extent can this secularized and personalized religiosity reject the fundamental components that have generally characterized the religious fact and yet itself remain genuinely religious? And does this rejection extend to the *wholly other*? If that were so, the logical skeleton of our argument would collapse, at least in part.

Some of those who have studied the *wholly other* and the sacred have negated and 'translated' it in practice into the concept of the transcendent, although it is not clear how operational this concept is for the history of religion. According to Luckmann, the social order transcends the individual in a variety of ways,[59] and the dimensions of religious reality in contemporary society must be located in the context of this transcendence (which is not necessarily metaphysical) of the social with respect to the individual. Luckmann asks whether that which religion institutionalizes can have its social and personal validity, and whether it can, at least analytically, be separated from the finally constituted religious institution.[60] In a word, does anything vital survive once religious reality becomes detached from institutionalized religion?

Luckmann regards the isolated individual as a sheer fiction: all individuals are linked by inter-subjective ties to the past and future, and this is the circumstance that makes the individual something more than a mere thing. The social order appears as something superordinate, almost as a spiritual order that transcends the individual and confers meaning upon his being. Religion in particular, as a social phenomenon, epitomizes this quality of the superordinate, even though it also lives within the individual. The individual becomes a person at that moment at which he transcends his biological nature, and this possibility is itself basic to the personal aspect of religiosity.[61] Subjective religiosity is thus grounded in the possibility of transcending contingency and human nature, especially when the latter is seen as biological reality.

These considerations lead us to ask whether we can still conceive of religion as grounded in the *wholly other* — in contrast with a vague religious moralism. As we translate the religious phenomenon into new dimensions (for instance, through personalization; or through the replacement of the symbol by the moral norm in the process of socialization), we abandon the idea of the *wholly other* as the distinctive feature of religious hierophany. But in doing so, do we not transform this hierophany into something that is religious in name only? Thus we concur with Luckmann in saying that if religion is to be considered as such it must 'transcend' the contingent, in the sense of having psychological connotations.

Religion develops from a set of circumstances in which the psychological experience of the *wholly other* originates. It is something distinctly set over against the profane, and if this is our criterion we shall not be persuaded into denying or ignoring the existence of religious crisis by the type of lexical acrobatics with the concepts of sacredness, religiosity, religion, etc., that have been engaged in by Sturn and Savramis.[62] The *wholly other* is the basis for distinguishing religious fact: the crisis of religion is the crisis of the *wholly other*. Even if we discarded such concepts as desacralizatiòn, dechristianization, and so on, we should be left with the objective problem that the sense of the *wholly other* is degraded and concealed in the profane in secularized industrial and post-industrial society.

When the analytical perspective of depth psychology is applied to the history of religion, we find a return to the concept of the *wholly other* by means of a broad analysis of images and symbols which . . . are not irresponsible creations of the psyche; they respond to a need and fulfil a function, that of bringing to light the most hidden modalities of being.[63] All religious symbolism develops in the context of an awareness of the *wholly other*, and all profane reality is itself shot through with religious symbolism and 'decayed' images. Undoubtedly, '. . . symbols never disappear from the *reality* of the psyche. The aspect of them may change, but their function remains the same.'[64] Eliade describes with great insight how the religious phenomenon both is and is not present through symbols and images, when he observes that

> The most abject 'nostalgia' discloses the nostalgia for Paradise. The images of the 'oceanic paradise' that we have mentioned haunt our novels as well as our films. (Who was it said of the cinema that it was the 'factory of dreams'?) We might just as well analyse the images suddenly released by any sort of music, sometimes by the most sentimental song; and we should find that these images express the nostalgia for a mythicized past trans-formed into an archetype, and that this 'past' signifies not only regrets for a vanished time but countless other meanings; it expresses all that might have been but was not, the sadness of all existence, which *is* only by ceasing to be something else; regrets that one does not live in the country or in the times evoked by the song . . . in short, the longing for something *altogether different* from the present instant; something in fact inaccessible or irretrievably lost . . .[65]

Thus, and this concept brings us back to Luckmann's discussion, it is justifiable to hold that, although the desacralization which is taking place in contemporary society alters the content of religiosity, it has not completely destroyed the essential component of spiritual life. Through the image and the symbol, through all of this decayed mythology, a nexus is preserved that connects religion with the secularized and desacralized world. Thus, in order to rediscover the religious fact, we must follow the river of spirituality which, over the centuries, has divided into smaller and smaller streams, finally finding its last receptacle in the depths of the individual, becoming totally privatized, or perhaps totally desacralized.

Thus the need for the *wholly other* survives, but 'how desecrated, degraded, and artificialized'.[66] It is thus essential, and here lies the importance of Luckmann's essay, to seek out and rediscover the mythology and the theology that are disguised in the chronicles of every day, in the degraded banality of the life of every being, in a word, in the context of a new secularized religion.

'Modern man,' remarks Eliade, 'is free to despise mythologies, but that will not prevent his continuing to feed upon decayed myths and degraded images.'[67] This is a fundamental concept, although, after all, it requires a measure of verification. But, once we have iden-tified, by means of images and symbols, the nexus of the *wholly others* that mark the progress of *homo religiosus* through time, *the necessity remains of historically locating these conditions and these situations specifically in the contemporary era.*

Thus, to return to the problem with which we are concerned, the argument must consider the condition of historical man located in his time, without however forgetting the psychic rhythms and states, the fundamental requirements and features of an individual who, in some of these very states, transcends time.

> Man is also aware of several temporal rhythms, and not only of historical time—his own time, his historical con-temporaneity . . . such historic awareness plays a relatively minor part in human consciousness, to say nothing of the zones of the unconscious which also belong to the make-up of the whole human being.[68]

But if, at bottom, it is the chain of the *wholly other* that securely binds together the various manifestations of the religious through space and time, and if, in society, taken as a unified whole, it is transcendence which most specifically characterizes the religious in industrial society, we are then confronted with the following problem: do industrial and post-industrial societies leave any space within themselves, and within the process of rationalization to which they are committed, for the transcendent *as a conscious, objective dimension of the wholly other*? That is: once the problem is thus posed, if we grant that the transcendent exists and that it is the locus of extra-ecclesial religiosity, does it, in the long run, have rights of citizenship in a post-industrial society oriented toward total rationalization?

(e) *The wholly other and one-dimensional society*

Luckmann's hypothesis posits both the privatization of religion and of the *wholly other*, and also the idea of society as an entity transcending the individual. This distinction appears to be quite contrary to what Marcuse suggests — namely that in post-industrial society, the contrast between private and public existence, and between individual and social needs, dissolves. Marcuse calls this new society, founded on the tertiary sector of the economy, a one-dimensional society, founded on the tertiary sector of the economy, a one-dimensional society, which differs from all previous societies. In this type of society, service rather than the supply of products, becomes a dominant concern: men have reached a cultural level beyond that at which they are merely the producers and consumers of goods. Many of what appear to be produced commodities are really no more than services produced to meet induced demand — evident, for example, in the mass media, the diversification of fashion to different age sets, the diversification of provision for various interest groups that have been stimulated. The tertiary society allows the individual to participate as something more than merely a worker: he is socialized in the context of this new dimension and acquires an integrated system of values (or of non-values) that characterize the entire consumer society.

In this new society, the *wholly other* itself takes on new forms. In so far as it remains a possibility for men, it implies in itself a criticism of the existing social order, and is itself a conception that transcends that social order. Yet it is more difficult for such implied criticism to persist: the social order itself is increasingly dictated — or claims to be dictated — by considerations of 'that which is rational'. We do not need to take up the question of whether the individual's felt-needs are (in whatever sense one confers on the words) 'true' or 'false'. What concerns us is whether in the context of a society in which most of the needs are what Marcuse terms 'false', namely 'the prevailing needs to relax, to have fun, to behave and consume in accordance with the advertisements, to love and hate what others love and hate . . .'[69], there is a still a place for the *wholly other* as a unitary religious fact. If the sense of the *wholly other* is itself to be degraded and fragmented in this type of society, may not, in the context of extra-ecclesial religiosity, the personalization and transcendence to which Luckmann refers, merely reflect further changes in the human psyche, until the *wholly other* will become so dessicated that it may be reduced virtually to biological levels, or to what Jung would call the archetype of the personality.

Clearly, it is abstractly possible that the tendency towards total rationalization and the construction of a one-dimensional world, is the produce of an impulse that also operates at the bio-psychological level. Psychic activity is correlated with biological processes, and even religiosity and the experience of the sacred are connected with such processes. The facility for perceiving the religious fact, the immediate religious experience, the subsequent elaboration, and symbolism, are all involved in the total psycho-physical condition. Yet, if the transformation of society were to affect the bio-psychological facts of personality in such a way that there was a 'jump' in the physical bases of personality, then, clearly, it would become materially impossible to place oneself *outside* the system; man would be a material part of the system, and would be biologically deprived of the possibility of striving towards transcendence. He would become incapable of certain experiences, in particular the experience of the *wholly other*. This would amount to something similar to an authentic biological mutation.

We may then ask whether there is a religious residue that is irreducible to its individual manifestations, and that is also uneliminable, even under the impress of the one-dimensional society. The work of Jung allows us to throw doubt on any inductive argument concerning the extinction of religion. Jung maintained that the archetypes, irreducible to contingent personal situations, reappear with persistent regularity and must belong to a kind of unconscious that is shared by all men. From the overlapping of the archetype and the *numinosum*, it is possible to argue that the sacred experience is itself 'primitive' and general. Whereas for Freud, the image of God is, from infancy, a projection of the father, for Jung, the earthly father is essentially the image of the celestial one. Yet, the totality of Jung's archetypes are rather similar to Freud's Id: the difference is that in the case of the archetypes, the range of apparently undifferentiated impulses at the basis of the personality displays a much greater variety, and one of the impulses in question is the religious impulse. According to Freud, the demands of the Id are irrenounceable. Zunini justly remarks that 'the sum of the archetypes is the sum of all the latent possibilities of the human psyche'.[70] Among these possibilities is the religious 'possibility'.

The problems and questions overlap and multiply, and the problems, which we have intentionally multiplied in order to show how difficult is their solution, are strictly related, not only to the theoretical considerations we have advanced, but also to the features that will characterize the society of which we are a part and to the confidence we ultimately have in man as a being who is not reducible exclusively to his biological and psychological significance.

On this point we are very close to Marcuse:

> the distinguishing feature of advanced industrial society is its effective suffocation of those needs which demand liberation — liberation also from that which is tolerable and rewarding and comfortable — while it sustains and absolves the destructive power and repressive function of the affluent society. Here, the social controls exact the overwhelming need for the production and consumption of waste; the need for stupefying work where it is no longer a real necessity; the need for modes of relaxation which soothe and prolong this stupefaction; the need for maintaining such deceptive liberties as free competition at administered prices, a free press which censors itself, free choice between brands and gadgets.[71]

These *liberties* are produced by a society that tends to rationalize and objectify thoughts and needs, to compress and obliterate the *wholly other*, since (at least apparently) the *wholly other* is alien to this society, with which even the process of privatization of extra-ecclesial religiosity must come to terms. It is also, and above all, extra-ecclesial religiosity especially that asserts and maintains itself *precisely in this type* of society.

Although it seems paradoxical, on the whole, religion, by virtue of being connected with the past, with the primordial instant, with something that transcends — or would transcend — contingent reality, exists largely apart from the great machine of industrial and post-industrial society. And thus, within certain limits, it is able to escape its hold. Yet if on the contrary, if Marcuse's argument is valid, privatized extra-ecclesial religion *could* have little prospect of survival.

At any rate, one must consider that the authentic religious dimension tends, or should tend in its intrinsic character, to transcend society, and to become an element of criticism and a term of comparison with respect to a society which, both internally and as a system, ceases to be capable of value judgments and thus of criticism and self-criticism. Exactly because it is characterized by the *wholly other*, the religious dimension *must be a critical reality*. Indeed, it can only be a critical reality capable of transcending the social and — to the extent that it does so — of supplying the individual with the means to develop his personality so as to make it capable of life and criticism which are autonomous with respect to the emergence of the one-dimensional society.

But, exactly because of its critical component, the religious dimension must also partake of the social. And here lies the danger that the 'person' (who psychologically and theoretically seeks to transcend the society in which he lives, and who sees it, in a certain sense, from the outside) may become a formally religious individual, but in fact one totally integrated with the society, religiously degraded, reduced to one dimension: that is, one who, together with other men, is unconsciously intent on destroying what depends on the *wholly other* for its own existence.

Private space, then, must survive so that an organic and adult religiosity can be formed and find a place within it.

But, according to Marcuse, and *to some extent* also in our own view

> Today this private space has been invaded and whittled down by technological reality. Mass production and mass distribution claim the *entire* individual, and industrial psychology has long since ceased to be confined to the factory. The manifold processes of introjection seem to be ossified in almost mechanical reactions. The result is, not adjustment but *mimesis*: an immediate identification of the individual with *his* society and, through it, with the society as a whole.[72]

At this point it seems that Luckmann's argument concerning privatization and transcendence is less valid than it had appeared at first, less acceptable. I do not suggest that Marcuse's thesis should be uncritically accepted, but undoubtedly it must at least be tested with reference to a wider argument.

This test seems to be necessary, although Marcuse admits of no discussion concerning his hypotheses when he says that

> the concept of alienation seems to become questionable when the individuals identify themselves with the existence which is imposed upon them and have in it their own development and satisfaction. This identification is not illusion but reality. However, the reality constitutes a more progressive stage of alienation. The latter has become entirely objective; the subject which is alienated is swallowed up by its alienated existence. There is only one dimension, and it is everywhere and in all forms. The achievements of progress defy ideological indictment as well as justification; before their tribunal, the 'false consciousness' of their rationality becomes the true consciousness. [73]

False consciousness and authentic consciousness in which there is no place for the *wholly other*? And thus, ultimately, a structural change in the psychology of the individual which is brought about by the changes produced by industrial and post-industrial society? Undoubtedly, and here Marcuse is partly right, modern science

> (a) . . . strengthens the shift of theoretical emphasis from the metaphysical 'What is . . .?' to the functional 'How . . .?', and (b) . . . establishes a practical (though by no means absolute) certainty which, in its operations with matter, is with good conscience free from commitment to any substance outside the operational context. In other words, theoretically, the transformation of man and nature has no other objective limits than those offered by the brute factuality of matter, its still unmastered resistance to knowledge and control. [74]

It seems, then, that the problem of extra-ecclesial religiosity restates in analogous terms the whole problem of ecclesiastical religiosity, albeit on a different scale and though we may finally conclude that the abandonment of religious practice does not, in fact, coincide with the abandonment of all religiosity.

Indeed, one may assert with reasonable assurance that on the whole the crisis of religion in our time, real as it is, takes on less serious dimensions than might appear from a simple analysis of the decline in traditional religious practice. The new dimensions of technology and science, of the city and of the technopolis, thus put forward, in analogous but also novel (because more open, and more dramatic) conditions, the problem of religiosity in its extra-ecclesial form.

As we have seen, we must ask ourselves also with respect to extra-ecclesial religiosity whether in our society the *wholly other* is still possible in the future. As we have noted above, given the current limitations of science, it is virtually impossible to answer this question in terms of the sciences of man. It would be a matter of establishing if and to what extent the evolution of which we have spoken can substantively modify the characteristics of the human individual. Among other things, this is a problem which, on the one side, goes beyond the boundaries of sociology toward the other sciences of man, from general biology to the biology of the brain, from endocrinology to general and social psychology. On the other it raises issues for philosophy and philosophical anthropology. Even posed in wider terms, the question would not receive an unequivocal answer.

Modern society tends, as we have seen, to translate everything into 'one dimension', which in and of itself excludes the religious, even extra-ecclesial religiosity. If speaking of religion is still to make sense, that religiosity must involve what Marcuse calls a 'transcendent project', which stands in contrast with this one-dimensional society. To exist at all, religion must move between two apparently contradictory poles. On the one hand, it must not oppose the development of society as such, and on the other, it must bring about a profound contradiction of it: on the one side it must become integrated into historical development, and on the other it must transcend it.

If this extra-ecclesial religiosity has the importance attributed to it by some students, Luckmann and Savramis, for instance, then it must be integrated in society to a relatively high degree. In practice, we do not have sufficient evidence to say whether in the real situation this is so. Its dimensions would have to be determined through the study of its expressions. We might, for example, try to discover whether a new image of God existed which was relevant to, and which expressed, some aspects of industrial and post-industrial society, and the extent of its diffusion. Clearly, the image of God is bound up with the image of the world as the tangible, attainable, and verifiable world in which man moves. The religious worlds of the Greek gods and of medieval Christendom were conceptually integrated with distinctive social systems, for which they were, in part, functional expressions. In the same way, the image of God required by a religion that is privatized, but that is integrated in a new form of society, must be an image (within certain limits) of that world, of the secularized and rapidly changing metropolis, of the new physical reality, of which, through technical-scientific progress, man seems to be a co-creator, and so on. A society in which the proportion of those involved with the tertiary sector of the economy has risen so dramatically, will not sustain images of God that were appropriate in societies where the vast majority were in primary economic activities.

Until not many years ago, religiosity in advanced countries had developed in the context of an industrializing and industrialized society, but as we move into a post-industrial stage we must expect religion, and the crisis of religion, to take new shape. The human — one might almost say, the redemptive — significance of religion changes with the changes in the general equilibrium of the vital rhythms as society shifts first from agriculture to industry, and then from industry to services. But there are other changes, too. Psychological attitudes to life change with changes in public health (particularly with respect to the precariousness of life); in the material conditions of life (and thus with respect to the frustrations associated with those conditions); and the cultural conditions (which affect the sophistication and enlightenment with which religious issues are approached). We need do no more than allude to changes in the infant mortality rates in advanced countries: from 160 per thousand births to 27 in the United States between 1900 and 1960, for example. Put another way, it is expected that in the year 2000 A.D., some 980 people in a thousand born alive will reach the age of twenty, compared with 450 in the year 1750.[75] Such changes remove the individual from psychological participation in the reality of death: they predicate a rapid evolution in the complex psychology that relates religion to the precariousness of existence. As the life span is less readily perceived as limited, images of physical survival rapidly penetrate the secularized society, and they may do so more deeply as time goes on. Already, in the United States, men expect to 'deep-freeze' the human body at death, in the expectation of resuscitating it at some future time. Such a prospect profoundly alters the conception of life and death, and the human meaning of religion.

Within certain not yet clearly defined limits, the religious experience has been bound up with a profound feeling of insecurity typical of the human species, an insecurity that expresses the perennial threat to existence. The diminution of this insecurity with the progress of science must have its consequences, since anxiety and insecurity have been among the primary origins of religious awareness, even though they are not necessarily its source. We know from Stouffer's research that a considerable proportion of soldiers involved in combat experienced an increase in faith in God, [76] even though war in general weakens traditional religiosity (by virtue of its disruption of settled life patterns). Vergote's studies show that on the whole people pray more in conditions of particular distress, and when confronted with death (especially their own). [77] If the correlation between religion and the precariousness of existence is so great, then undoubtedly the recession of the image of death through technological-scientific advance cannot but exercise a profound influence. Naturally, this can happen both by diminishing the appeal of religion, thus weakening the sense of the religious, and by connecting the sense of the religious to other presuppositions less immediately connected with aspects of the human condition, thus profoundly changing their significance. Thus, some of the psychological motivations of the religious, as it was understood until yesterday, to a large extent until today, and in some measure until tomorrow, threaten to be superseded. And we must suppose that extra-ecclesial religiosity will be most subject to these changes, since it is a religiosity that is not organizationally protected.

Of course, the need for security will continue. It is not out of the question that the search for security will not continue to be a search for God or for some transcendent reality. It is also possible, even within the narrow limits of psychological research, that what Bergson calls 'the true source and true origin of religion' is to be found in something with respect to which such needs as those for survival and for security are only occasional manifestations. Extra-ecclesial religiosity has not lessened the importance of the problems that concern the sociology of religion: it has indeed posed them in a more immediate and dramatic way. The human soul appears more naked, thus deprived of its superstructure, and exposed, almost defenceless, to the psychological assault of the new world.

2. THE END OF THE SACRED AND OF RELIGION?

We have examined five groups of evidence concerning the survival of religion. First, the statistical evidence, viewed in historical perspective, indicated decline and its continuance. Second, we considered the contrast between non-religious (scientific) and religious knowledge, and concluded that the evidence was not as unambiguous and definitive as has sometimes been maintained. Third, we found historical arguments, and in particular that concerning the anti-historicism of religion, less persuasive and definitive than might have been expected. Fourth, with respect to extra-ecclesial religiosity as evidence for the survival of religion, we found the arguments inadequate. And fifth, we recognized that the broad considerations concerning the consumer society of the post-industrial world and its (Marcusian) one-dimensionality afforded disruptive prospects for religion, although once again, these were not completely convincing. Thus, although we recognize in the evidence a systematic tendency towards the loss of the sense of the sacred, and the extinction of religion, the extent and the complexity of the phenomenon, do not permit us to be unequivocal.[78] There survive, however latent they may be, factors that are capable of turning the ideological and psychological consequences of the process of technological and scientific evolution into other directions than those that might be regarded as the most expectable developments. Even though modern society appears to be becoming increasingly impoverished with respect to the phenomenal component of religion, evident even in the evolution of extra-ecclesial and secular forms, none the less we cannot with certainty presuppose an impoverishment *tout court* of the sacred.

The general rational arguments overlook the psychological reality of the experience of the *wholly other*, but even when we turn to individual psychology or to the relations of the individual and the group, we do not encounter the intimate essence of the religious fact.

The manifestations on which our analyses are based often have no more than a symbolic value, and can take us only so far. Since the human psyche is a synthesis of both conscious and unconscious aspects, we may ask whether the external disappearance of the sense of the sacred and the religious corresponds to an absolute disappearance. What we know is that there is a decay in the social manifestations of the sense of the sacred. At the same time, the individual's consciousness of having a sense of the sacred may also be expected to decay. But what occurs in the unconscious? May not this concern for the sacred persist in the depths of the ego, ready to re-emerge into consciousness, and perhaps also in the social sphere, once the influence of contemporary circumstances have weakened? There remains uncertainty about this, of course, which marks our whole inquiry into the deeper issues in this field.

One might maintain the thesis that in industrial society, the sacred and the religious tend more and more to become a sort of unexpressed potentiality instead of the active, manifest elements that they were until relatively recently. Indeed, if we adopt the concept of archetype developed by Jung, Jacobi, and others, we might be led to consider the social decline of the sacred as a reversible phenomenon. [79] Nor need the concept of the archetype be regarded as beyond the appropriate scope of the social sciences: a variety of scholars in various disciplines have given clues towards an adequate interpretation of this concept, including Hediger, Portmann, Lorenz, and Laverdes. Lorenz writes of 'innate schemata' that are independent of experience, although clearly does not imply that there are innate images in the human psyche in the Platonic sense, but only that the human psycho-physical structure is oriented towards certain particular manifestations of awareness and cognitive acquisitiveness in the presence of determinate stimuli. Jacobi observes that

> It has been remarked in many quarters that, from the standpoint of our present scientific knowledge, acquired characteristics or memories cannot be inherited. Those who have raised this argument have assiduously overlooked the fact that Jung's archetypes are structural conditions of the psyche, which in a certain constellation (of an inward and outward nature) can bring forth certain 'patterns' — and that this has nothing to do with the inheriting of definite images. [80]

Thus, one might maintain that the innate scheme that potentially favours the experience of the sacred may survive this phase of development of consciousness of the sacred in the human psyche.

Even if one does not accept the concept of the archetype, the possible validity of these observations is suggested by the history of the psyche of modern man: the spontaneous re-discovery of myths, of archetypes, of archaic symbolism, is a frequent occurrence. In this context, Eliade remarks that depth of psychology has freed the historian of religion from his last hesitations. A deep analysis of symbolism might help us to understand what survives within the psyche of desacralized man. From the beginning symbolism has appeared as a creation of the psyche, and thus (and I believe that this is also Eliade's position) a study of symbols in their manifestations does not exclude the possibility of discovering an unconscious sacred motivation even in the most desacralized and apparently secular symbolisms and myths. It could be that a secular, or an atheist, symbolism might conceal the development of a new unconscious sacred symbolism capable of acquiring vast social dimensions.

Whatever may be the case in this respect, there is another aspect of this problem that may leave us less certain about the reversibility of the decline of religiosity. The religious crisis is the consequence of the interaction of (mainly individual) features typical of previous phases of civilization, and the new features produced by industrial society. The antithesis between these two groups of factors leads to a crisis of the sacred. But after some time the features arising from earlier conditions of society will disappear. What might then happen? We do not know how the psyche will react to the new conditions. Our review of the various levels of inquiry relevant to the problem of religion in contemporary society, do not allow us to say where the process of secularization will terminate, or whether there will be any substantial reversal of the current tendency. All that can be said with certainty is that the decline of the sacred is intimately connected with the changes in society and human psychology. It cannot be considered as merely a contingent fact: it is associated with the collapse, whether temporarily or finally, of traditions, cultures, and values.

From the religious point of view, humanity has entered a long night that will become darker and darker with the passing of the generations, and of which no end can yet be seen. It is a night in which there seems to be no place for a conception of God, or for a sense of the sacred, and ancient ways of giving significance to our own existence, of confronting life and death, are becoming increasingly untenable. At bottom, the motivations for religious behaviour and for faith persist—the need to explain ourselves and what surrounds us, the anguish, and the sense of precariousness. But man remains uncertain whether somewhere there exists, or ever existed, something different from uncertainty, doubt, and existential insecurity.

Notes

INTRODUCTION

1. For reasons of space he does not expound and discuss the Marxist positions: but this represents only a postponement of that task.

THE THEME

1. Lewis Mumford, *The Condition of Man*, London: Secker and Warburg, 1944, p. 11.
2. *Ibid.*, p. 12.
3. *Ibid.*, p. 3.

CHAPTER 1

1. See P. van Hooydonk, 'Critical Considerations on "La Sociologie Religieuse" ', *Social Compass*, VII, 5, (1961), pp. 387–406.
2. See Camillo Pellizzi, 'Caproni, Parruche e Altro', *Rassegna Italiana di Sociologia*, II, i, (1961), pp. 99–112.
3. Dupréel is among those whose Weltanschauung affects his view of this problem. He sees religion as a way of making sense of the 'interval of phenomena' that science has as yet been unable to explain. The task of the sociology of religion is the analysis of social groups and acts the existence of which and the transformations of which are the result of the dynamics of this 'interval'. Apart from being superficial, this definition of research is based on ideological presuppositions. Other definitions of religion (and thus by implication of the object of the sociology of religion) are no more convincing or useful. Croce sees in religion the partial perception of 'invisible forces' (not a fruitful sociological concept); Croce tells us that religion is an 'imaginative and therefore immature and contradictory form of philosophy,' a definition that is very similar to Dupréel's. For William James, religion represents, 'the feelings, acts, and experiences of individual men in their solitude, so far as they apprehend themselves to stand in relation to whatever they may consider the divine', *The Varieties of Religious Experience*, New York: Crowell-Collier 1961 edn., p. 42. This is a subjective definition which has no utility for us, as we shall see below, when we discuss the work of Howard Becker. These expressly

philosophical definitions may well possess some validity, but they remain at the margin of our problem.

4.   Jack Goody, 'Religion and Ritual; the Definitional Problem', *The British Journal of Sociology*, XII, 2, (1961), pp. 142–64.

5.   In this connection see Schmidt, *The Origin and Growth of Religion. Facts and Theories*, (H. J. Rose, trans.). London: Methuen & Co., 1930.

6.   He observes that

>   All known religious beliefs, whether simple or complex, present one common characteristic: they presuppose a classification of all things, real and ideal, of which men think, into two classes or opposed groups, generally designated by two distinct terms which are translated well enough by the terms *profane* and *sacred*. This division of the world into two domains, the one containing all that is sacred, the other all that is profane, is the distinctive trait of religious thought; the beliefs, myths, dogmas and legends are either representations or systems of representations which express the nature of sacred things, the virtues and powers attributed to them, or their relations with each other and with profane things. But by sacred things one must not understand simply those personal beings which are called gods or spirits; a rock, a tree, a spring, a pebble, a piece of wood, a house, in a word, anything can be sacred. A rite can have this character; in fact, the rite does not exist which does not have it to a certain degree. There are words, expressions and formulas which can be pronounced only by the mouths of consecrated persons; there are gestures and movements which everybody cannot perform.

E. Durkheim, *The Elementary Forms of Religious Life*, (J. Swain, trans.), London: Allen and Unwin, 1915, p. 37.

7.   From a certain perspective, Durkheim's viewpoint may thus be seen as paralleling, and at the same time contrasting with, that of Comte. For Comte sociolatry is at the final stage of evolution, while for Durkheim it lies at the beginning. For the latter, primitive beliefs, such as the belief in the group totem, in mana, in the orenda, are already in themselves expressions and manifestations of the cult of society, in the same way that rituals and religious gatherings represent the mystic sublimation of the various 'forces' whose integration constitutes society.

8.   Cf. Talcott Parsons, *Essays in Sociological Theory*, Glencoe, Ill.: Free Press, 1954, p. 202.

9.   See W. DeVries, 'Magic and Religion', *History of Religion*, I, 2, (1962), pp. 214–21.

10.   E. E. Evans-Pritchard, *Witchcraft Oracles and Magic Among the Azande*, London, 1937.

11.   Some sociologists have virtually ignored the religious dimension in society, giving only brief attention to churches and other religious and para-religious organizations. Thus, to give one example, for Ferdinand Tönnies, religion is an appendix to sociology, something that

can be ignored, since without it the fundamental structure of his sociology would not lose anything essential. But since religious life is an essential component of social life, Tönnies' neglect of it sub-stantially weakens his approach. See J. Leif, *La Sociologie de Tönnies*, Paris: Presses Universitaires de France, 1946. Of Tönnies' own work c.f. especially *Community and Society* (trans. C. P. Loomis), East Lansing, Mich.: Michigan State University Press, 1957.

12.   These approaches do not provide adequate conceptualization of the socio-religious problem. The same can be said of others, such as Vilfredo Pareto and Toniolo. See V. Pareto, *Trattato di Sociologia Generale*, Milan: Edizioni di Comunità, 1964; Luigi Sturzo, *La Società Sua Natura e Leggi*, Bergamo, 1949; *Del Metodo Sociologico, Riposta ai Critici*, Bergamo, 1949; *La Vera Vita, Sociologia del Soprannaturale*, Rome, 1974; G. Toniolo, *Opera Omnia*, edited by the Comitato Opera Omnia di G. Toniolo, Vatican City, 1940.

13.   For further discussion see, in particular, the introduction and the second part of my book, *Il problema della Logica nelle Scienze Umane*, Padua: Marsilio Ed., 1964.

14.   Cf. Gabriel le Bras, 'Secteurs et Aspects Nouveaux de la Sociologie Religieuse', *Cahiers Internationaux de Sociologie*, 1, 1946, p. 65 ff. Le Bras rightly observes that it does not make sense to set limits to religious sociology 'puisqu'elle (religion) embrasse tous les temps, tous les pays, tous les songes des hommes sur l'eternel et l'infini.'

15.   Cf. A. Faggiotto, *Filosofia e Religione*, Padua: Liviana Ed., 1951–52.

16.   To group the various approaches into schools would bring with it the imprecision which chararizes all such schematizations, even though it would enable us to identify the basic arguments on which the various theories are grounded.

17.   There is a formidable number of approaches with philosophical, political, and ethnological foundations, which must be taken into account in any socio-religious inquiry. In merely listing the schools, one realizes that many authors approach our problems from an ideological standpoint or from disciplines with limited methodological equipment. Without seeming to realize the enormous diversity of the field he surveys, P. Honigsheim makes a detailed list of schools and approaches which deal with socio-religious problems. (Cf. P. Honigsheim, 'Sociology of Religion: Complementary Analyses of Religious Institutions', *Modern Sociological Theory in Continuity and Change*, New York: Dryden Press, 1957, pp. 450–81.)

Beginning at the end of the First World War, Honigsheim distinguishes seven basic schools of religious sociology: (1) the socialist school of a more or less orthodox Marxian character; (2) the Dar-winian evolutionary; (3) the positivistic (Comte, Durkheim, and their schools); (4) the Catholic, first through its Platonic-Augustinian representatives such as Frohschammer, Günther, Knoodt, Vogelsang, and secondly through the neo-thomists and scholastics in general; (5)

the psychoanalytic; (6) the anthropological, with special reference to Gräbner, Schmidt, and their Latin-American followers; and (7) the German neo-Kantian, with special reference to Jellinek, Troeltsch, and Weber.

18. Among values, Becker includes also the categories of sacred and secular.

19. Cf. Roger Caillois, *L'homme et le Sacré*, Paris: Gallimard, 1950, p. 11.

20. In spite of our qualifications, we have been charged with attempting an exhaustive definition of the sacred.

21. We hereby give an implicit answer to the objections raised by Franco Demarchi in his long article 'Profilo Sociologico della Dinamica Religiosa', *Humanitas*, 10, 1961, pp. 788–809.

22. R. Caillois, *L'homme et le Sacré, op. cit.*, p. 17.

23. *Ibid.*, p. 25.

24. Cf. Gordon W. Allport, *The Individual and His Religion*, New York: Macmillan, 1950.

25. *Op. cit.*, p. 26.

26. *Ibid.*

27. Cf. C. Pellizzi, *op. cit.*

28. With respect to these considerations and some of the previous ones, cf. the excellent book by M. von Mankeliunas, *Psicología de la Religiosidad*, Madrid: Religión y Cultura, 1961.

29. Cf. W. H. Clark, *The Psychology of Religion. An Introduction to Religious Experience and Behavior*, New York: Macmillan, 1958.

30. Cf. Mircea Eliade, *Trattato di Storia delle Religioni*, Turin: Einaudi, 1954, p. xi. This reference is to Ernesto di Martino's preface to the Italian edition.

31. Mircea Eliade, *Traité d'histoire des religions*, Paris: Payot, p. 16 ff.

32. *Ibid.*, p. 20.

33. Cf. Faggiotto, *Filosofia e Religione, op. cit.*

34. Cf. Rudolf Otto, *The Idea of the Holy*, London: Oxford University Press, 1923.

35. This validity is not affected by the fact that a number of Otto's theses on the origin of religion are debatable. Although we maintain that his approach is generally useful on the level of the psychology of religion, we do not intend to give him equal support in all areas. It is appropriate to point out here that he has made a certain contribution to a detailed psychological view of the religious fact. (The first edition of the volume was published at Breslau in 1917 under the title *Über das Irrationale in der Idee des Göttlichen und sein Verhältnis zum Rationalen*).

36. Otto, *op. cit.*, p. 12.

37. *Ibid.*, p. 13.

38. *Ibid.*, p. 20. This awareness of a super-power may well be summarized in the words of the Moslem contemplative, Bajesid Bostani.

'then the holiest God revealed to me his secret and revealed in me all his glory. And then as I was contemplating, no longer with my own but with his eyes, I saw that, compared with his, my own light was naught but darkness and shadow. And also my greatness and my power were as nothing in comparison to him. And when I looked upon the works of piety and example which I had offered in his service with a truthful eye, I saw that they came, not from myself, but from him.'

Cf. Tezkereh-I-Evlia, *Tadhkiratu l'avliya*, (Memoirs of the friends of God), French translation, Paris: Courteille, 1880, p. 132. This Italian translation is in Ernesto Buonaiuti, *La Vita dello Spirito*, Rome: De Carlo, 1948.

39. M. Eliade, *op. cit.*, p. 27.
40. R. Otto, *op. cit.*, p. 61.
41. *Ibid.*, p. 119.
42. *Ibid.*, pp. 29–30.
43. M. Eliade, *op. cit.*, p. 25.
44. Thus for example:

A cultural stone manifests, at a certain moment of history, a certain modality of the sacred: this stone shows that the sacred is something different from the surrounding cosmic setting, that, like a rock, the sacred "is" absolute, invulnerable, static, and immune from becoming. This ontophany (with its religious projection) of the cultual stone may become modified in its form during the course of history. The same stone may be worshipped later, not because of what it immediately reveals (no longer as an elementary hierophany, etc.), but because it has become integrated into a sacred space (a temple, altar, etc.) or because it is considered to be the epiphany of a god, etc. The stone remains something different from its surroundings; it continues to be sacred in virtue of the primordial hierophany which picked it out. Nevertheless, the value given it changes with the religious theory within which the hierophany becomes integrated.

M. Eliade, *op. cit.*, p. 35.

45. *Ibid.*, p. 35.
46. *Ibid.*, p. 24.
47. *Ibid.*, p. 26.
48. M. Eliade, *Images et Symboles*, Paris: Gallimard, 1952, p. 70.
49. M. Eliade, *Traité d'histoire des religions, op. cit.*, p. 32.
50. One may question the thesis of Bergson when he maintains that

there is no religion without rites and ceremonies. The religious representation is above all an occasion for these religious acts. They doubtless emanate from belief, but they at once react on it and strengthen it: if gods exist, they must have their worship; but since there is worship, then there must be gods. This solidarity of the god with the homage paid him makes of religious truth a thing apart, having no common measure with speculative truth, and depending, up to a certain point, on man. Henri Bergson, *The Two Sources of Morality and Religion*, (trans. R. A. Audra & C. Brereton), London: Macmillan, 1935, p. 171.

51. Cf. Thomas Luckmann, Paper at the Symposium on Unbelief, Rome, 1969, p. 13: published in R. Caporale and A. Grumelli, *The Culture of Unbelief*, Berkeley and Los Angeles: University of California Press, 1971.

CHAPTER 2

1. Of this author cf. *Religion, Society and the Individual*, Macmillan, New York, 1957; 'Present Status of the Sociology of Religion', *Journal of Religion*, XXXI (1951), pp. 194–210; 'Areas for Research in the Sociology of Religion', *Sociology and Social Research*, XLII, 6, (1958), pp. 466–72.

2. The evolution of science exercises a profound influence on human thought and human attitudes in general, although this influence may be felt only in the long run. As Whitehead justly observes, such changes take place cyclically.

    General climates of opinion persist for periods of about two to three generations, that is to say, for periods of sixty to a hundred years. There are also shorter waves of thought, which play on the surface of the tidal movement. We shall find, therefore, transformations in the European outlook, slowly modifying the successive centuries. Alfred North Whitehead, *Science and the Modern World*, London: Cambridge Univ. Press, 1926, p. 24.

    Naturally, the sociologist of religion is primarily interested in the longer waves which characterize an entire phase in the development of human history.

3. M. Pfliegler, *Die religiöse situation*, Graz-Salzburg-Vienna: Verlag Anton Pustet, 1948. This work, which is not sociological, shows extreme sensitivity toward the most recent religious crisis.

4. Cf. our essay 'L'oggetto della sociologia religiosa', *Notiziario di Sociologia*, I, 4, (1958), pp. 1–7. Here are proposed in embryonic form the concepts developed in the first chapter of this book.

5. Jean Chelini, *La ville et l'Église*, Paris: Éditions du Cerf, 1958.

6. See S. S. Acquaviva, *op. cit.*, pp. 6–7.

7. Cf. J. Chelini, *op. cit.*

8. Concerning the standardization of methods of research in the sociology of religion cf. also Edvard Vogt, 'Religious Sociology and the Standardisation of its Methods', *Euntes Docete*, VIII, 2, (1955), pp. 205–21. See also S. S. Acquaviva, 'L'oggetto della sociologia religiosa', *Notiziario di sociologia*, I, 4, (1958), pp. 1–7; *idem*, 'Religione e irreligione nell'età postindustriale', *Studi di Sociologia*, 1968; and the volume *idem, Religione e irreligione nell'età postindustriale: diabattito su l'eclissi del sacro nella società industriale*, Rome: AVE, 1971.

9. P. Deffontaines, 'Introduction à une géographie des religions', *Chronique sociale de France*, (1934), p. 77 ff., and *Géographie et Religion*, Paris: Gallimard, 1948.

10. Sabino S. Acquaviva, 'La sociologia della religione', *Questioni di sociologia*, Brescia: La Scuola, 1966.

11. On this topic cf. also G. Le Bras, 'Mesure de la vitalité du Catholicisme', *Cahiers internationaux de sociologie*, VIII (1950), p. 6 ff.

12. Given the nature of our study we omit consideration of the more intense forms of religiosity, such as extreme devotion or holiness, which, at least for the last few centuries, affect only a very limited section of society.

13. It is difficult to distinguish between those who cling to the great rituals of devotion to tradition or a passion for their folkloristic elements, and those who experience them as expressions of their religion.

14. Cf. J. Chelini, *op. cit.*, p. 219; Morcillo Gonzáles, *El precepto de la Misa en la diócesis de Bilbao*, 1952, p. 3; *El complimiento pascual en la diócesis de Bilbao*, 1954, p. 6.

15. A. Desqueyrat, *La crise religieuse des temps nouveaux*, Édition Spes, Paris, regards as atheists a much broader category of people, including those who concede the probability of the existence of God, and those who certainly believe in 'something' beyond the known world.

16. The distinction is from Jacques Maritain, *Il significato dell'ateismo contemporaneo*, Brescia: Morcelliana, 1950, p. 9. On distinctions within atheism see also the article by Giulio Girardi, 'Pour une définition de l'athéisme', *Salesianum*, XXV, 1, (1963), pp. 47–74.

17. Cf. Jean Lacroix, *Le sens de l'athéisme moderne*, Tournai: Casterman, 1964, p. 15.

18. *Ibid.* An international symposium on atheism reached analogous conclusions, namely that, socio-psychologically atheism is not an entity: it is more appropriate to acknowledge a number of atheisms. The explanation of the origin and significance of atheism varies. Atheism may be axiological (that is, integral humanism which excludes every 'alienation'); epistemological (agnosticism with respect to any type of transcendence); or semantic (which excludes the concept of God as meaningless). Cf. 'Colloque international romain sur l'athéisme', *Lumen Vitae*, 4, (1963), pp. 773–4.

19. François A. Isambert, 'L'analyse des attitudes religieuses', *Archives de sociologie des religions*, 11, (1961), pp. 35–52. Jacques Maître, 'Structure et mesure en sociologie du catholicisme', *Archives de sociologie des religions*, II, (1961), pp. 53–70.

20. Cf. T. Luckmann, *Das Problem der Religion in der modernen Gesellschaft*, Freiburg: Rombach, 1963.

21. T. Luckmann, *op. cit.*, p. 15.

22. Cf. D. Martin, 'Toward Eliminating the Concept of Secularization', in J. Gould (ed) *Penguin Survey of the Social Sciences*, Harmondsworth:

Penguin, 1965. David Martin's article is polemical, but acutely observes the way in which the idea of secularization is used in anti-religious ideology.

23. On the problem of the intensity of practice in France, there is now an extensive literature. See, J. Maître, 'Les denombrements des catholiques pratiquants en France', *Archives de sociologie des religions*, II, 3, (1957), pp. 72–95; L. J. Lebret, *La France en transition (étapes d'une recherche)*, Paris: Éditions Ouvrières, Économie et humanisme, 1957. *Informations Catholiques Internationales* has published a brief essay on religiosity among young people (18–30 years) in France. The statistics are very detailed, and warrant close analysis. Of the young people interviewed (1,524), 18 per cent have no religion, and 14 per cent either do not believe in God or have no opinion on the subject. In the same sample, 35 per cent attend church regularly, and 36 per cent say that they never pray. These figures agree with those published by other French scholars. Cf. *Informations Catholiques Internationales*, 86, 1959, pp. 11–20, unsigned.

Of other studies, see: F. A. Isambert, 'L'attitude religieuse des ouvriers français au milieu du XIXᵉ siècle', *Archives de sociologie des religions*, III, 6, (1958), pp. 7–35; M. Vincienne and Courtois, 'Notes sur la situation religieuse de la France en 1848', *Archives de sociologie des religions*, III, 6, (1958), pp. 104–18; J. Hours, 'Lyon, ville de foi chrétienne', *Revue de psychologie des peuples*, 2, (1958), pp. 176–86; J. Labbens, 'La pratique religieuse dans la ville de Saint Irénée', *Chronique social de France*, 6, (1958), pp. 293–301; *L'Archdiocèse de Lyon. Situation démographique et religieuse*, Institut de Sociologie, Lyon, 1958; M. Desabie, *Le recensement de la pratique religieuse dans la Seine*. 14 Mars 1954, Paris: INSEE, 1958; *La Pratique dominicale dans les zones urbaines de Saône-et-Loire*, vol. II and III, Direction des Oeuvres, Autun, 1958; M. Debrel, 'Ivry, Ville marxiste et présence de l'Église', *Parole et Mission*, 10, 1958, pp. 367–82; M. Desabie, 'Sociologie religieuse dans la Seine. Recensement du 14 Mars 1954', *Revue de l'Action Populaire*, n. 4, 1958, pp. 815–23; F. A. Isambert, 'L'abstension religieuse de la class ouvrière', *Cahiers internationaux de sociologie*, XXV, 2, (1958), pp. 116–34.

24. S. Ligier, *Recherches sociologiques sur la pratique religieuse du Jura*, Vols, Lons-le-Saunier, 1963; J. Perrot, *Grenoble, essai de sociologie religieuse*, Grenoble: Centre d'études des complexes sociaux, 1953; L. Gros, *La pratique religieuses dans le diocèse de Marseille*, Marseilles: Éditions Ouvrières, 1953; J. Chelini, *Genèse et évolution d'une paroisse surburbaine marseillaise*, Le Bon Pasteur, Marseilles: Imprimerie Saint-Leon, 1953; *Semaine Catholique*, 4 March 1955; *Bulletin Paroissial de Nancy*, March-April, 1954; Y. Daniel, *Aspects de la pratique religieuse à Paris*, Paris: Éditions Ouvrières, 1953; *Semaine Religieuse de Paris*, CX (1963), n. 5693, pp. 617–43. See also

J. Labbens, *Les 99 autre . . . ou l'Église aussi recense*, Lyon: Vitte, 1954; J. Labbens, *La pratique dominicale dans l'agglomération lyonnaise*: I. *L'equipement religieux*, 1955; II. *Paroisses et chapelles*, 1956; III. *L'instruction, la ville et les pratiquants* (in collaboration with R. Daille), 1957; P. Minon, *Le peuple liègois, structures sociales et attitudes religieuses*, Liège: Secrétariat Interparoissial, 1955, p. 127; P. Winninger, 'Éléments de geographie religieuse de l'agglomération strasburgeoise. Le Catholicisme', *Bulletin de l'association géographique d'Alsace*, 3, 1956, pp. 16–20; P. Gouyon, *La pratique religieuse d'une petite ville girondine, Libourne*, Libourne, 1957; J. Paquet and L. Rhety, *La pratique dominicale dans les zones urbaines de Saône et Loire*, I. Direction des Oeuvres, Autun, 1956; J. Verscheure, 'Aspects méthodologiques d'une enquête ménée dans le diocèse de Lille sur la pratique religieuse', *Lumen Vitae*, VI, 1–2, (1951), p. 239 ff.; J. Verscheure, *Lille, pratique dominicale. Aspects sociologiques*, 1956; Verscheure, Deprost, Traulle, *Aspects sociologiques de la pratique dominicale, Diocèse de Lille*, Centre diocésain d'études socio-religieuses, 1961; A. Aubert, *Enquête de sociologie religieuse d'Arles-ville*, mimeographed; P. Gouyon, *La pratique religieuse de l'agglomération bordelaise*, Maison des Oeuvres, Bordeaux, 1957; L. M. Luchini, *L'agglomération dijonnaise. Essai de sociologie*, Dijon: Secrétariat de la Mission, 1959; Anon., *La Haute Marne, le diocèse de Langres, Conclusions d'une enquête de sociologie religieuse*, Langres: Secrétariat de l'Evêché, 1959; *Le diocèse de Versailles. Sondages historiques. Recensement de pratique religieuse de 1954*, Conclusions Pastorales, Evêché de Versailles, Versailles, 1959; 'Le recensement diocésain de pratique dominicale en 1962', *Semaine religieuse de Versailles*, 13 and 20-9-63, nn. 30–31; Th. Gelebart, *La pratique dominicale à Landernau d'après la consultation paroissiale du 20 octobre 1957*, Landernau, 1959; O. d'Allerit, 'Une enquête de sociologie religieuse en milieu rural: Vendenheim et Lampertheim', *Paysan d'Alsace*, Strasbourg, 1959, pp. 523–57.

25. Data on religious practice in Nice are to be found in Anon., *Diocèse de Nice. La pratique dominicale. Enquête de sociologie religieuse*, 1954, Nice: Direction des Oeuvres, 1959; M. Quoist, *La ville et l'homme*, Éditions Ouvrières, 1952: (this study concerns only the proletariat in Rouen); R. Daille, *Pratique dominicale dans l'agglomération de Roanne*, Lyon: Institut de Sociologie, 1957; P. Leclercq, 'Pratique religieuse à Metz et dans les environs durant le XIXᵉ siècle', *Revue ecclésiastique du diocèse de Metz*, 4 and 11, (1958): (this article gives figures on practice in the diocese during the nineteenth century. Practice, which was formerly low, revived during the empire and the restoration (60 per cent) falling to 30 per cent between 1830 and 1848. There was a considerable comeback (50 per cent) during the second republic and the second empire which continued during the German

occupation, finally reaching 70 per cent. With the restoration of France after the First World War, it declined rapidly, stabilizing at around 33 per cent in 1930.) *Sociologie et pastorale, Diocèse de Poitiers*, Poitiers, 1959: (Religious practice in a good part of the diocese was fairly high. In the canton of Châtillon there was a practice rate of 50 per cent among managerial staff and office workers, of 82 per cent among manual workers, and 97 per cent among farmers, but in general the average practice rate was below 40 per cent); R. Daillè, *La Pratique dominicale dans l'archiprêté de Rive de Gier*, Lyon: Institut de sociologie, 1959; A complete picture of French surveys up to the 1950s has been given by M. J. Maître sponsored by the 'Groupe de Sociologie des Religions' of Paris. On general problems cf. also F. Malley, 'La pratique religieuse dans les grandes villes françaises', *L'Actualité religieuse dans le monde*, 52, (1955), p. 17 ff. and also J. Maître, 'Les dénombrements des catholiques pratiquants en France', *Archives de sociologie des religions*, II, 3, (1957).

26. Cf. *Coutances, sociologie et pastorale*, Coutances, 1958.
27. Cf. F. G. Dreyfus, 'Les Protestantisme Alsacien', *Archives de sociologie des religions*, II, 3, (1957). See also F. G. Dreyfus, 'Sociologie et pratique religieuse', *Revue d'histoire et philosophie religieuse*, 35, (1955), pp. 210–24.
28. J. Chelini, *op. cit.*, p. 94.
29. *Op. cit.*, p. 228.
30. Concerning the problem of practice in metropolitan Paris cf. also Y. Daniel, *Aspects de la pratique religieuse à Paris, op. cit.*
31. G. Le Bras, *Études, op. cit.*, p. 151.
32. G. Le Bras, *Études, op. cit.*
33. See Ch. Bettelheim, S. Frere, *Auxerre en 1950*, Paris, Colin Éd., 1950.
34. On this theme, Chelini remarks that

> In our towns, the majority of first marriages (from 50 to 85 per cent) is still celebrated with a religious ceremony and in those countries with civil legislation connected to canon law the religious marriages are practically the totality. On the contrary, in the majority of European and American towns, where divorce is admitted, there is a percentage of 10 to 20 per cent of religious marriages which are dissolved and that is because there is a high percentage of second-marriages and a proportional decrease of catholic marriages. The possibility to dissolve a religious marriage is therefore a proof for the married couple: it is no longer absolutely irrevocable. . . . This devaluation of religious marriage strongly highlights the progressive paganization of city customs.

Research among Protestants supports analogous conclusions about the influence and the diffusion of mixed marriages. Marriages between Lutherans and non-Lutherans increased significantly in America between 1936 and 1950, especially following the Second World War. Twice as many women as men married non-Lutherans: over 50 per cent of the marriages were with other Protestants, 20 per cent with Catholics, and the rest with persons not belonging to any church. The consequences of the increase in mixed marriages are analogous to those reported by Chelini for France and for the Catholic world in general: among other things, a decline in attachment to the church. Cf. J. H. S. Bossard and C. L. Harold, 'Mixed Marriages Involving Lutherans. A Research Report', *Marriage and Family Living*, XVII, 4, (1956), pp. 308–11. On the same problem of mixed marriages cf. also J. H. Locke, G. Sabagh and M. M. Thomas, 'Interfaith Marriages', *Social Problems*, IV, 4, (1957), pp. 329–33.

35. A more up-to-date picture of the distribution of religious practice in France is given in F. Boulard and J. Remy, *Pratique religieuse urbaine et regions culturelles*, Economie et Humanisme, Paris, 1968. These newer data in no way invalidate our thesis. Cf. pp. 49–50, 70–7.

36. Cf. E. J. Ross, 'La sociologie religieuse aux États-Unis', *Actes du IV Congrès international de sociologie religieuse*, Paris: Éditions Ouvrières, 1955, pp. 131–49.

37. Michael Argyle, *Religious Behaviour*, Glencoe, Ill.: Free Press, 1959, p. 29.

38. *Ibid.*, pp. 32 ff.

39. Public Opinion News Service, July 1954.

40. B. Lazerwitz, 'Some Factors associated with Variations in Church Attendance', *Social Forces*, XXXIX, 4, (1961), pp. 301–9. See also D. H. Heat, 'Secularization and Maturity of Religious Beliefs', *Journal of Religion and Health*, 1969, 8, pp. 334–58; J. Honders, *La vie religieuse aux États-Unis*, Brussels: Coll. Études Religieuses, 1957; F. Houtart, *Aspects sociologiques du catholicisme americain*, Paris: Éditions Ouvrières, 1958; J. W. Saatman, 'Protestantism americain', *Nouvelle revue theologique*, May 1956; Jean Marie Jammes, 'La dechristianisation ouvrière et le cas americain', *Masses Ouvrières*, CXXXIV, (1957), pp. 56–78.

41. J. Chelini, in *Signes des Temps*, November, 1961, 11, pp. 11–15, but see also C. Y. Glock, 'Y a-t-il un reveil religieux aux États-Unis?' *Archives de Sociologie des Religions*, 12, (1961), pp. 35–52.

42. See, R. Hoge, 'Religious Commitments of College Students of Five Decades', *Jahrbuch für Religionssoziologie*, 7, (1971), pp. 184–211.

43. See, J. P. Alston, R. C. Hollinger, 'Correlates of Perceived Secularization', *Journal for the Scientific Study of Religion*, XI, 4, (1972).

44. R. Stark and C. Y. Glock, *American Piety*, Berkeley and Los Angeles: University of California Press, 1968, pp. 204 ff.

45. See, H. M. Ramirez, *Sociologia Religiosa de Chile*, Editiones Paulinas, 1957.

46. See, 'La situation sociologique de l'Église au Chile', *Pro Mundi Vita—Centrum Informationis*, 1, pp. 3–5.

47. 'Causas de las escasez sacerdotal en Chile', *Mensaje*, 130, (1964), pp. 307–10.

48. Tiago G. Colin, 'Aspects socio-religieux et sociographiques du Brésil', *Social Compass*, V, 5-6, (1957-8), pp. 200-36, esp. pp. 233 and 227. See also, A. Rolim, 'Quelques aspects de la pratique religieuse au Brésil', *Social Compass*, 14, (1967), pp. 457-68.

49. *Lumen Vitae*, 1, (1962), p. 141.

50. F. Houtart, *L'Église latino-americaine à l'heure du concile*, Freiburg: Feres, 1963; *Pro Mundi Vita*, 1966, 11.

51. *Pro Mundi Vita*, 14, 1965.

52. See, *Pro Mundi Vita*, 17, 1967; G. Perez and I. Wüst, *La Iglesia in Colombia*, Bogotà: Feres, 1961.

53. *Pro Mundi Vita*, 7, 1965.

54. F. Houtart, *op. cit.*

55. The results of studies conducted by the Vienna Institute of Socio-Religious Research were summarized in *Social Compass*. Cf. E. Bodzenta, 'Forschungen in Österreich, Ergebnisse und Methoden', *Social Compass*, VI, 4-5, (1959), pp. 142-54. During that period the practice rate reached an average of 60 per cent in the Tyrol (with high points over 80 per cent) and a few other areas; in the areas of Linz, Skt. Pölten, Vienna-Nordteil, and Burgenland it reached 40-50 per cent; in Innsbruck, Salzburg, in Styria and in Carinthia between 30 per cent and 40 per cent; in Vienna, Graz, Linz, Klagenfurt, and in the southern parts of the diocese of Vienna it was below 20 per cent.

56. Various authors, *Sozialstruktur und religiöse Praxis in einer industriellen Mittelstadt*, Icares, Abteilung Österreich, Bericht 29, Vienna, 1957.

57. Cf. E. Bodzenta, *Die Katholiken in Österreich*, Vienna: Herder, 1962. Recent data on Austria (1968) can be found in H. Bogensberg and P. Zulehner, 'Austria', in H. Mol, *op. cit.*, pp. 47-66.

58. A. Collard, 'La première carte de la pratique religieuse en Belgique', *Lumen Vitae*, VII, 4, (1952), p. 644; *Carte de la pratique dominicale en Belgique par localité*, Mons: Éditions du Dimanche, 1952. On the problems of religious sociology in Belgium cf. N. De Volder, 'La sociologie religieuse en Belgique', *Actes du IV Congrès international de sociologie religieuse*, Paris: Éditions Ouvrières, 1955; and also P. Chalon, 'Implantation de la sociologie religieuse en Belgique', *Social Compass*, VI, 4-5, (1958-9), pp. 155-64.

A 1966 survey showed average religious practice for all Belgium of 35.8 per cent of the obligees. Cf. F. Houtart, 'Belgium', in H. Mol, *op. cit.*, pp. 67-82.

59. Cf. F. Groner, *Kirchliches Handbuch, Amtliches statistisches Jahrbuch der Katholischen Kirche Deutschlands*, vol. XXIII, Cologne, 1944-51 and XXIV, Cologne, 1952-6. See also B. Häring, *Macht und Ohnmacht der Religion, Religionssoziologie als Anruf*, Salzburg: Otto Müller, 1957.

60. Cf. F. Groner, 'Kirchliche Statistik Deutschlands für das Jahr 1957', *Amtliche Zentralstelle Deutschlands für kirchliche Statistik des*

katholischen Deutschlands, Cologne, 1958; and F. Groner, *Kirchliches Handbuch 1957-61*, Cologne: Bachem, 1962 and later year-
books.

61. N. Greinacher, 'Dévolution de la pratique religieuse en Allemagne
    après la guerre', *Social Compass*, X, 4-5, (1963), pp. 345-55.
62. Cf. R. Wilhelm, 'Germany: Democratic Republic', in H. Mol (Ed.),
    Western Religion, The Hague: Mouton, 1972, pp. 13-28.
63. See P. Zieger, *Kirchliche Statistik (Gliederung, Pfarrstellen und
    Geistliche Kräften der evangelischen Landeskirchen nach dem Stand
    von 31-12-1958)*, Gerd Mohn, 1958: extract from *Kirchliches Jahr-
    buch für evangelische Kirche in Deutschland*, 1958.
64. These figures are taken from Conor K. Ward, 'Church Attendance in
    Great Britain', Sociologia Religiosa, III, (1959).
65. Derived from Robert Currie and Alan Gilbert, 'A Statistical Survey of
    Church Membership in Britain and Ireland since 1700' cited in B. R.
    Wilson, *Contemporary Transformations of Religion*, Oxford:
    Clarendon Press, 1976.
66. W. F. Pickering, 'Quelques resultats d'interviews religieuses', Vocation
    de la Sociologie religieuse. *V Conference internationale de Sociologie
    religieuse*, Paris: Casterman, 1958, pp. 54-78; and Louis Harris
    International Speedsearch, *Spiritual Attitudes Survey*, 1974.
67. See B. R. Wilson, *op. cit.*, and also *idem*, *Religion in Secular Society*,
    London: Watts, 1966.
68. See 'New Forms of Ministries in Christian Communities, *Pro Mundi
    Vita*, 50, (1974), pp. 84-6, 89. For a general bibliography, see David
    Martin, *A Sociology of English Religion*, London: SCM Press, 1967;
    and *A Sociological Yearbook of Religion in Britain*, London: SCM
    Press, 1970-5.
69. G. H. L. Zeegers, 'Sociologie religieuse dans le contexte d'une socio-
    logie générale aux Pays-Bas', *Lumen Vitae*, VI, 1-2, (1951), pp. 43ff.
70. Cf. P. van Hooydonk, 'De religieuse practijk van de katholieke
    bevoking in de stad Groningen en in het bijzonder in de Ooster-
    parkbuurt', *Social Compass*, V, 3, (1957), pp. 89-119.
71. Cf. Roger Vekemans, 'La sociographie de catholicisme aux Pay-Bas',
    Archives de sociologie des religions, II, 3, (1957), pp. 129-36.
72. Dutch Catholicism has suffered less than Protestantism. While
    Protestants fell from 59.1 per cent in 1830 to 42.6 per cent in 1947, the
    Catholics accounted for a growing proportion of the population (40.4
    per cent in 1960).
73. See Th. M. Steeman, 'L'Eglise d'aujourd'hui: une exploration de la
    Hollande Catholique en 1966', *Social Compass*, XIV, 3, (1967).
74. For Czechoslovakia see the journal *Wort und Wahrheit* which contains
    two articles by Observator, 'Kirche in der CSSR. Zwischen Unterdrück
    und Selbstbehauptung in atheistischer Umwelt', 20, 1965; and 'Von
    Hus bis beute. Erbe und Zukunft des tschechischen Katholizismus',
    1967, n. 22.

216 THE DECLINE OF THE SACRED

75. Cf. E. Kadlecova, 'Czechoslovakia', in H. Mol, *op. cit.*, pp. 117–34.
76. See G. Castellan, 'Eléments d'une sociologie religieuse en Yougoslavie socialiste', *Annales*, 4, (1959), pp. 694–709. See also A. Fiamengo, 'Yugoslavia', in H. Mol, pp. 587–99.
77. Cf. CSEO, 'La vita della chiesa nei paesi del'Est', March 1967, p. 40.
78. For Bulgaria cf. J. Ochavkov, 'Les resultats d'une étude sociologique de la religiosité en Bulgarie', *Revue française de sociologie*, VII, 4, (1966), pp. 456–71. See also J. Ochavkov, 'Bulgaria', in H. Mol, *op. cit.* and 'Religioznata psikhika ineinoto preodoliavane v Bulgaria' (Religious Psychology and its waning in Bulgaria), *Novovreme*, 7, (1966).
79. See Stanislaw Ossowski, *Przeglad Kulturalny*, 1958, 29; and 1961, 46; and *Nowa Kultura*, 32, 39, 47, (1958); and 2, 1961. There is a complete synthesis in *Questitalia*, V, 48, (1962), pp. 31–6. But for a more optimistic view, see the article by Leszek Kolakowski, and the synthesis of his ideas in *Frankfurterhefte, Zeitschrift für Kultur und Politik*, XVI, 11, (1961), pp. 740–4; and Eugen Kogen, 'Kirche und Heimat: Bermerkungen zu den Thesen eines Warschauer Philosophen', *Frankfurterhefte*, XVI, 11, pp. 727–30, and 12, (1961), pp. 807–11.
80. Anna Pawelczynska, 'Les attitudes des étudiants Varsoviens envers la religion', *Archives de sociologie des religions*, 12, (1961), pp. 107–32.
81. J. Maître, 'Un sondage polonais sur les attitudes religieuses de la jeunesse', *Archives de sociologie des religions*, 12, 1961, pp. 133–43.
82. CSEO, *La Vita della chiesa nei paesi dell'Est*, April 1967, p. 80.
83. Cf. 'Études de sociologie religieuse en cours en Pologne', *Social Compass*, XI, (1964), 3–4. To mention just one datum: in the diocese of Tarnow, with about 1 million inhabitants, average religious practice is above 70 per cent, while attendance at catechism instruction varies between 80 per cent and 100 per cent. See also J. Majka, in H. Mol, *op. cit.*, pp. 403–425.
84. For Hungary see the publications of the Ungarisches Kirchensoziologisches Institut of Munich, which in collaboration with the Ungarisches katholisches Institut für kirchliche Sozialforschung of Vienna, published in 1965 an excellent synthetic study, *Beiträge zur Lage der katholischen Kirche in Ungarn 1964*. See also E. Andras, 'Die Lage der Kirche in Ungarn im Jahre 1966', *Orientierung*, 1966. More recent data on Hungary are in *Social Compass*, 5, 1968. Cf. among others J. F. Bango, 'Convictions religieuses de la jeunesse hongroise scolaire et étudiante', *Social Compass*, XV, 5, (1968).
85. Ivan Varga, 'Hungaria', in H. Mol, *op. cit.*, pp. 277–94. See also 'Ifjüsag, vallasossag, szekularizacio' (Youth, religiosity, secularization), *Vilagosag*, 2, (1968).
86. For further information on socio-religious issues in Spain, see the bibliography.
87. See, M. F. Falcão, 'Sondagem â assistência a Misâ domincal no

patriarcado de Lisboa', *Novellae Olivarum*, 1956, 25, pp. 68-85; Cf. A. Querido, 'Elements pour une sociologie du conformisme catholique au Portugal', *Archives de sociologie des religions*, IV, 7, (1959), pp. 144-51; C. M. Gonzáles, *El precepto de la Misa en la diócesis de Bilbao, cit.*; *El cumplimiento pascual en la diócesis de Bilbao, cit.*; O. Argos, 'La asistencia a la misa en la Diocesis de Santander', *Bolletin del Obispado*, 1959.

88. A. Aparicio, 'Beja terra de missao', *Boletim de Informaçao Pastoral*, I, (1959), pp. 19-23. Sunday practice is 2.7 per cent; Cf. Anon., 'Em vias de decristianizacao as regioes mais praticantes de Portugal', *Boletim de Informação Pastoral*, II, 7, (March-May 1960), pp. 16-20.

89. J. M. Vasquez, *Así viven y mueren, op. cit.*

90. See, R. Duocastella, 'Geographie de la pratique religieuse en Espagne', *Social Compass*, XII, 4/5, (1965), pp. 253-302.

91. All these authorities agree that Spanish society is only nominally Catholic in that dechristianization has already gone very far. Cf. F. Malley, 'Quelques sondages sur la pratique religieuse à Barcelone', *L'actualité religieuse dans le monde*, 22, 1954. See also, the local study, J. M. de la Rica Basagotti, *La parroquia de Nuestra Señora de la Mercedes de las Arenas*, Bilbao: Università di Deusto, 1957.

92. The same may be said concerning the decline in the number of seminarians. The author indicates the fall in the number of clergy in areas which, during the civil war, were held by the anti-Franco republicans. Cf. R. Duocastella, 'Problemas sacerdotales en España', *Cuadernos del Centro de Estudios de sociologia aplicada*, (1959), 1, Madrid. See also, R. Duocastella, 'Sociologia religiosa de las migraciones interiores. Las Migraciones en España', *Documentación social*, vol. 4, p. 45.

93. From P. Americh, in H. Mol, *op. cit.*, pp. 459-77.

94. See J. Aubrey, 'Renaissance catholique en Écosse', *Études*, 1, 1957, pp. 73-90; J. Highet, 'Great Britain: Scotland', in H. Mol., *op. cit.*, pp. 249-69.

95. Daphne D. C. Pochin Mould, 'The Church in Ireland', *Carmel in the World*, II, 3, (1962), pp. 202-11.

96. See Conor Ward, 'Ireland' in H. Mol., *op. cit.*, and more especially *Pro Mundi Vita*, 'New Forms of Ministries . . .' 50, (1974), pp. 84-6, 89.

97. See, H. Chatelain, 'Les conditions d'une sociologie des religions en Suisses. Remarques preliminaires sur une sociologie du protestantisme', *Archives de sociologie des religions*, III, 5, (1958), pp. 151-6.

98. See E. Perret, 'La pratique du culte à Genève', *Bull. du Centre protestante d'études*, 1963, n. 2-3. More recent data, which do not change the picture, may be found in R. J. Campiche, 'Switzerland'; in H. Mol, *op. cit.*, pp. 511-30.

99. On this topic cf. especially Sidney and Beatrice Webb, *Il communismo*

sovietico: una nuova civiltà, Turin: Einaudi, 1950, vol. II, p. 621 ff. Cf. also J. F. Hecker, *Religion and Communism*, London: Chapman and Hall, 1933. See also H. Peltier, 'Souvenirs et réflexions sur le christianisme en URSS', Études, Dec. 1958, pp. 293–308; Anon. 'La réaction religieuse des Russes soviétiques à l'Exposition de Bruxelles', *Irénikon*, XXXII, 1, (1959), pp. 48–57.

In Estonia around the beginning of the sixties only about 25 per cent of babies were baptized in the Lutheran church, although 70 per cent of the population were, at least nominally, Lutheran. Cf. *Ordine Civile*, II, 1, (1960), p. 16. Grünwald's book is a true mine of information on the state of religion in the USSR. Among the interesting figures given is the probable percentage of practising workers which is set at not more than 10 per cent. Cf. C. de Grünwald, *La vie religieuse en URSS*, Plon, Paris, 1961, and Puskareva, Snesarev, Smeleva, 'Religiozno-bytovye perežitki i puti ik preodolenija', *Kommunist*, 8, 1960, pp. 86–95.

100. For a bibliography, see *Religionsosiologien I Norden*, 4, 1961, (edited by Edvard Vogt).

Precise figures for Sweden appear in Berndt Gustafsson, 'Staatskirche und Entkirchlichung in Schweden', part of the volume *Probleme der Religionssoziologie*, Sonderheft 6, 1962, of the *Kölnerzeitschrift für Sociologie und Sozialpsychologie*, pp. 158–65.

101. Anon. 'L'Église et la société sécularisée: l'expérience scandinave', *Pro Mundi Vita*, (1969), 29, pp. 1–28.

102. E. Vogt, 'The sociology of Protestantism in Norway', *Fifth Colloquium on the Sociology of Protestantism*, Sigtuna, Sweden, 20–24 April 1965; and especially E. Vogt, 'Norway', in H. Mol, *op. cit.*, pp. 389–405.

103. See, J. Thorgaard, 'Denmark', in H. Mol, *op. cit.*, pp. 135–41.

104. P. Seppänen, 'Finland', in H. Mol, *op. cit.*, pp. 143–73.

105. S. Burgalassi, *Italiani in Chiesa*, Brescia: Morcelliana, 1967; *Sociologia delle religioni in Italia dalle origini al 1967*, Rome: Ed. Pastorali, 1967.

106. A. Leoni, *Sociologia e geografia religiosa di una diocesi*, Rome: Università Gregoriana, 1952. (See *Sociologia religiosa*, III, 3, (1959), under 'Documenti' for studies, essays, reviews, which discuss this volume.)

107. S. S. Acquaviva, 'Alcune note introduttive al problema dello stato della pratica religiosa nella regione di Alessandria: dati statistici e sociologici', *Sociologia religiosa*, I, 1, (1957), pp. 141–47.

108. S. S. Acquaviva, 'Dati sociologico-religiosi della regione polesana', *Sociologia religiosa*, II, 2, (1958), pp. 139–47.

109. S. S. Acquaviva, 'Appunti metodologici per la preparazione di una ricerca sociologico-religiosa su un'area sufficientemente estesa', *Studia Patavina*, III, 3, (1956), pp. 495–502. The study of Leoni refers to the same area: see S. S. Acquaviva, 'Un primo contributo alla sociologia

storico-religiosa del Padavano', *Studia Patavina*, III, 1, (1956), pp. 140–53.

110. S. S. Acquaviva, 'Vieste e Manfredonia', *Sociologia religiosa* II, 2, (1958), pp. 145–46. We have returned more recently to the problem of religious practice in the Gargano with a large survey on the crisis of traditional culture, and religion, in this region. The survey includes also Voeste and Manfredonia, see G. Eisermann and S. S. Acquaviva, *La Montagna del sole*, Milan, 1971. In the sample interviewed there was a regular mass attendance of 43.97 per cent. 37.69 per cent of the sample said they attended mass sometimes, and 17.34 per cent said that they never attended. 21.38 per cent of the sample said that they never took communion.

111. A. Bagnoli, 'Insegnamento di una statistica e relievo statistico sulla frequenza alla messa', *Bollettino diocesano di Volterra*, XXXII, (1952), pp. 101–4 and 122–7. In the diocese practice went from a maximum of 48.29 per cent to a minimum of 9.6 per cent.

112. For information on Italy in the 1940s and 1950s, see A. Leoni, 'La situazione religiosa in Italia', *Realta sociale d'oggi*, VIII, 11–12, (1953), pp. 705–25, esp. p. 716. For its size, Rome has a high per-centage of its population professing belief in God — 92.2 per cent; some 4.3 per cent are in doubt, and 2.5 per cent do not believe. The remainder either did not answer or had not considered the problem. See E. Pin and C. Cavallin, *La reliosità dei Romani*, Rome: CIRIS, 1970. For the rural parishes studied, the average percentage is 33.7 per cent. See, various authors, *L'anima religiosa del mondo d'oggi*, Rome: A.C.I., 1957, p. 212. In Poggetti (Maremma, Tuscany), 20 per cent of women and 0 per cent of men practised. These figures are similar to those for Volterra. See, various authors, *Le inchieste del notiziario passionista*, 4, (1957), p. 8. In Ascoli Piceno, the practice rate appears to have been about 64 per cent. See the interesting analysis by B. Riccitelli, *Frequenza alla Messa festive, analisi di un'inchiesta*, Ascoli Piceno: C.C.D., 1962.

For Bologna, an average practice rate of 30.16 per cent of the obligees was reported. A fairly complete summary of the Bologna survey is to be found in 'Pratica religiosa e atteggiamento politico a Bologna', *Questitalia*, 56–7, (1962), pp. 36–49. On the general state of religious practice in Italy, see our essay, S. S. Acquaviva, 'Sociologie religieuse et sociologie des religions en Italie', *Archives de sociologie des religions*, 12, (1961), pp. 81–8. See also, A. M. Seronde, M. Soultrait, R. Nouat, J. Rovan, P. Lengrand, E. Cassin, J. Besson, *La Calabre, Une région sous-développée de l'Europe méditerranéenne*, Paris: Colin, 1960.

113. Data on Italian religiosity in more recent years may be found in Giuseppe Zanchi (Ed.) *Dove va le religione in Italia*, Città Nuova, Incisa Val d'Arno, 1971, which contains summaries of a number of surveys.

114. Useful historical data were collected by Quirino Principe for the Centro Studi di Sociologia Religiosa in Padua. These show that for the period 1744–53, there was a practice rate of 99.57 per cent in the city of Padua and of 99.91 per cent in the surrounding countryside. See, Q. Principe, 'Diocesi di Padova, Practica religiosa (1744–53)', *Sociologia religiosa*, III, 3, (1959), pp. 151–66.

For the Italian situation as a whole, see S. Burgalassi, 'Aspetti e tendenze sociologiche in Italia: l'eucarestia e i fedeli', *Studi di sociologia*, II, 4, (1964), pp. 147–69.

115. See the essay by Cleto Corrain, 'Le tradizioni del periodo natalizio e i giorni dei presagi nel Polesine', *Lares*, XXIII, (1957), 1–2. Most of the information was collected from very old people, since young people preserve traditions usually for folkloristic motives rather than from religious conviction. Superstitious traditions decay together with those which are bound up with official religiosity. Analogous themes have been dealt with by Battaglia (formerly professor of Anthropology and Ethnology at the University of Padua) from whose enormous production see, R. Battaglia, 'La vecchia col fuso e la filatura del lino nelle tradizioni popolari', *Ce Fastu?*, XXXV, 5–6, (1949); 'Religiosità popolare italiana', *Lares*, III, 2, (1932). From Battaglia's many essays it is clear that popular religiosity is now nothing but an immense ruin.

On the survival of the more archaic forms of magic, superstition, and popular religiosity cf. also E. De Martino, *Sud e magia*, Milan: Feltrinelli, 1959, and the older and polemical work by Th. Trede, *Das Heidentum in der römischen Kirche. Bilder aus dem religiösen und sittlichen Leben Sud-Italiens*, Gotha 1889–91, 4 vols.

116. For a first approach to the subject, on a purely informational level cf. D. Grasso, 'La crisi delle devozioni', Stella Matutina, LV, nn. 7–8, pp. 199–202.

117. Cf. *Pro Mundi Vita*, 18, (1971), special note, pp. 1–26. In Italy in 1957–8, there were 100 admissions to all the seminaries of Trento. According to a 1970 study done by the diocese, this number had fallen to 19. Cf. *Ricerca socio-religiosa*, 3, (1971), pp. 18–19. The conclusions are the same in P. De Sandre and G. Guizzardi, *Struttura e dinamica delle vocazioni sacerdotali delle Venezie*, Padova, 1969, p. 31. Within a few years the number of Catholics in the world has risen by 100 million, while there has been a 14 per cent decrease in the number of priests. Cf. A. Favale, E. Gozzelino, *Il ministero presbiteriale. Fenomenologia e diagnosi di una crisi*, Turin: Elle Di Ci, 1972, pp. 308.

118. The data were not selected in a statistically representative way, and thus it is not a sample in the proper sense of the term. Furthermore the testing of the theory continues in smaller surveys conducted within other religions. See Paolo De Sandre, *Sociologia della religiosita*, Rome: Ave, 1967.

CHAPTER 3

1. On archaic societies, see R. Allier, *Les non-civilisés et nous*, Paris, 1927; *La psychologie de la conversion chez les peuples non civilisés*, Paris, 1925; also R. Bastide, *Élements de sociologie religieuse*, Paris, 1912; D. Descamps, *État social des peuples sauvages*, Paris, 1935; R. H. Lawy, *Traité de sociologie primitive*, Paris, 1935; L. Lévy-Bruhl, *Les fonctions mentales dans les sociétés inférieures*, Paris, 1910; T. Pattent, *The Social Basis of Religion*, New York, 1911.

2. Among the works concerned with primitive peoples which deal, directly or indirectly, with questions bearing on the sociology of religion, see E. De Martino, *Il mondo magico*, Turin: Einaudi, 1948; M. Eliade, *Traité d'histoire des religions*, Paris: Payot, *Le chamanisme et les techniques archaiques de l'extase*, Paris: Payot, 1951; E. Durkheim, H. Hubert, M. Mauss, *Le origini dei poteri magici*, Turin: Einaudi, 1951.

3. Cf. P. Tacchi Venturi, Storia delle religioni, Turin: Utet, 1945, vol. I.

4. Cf. L. Levy-Bruhl, *Les Carnets*, Paris: Presses Universitaires de France, 1949; English translation by Peter Rivière, Oxford: Blackwell, 1975.

5. On primitive mysticism see Mircea Eliade, *Le Chamanisme et les techniques archaiques de l'estase*, Paris: Payot, 1951.

6. M. Eliade, *Traité d'histoire des religions*, Paris: Payot, p. 38.

7. Gaston Bouthoul, *Traite de sociologie*, Paris: Payot, 1946, p. 211. The author observes that among primitive peoples the concept of religion as a discrete phenomenon in the sense in which it is understood in more advanced societies, does not in fact exist.

8. See M. Eliade, *Le Chamanisme . . . op. cit.*

9. Although less rigidly fixed, differences in property, rank, and occupation are to be found in Buddhist societies, and are frequently justified in religious terms.

10. Recent caste divisions are generally survivals of more archaic social structures.

11. According to Kluge, the word *ghilda* is a derivative of *Geldan* or *Gildan*, which in old German means to sacrifice (*opfern*). In the eleventh century, a 'gulda' was a gathering for a sacrificial banquet. Amire traces these guilds to the ancient *Bundbrüderschaften* of early Germanic history. In spite of their social, political, and economic interests, the religious goal is always the predominant one in these guilds.

12. A. Faggiotto, 'Remoti indizi della Magna Mater nell'Estremo Oriente', *Atti dell'Accademia Patavìna di Scienze, Lettere ed Arti*, LXVI, 1953–4.

13. C. Dawson, *Progress and Religion*, London: Sheed and Ward, 1945, p. 116.

14. Before it became individuated, Greek religion was first a feature of the state, of social groups, of the tribe, and of the family.

15. On heresy, see, among others, W. Bousset, *Hauptprobleme der Gnosis*, Göttingen, 1907. On the Albigensians, see C. Schmidt, *Histoire et doctrine de la secte des Cathares ou Albigeois*, Paris, 1894; I. Doellinger, *Beiträge zur Sektengeschichte des N. A.*, Munich, 1890. On Arnold of Brescia there are a great many sources, from Guadagnini, *Apologia e Vita di Arnoldo*, Pavia, 1790, to the more recent G. Volpe, *Movimenti religiosi e sette ereticali nella società medioevale italiana (sec. XI-XIV)*, Florence, 1924, which is also useful for a comprehensive view of heresy in Italy. On John Ball, see especially C. Oman, *The Great Revolt of 1381*, Oxford, 1906. On Thomas Münzer, see E. Bloch, *Th. Münzer Theologie der Revolution*, Berlin, 1922. More specifically on the Anabaptists: G. Piscel, *Il regno degli Anabattisti*, Rome 1928; *Mennonitisches Lexicon*, Frankfurt am Main, 1908; *Gedenkschrift zum 400-jährigen Jubiläum der Mennoniten oder Taufgesinnten, 1525-1925*, Ludwigshafen am R., 1925. Concerning the peasants see the very old but impressive W. Zimmermann, *Allgemeine Geschichte des grossen Bauernkrieges*, Stuttgart, 1841-3, (I have used the third edition which has been revised from a socialist point of view). Also useful among more recent works is W. Stolze, *Der deutsche Bauernkrieg*, Halle, 1908.
16. W. H. C. Frend, *The Donatist Church. A Movement of Protest in a Town of North Africa*, Oxford, 1957.
17. One index of the social and religious turmoil in Italy during this period is given by the revolution which broke out in Naples when Campanella published his *Città del Sole*. The Calabrian plot was intended to realize Campanella's utopia, and was a very serious event involving people from every social rank, including nobles and monks.
18. See C. Violante, *La società milanese nell'età precomunale*, Laterza, Bari, 1953, p. 179; R. Manselli, 'Per la storia dell'eresia nel secola XII', *Bollettino Istituto storico italiano per il Medio Evo e Archivio Muratoriano*, n. 67; Ilarino da Milano, 'Le eresie populari del secola XI', *Studi gregoriani*, 1947, n. 2, pp. 43-89; G. Volpe, *op. cit.*
19. Earlier risings in Spain may not, however, be entirely ignored. The Spanish peasants broke into violent revolt in Majorca in 1391, and again in 1451, when revolts also occurred in Valencia, Castilla, Navarra, and Catalonia. Under pressure of these revolts, and for financial reasons, the kings of Aragon, John I and more especially Martin I, showed themselves favourable to the idea of freeing the serfs, but this was prevented by the nobility. The tense situation led to the revolts of 1462 and 1482. In 1486, Ferdinand the Catholic decreed the abolition of serfdom against a monetary payment, and abuses of feudal power, such as *jus primae noctis*, were abolished.
20. Among the heretical sects of this period we should mention the Anabaptist community of the Moravian Brothers, who practised full communion of goods. Doni (Mondi Celesti, 1562), Vairasse (Historie des Sevarambes, 1677), and Morelly (Iles flottantes, also called

Basiliade, 1753), are among the many Utopian writers who bear
witness to the fact that the communistic ideal was not entirely
forgotten during the period preceding the French revolution. Morelly
argues, in *Le Code de la Nature* (1755), for the necessity of communistic legislation that would result in true well-being for everyone.
Brissot de Warwille (1754–95) also took a communistic position,
and held that private property amounted to theft.

21. de Lagarde grasps the significance of certain desacralizing expressions
of the thirteenth century, when he remarks:

> Later on, studying the life of free cities, we will notice that the
> economic transformations themselves constitute a new barrier
> between clergy and laic societies in formation at that time. It is not
> surprising, therefore, that the XIII century has offered the ground
> for the culture of the 'bacilli' of the new and more elastic condition
> of Eastern society (. . .). The more vigorous is the reaction of the
> organism against the infection, the stronger is the virulence of
> germs; and this is the way the modern world is, with its sclerotic
> lungs and its attitude towards violence precluding the total un-
> derstanding of these remote struggles, and this may lead to an
> underestimation of the importance of events.

G. de Lagarde, *Naissance de l'espirit laïque au déclin du Moyen Age*,
(1) *Bilan du XIIme siècle*, Paris: Nauwelaerts, 1956, p. 188.

22. L. Mumford, *The Condition of Man*, London: Secker and Warburg,
1944, p. 108.

23. *Ibid*.

24. On this, see Guiseppe Toffanin, *Il secolo senza Roma*, Bologna:
Zanichelli, 1957.

25. G. Toffanin, *Storia dell'umanesimo*, Napoli-Citta di Castello, Perella,
1933; *Il secolo senza Roma, op. cit.*; *L'uomo antico nel pensiero del
Rinascimento*, Bologna: Zanichelli, 1957.

26. Of course, the decline is not as simple and universal as this discussion
might appear to suggest. The complex diversity of the routes through
which the various European countries moved towards these consequences, albeit at different times, is demonstrated by the example of
France. See H. Pirenne, 'De L'État de l'instruction des laïques à
l'époque mérovingienne', in *Histoire Économique de l'Occident
Médiéval*, Paris, 1951.

27. The transposition of culture from the monasteries to lay settings began
in the twelfth century, with such figures as Goffredo da Viterbo, who
preceded Petrarch by two centuries, and who began the transcription
of essentially classical manuscript texts.

28. But does Averroism represent a real tendency toward irreligiosity? The
problem is a complex one, but to indicate the irreligious character of
these currents it will be sufficient to recall what Boccaccio has to say
about the Averroist, Cavalcanti: 'and since he held many of the
opinions of the Epicureans, it was said among the common folk that

all his speculations were nothing but a search for a proof that God does not exist.' (*The Decameron*, VI, 9)

29. Cf. S. S. Acquaviva, *Automazione e nuova classe*, Bologna: Il Mulino, 1969, (3rd edition).

30. R. Tremelloni, *Storia dell'industria italiana contemporanea*, Turin: Einaudi, 1947.

31. On the technology of the Middle Ages cf. also: Lefebvre des Noëttes, *L'attelage, le cheval de selle à travers les âges*, Paris, 1931, and 'Le gouvernail: contribution á l'histoire de l'esclavage', *Mémoires de la société des Antiquaires de France*, 1932, vol. LXXVIII, etc.

32. On this theme cf, among others, W. Cunningham, *The Growth of English Industry and Commerce in Modern Times*, Cambridge-1915–21, (6th edition).

33. L. Mumford, *op. cit.*, p. 139.

34. The philosophical world had become something which could not even have been conceived before the year 1000. The philosophers were ready for any adventure. Averroës, Ockham, Nicholas of Cusa, Pomponazzi, prepared the libertine currents of the sixteenth century. Pomponazzi (1462–1524) in particular seems to have been firmly rooted in 'impiety'.

35. L. Mumford, *op. cit.*, p. 165.

36. In the twelfth century there appeared in France the first elementary schools clearly outside the influence of the priests and monks. In this respect, see G. de Lagarde, *Naissance, etc.*, *op. cit.*, p. 181; and H. Pirenne, *Les villes du Moyen Age*, p. 201.

37. G. de Lagarde, *op. cit.*, p. 202.

38. *Ibid.*, p. 187.

39. The élite irreligiosity of the twelfth and thirteenth centuries was socially less significant than the succeeding literary irreligiosity of the fourteenth and fifteenth centuries. The former was an irreligiosity of the few, of the élites, whereas the latter was more diffuse as literature, the dangerous vulgarizer of previously elaborated ideas, penetrated further among the masses.

40. Others also postulate various phases in the decline of religiosity. To give only one example, let us refer to Dardel's observation that:

> The problem of the 'universes of the mind' must today be a primary preoccupation of history. It is the problem which Lucien Febvre successfully broached in his *Probleme de l'Incroyance au XVIᵉ Siècle*, which appeared in 1942. Anachronism is the common fallacy of seeing Rabelais as an unbeliever in the style of a Voltaire or a Renan. Blindly, the allusion is made to an atheist rationalism, when in fact the sixteenth century was still imbued with the magical mentality, with occult practises, and with drifting philosophies in which the vestiges of Catholicism intermix with the 'winds of Lutheranism'. Rabelais sees a horizon where belief and unbelief coexist and mingle, and where our rational impossibilities no longer

come into play, since rationality is still dominated by mythology. To understand this one must free oneself of nineteenth-century ways of thinking and feeling, and follow the sinuous path — a path still half medieval — that the sixteenth century followed to reach its 'truth'. (Cf. Eric Dardel, L'histoire et notre temps', *Diogene* 21, 1958, pp. 14–31, in particular p. 29.)

41. Cf. A. N. Whitehead, *op. cit.*, p. 262.

42. In this regard see G. Muratori and D. Bighi, 'Andrea Vesalio, G. B. Canano e la rivoluzione rinascimentale dell'anatomia e della medicina', *Acta Medicae Historiae Patavinae*, X, (1964), pp. 41–96.

   For a comparison with medieval medicine, see *Medicina, Testi dell'alto medioevo*, (L. Firpo ed.), Turin, 1972, which includes among other things, the *Regimen Sanitatis Salerni* of the Salerno school and the *Fasciculus Medicinae*.

43. De Zwaan analysed the connections between religion and medical practice in Assyria, Babylonia, ancient Egypt, ancient India, and in Europe during the Middle Ages. See J.P. Kleiweg de Zwaan, 'Het betrekking tussen geneeskunst en godsdienst, cultur historisch beschouwd', *Mens en Maatschappij*, XXXI, 3, (1956), pp. 163–78, and XXXI, 5, (1956), pp. 287–305.

44. G. Toffanin, *op. cit.*, p. 133 (in a note).

45. Nor must the influence of scientific progress on other milieux be ignored. An example of this penetration into unlikely settings, comes from an anonymous eighteenth century French manuscript dealing with the attributes of divinity. In its footnotes is to be found an astonishing mass of references to technical and scientific concepts. Even the religious milieu was assimilating such concepts and themes. See *Perfections de Dieu*, MS. no. 1801, Orléans, mid eighteenth century, (first published by Éditions de Fontanelle, under the editorship of René-Jean Hesbert, in 1949).

46. For a rapid survey of the thought of Guiseppe Toffanin, an original and polemical scholar, see Bruno Lucrezi, 'Umanesimo di Toffanin', *Padova*, 1965, 1, pp. 34–5. Toffanin may be seen at his most lively in his 'A proposito dell'ultimo libro del prof. Garin', *Sophia*, XXX, 1–2, (1962), pp. 126–37.

47. See, among others, Antonio Corsano, 'Filosofia, scienza e tecnica nella crisi del pensiero rinascimentale', *Rivista di filosofia*, XL, 1, (1949), pp. 33–61.

48. Later, various creators and elaborators of rationalistic ideas come from a technological-scientific background. Comte was a tutor at a Polytechnic school, Herbert Spencer an engineer who contributed to the building of the first English railway, and Henri Poincaré also an engineer and a teacher of mathematics and physics. Wilfredo Pareto was also an engineer.

49. Mumford refers to a study of Winwood Reade who, in his *The Martyrdom of Man*, clearly formulates the new ideals of the age of

technology in the first phase of its development.

At the climax of that work he predicted three inventions: a fuel substitute for coal, aerial locomotion, and the synthetic composition of food. What further triumph was then left for man? The extinction of disease and the achievement of immortality. And then? Having reached the topmost peak of utilitarian fantasy, Reade could go no further: man's final task consisted in a cosmic return to the old theme of colonization: he would migrate into space and would finally, by becoming the architect of systems and the manufacturer of worlds, achieve the ultimate power and perfection of deity itself. The elaboration of that fantasy, with variations, was left to Mr. H. G. Wells: but its emptiness should be plain — it created a religious myth out of matter and motion and reduced the condition of man to that of an enlightened locomotive engineer. Mumford, *op. cit.*, p. 307.

50. Cf. C. Dawson, *op. cit.*, p. 190.

51. On this theme, see Bernard Fäy, *La massoneria e la rivoluzione intellettuale del secolo XVIII*, Turin: Einaudi, 1945, (2nd edition), p. 77. Among other authors, see Trevelyan, who goes into the problem of the diffusion of bourgeois and irreligious ideas in Great Britain. Cf. G. M. Trevelyan, *English Social History (A Survey of Six Centuries, Chaucer to Queen Victoria)*, London: Longmans Green, 1944.

52. Thus, we omit, for example, the problem of the secularization of state and of other institutions, which is at the same time a consequence and a cause of the declining sense of the sacred. In this connection we need only mention the secularization of schools, which has developed considerably over the last century. Prior to 1859 in Italy, 'The schools undertook to see that religious practices should be carried out, insisted that their students attend mass, confession, communion, etc., and directly oversaw the regular performance of such duties.' Cf. Aristide Gabelli, *L'istruzione in Italia*, Bologna: Zanichelli, 1891, vol. I, chap. 2, 'L'insegnamento religioso nelle scuole pubbliche', p. 52.

53. Cf. G. Le Bras, *Études de sociologie religieuse, op. cit.*, vol. I, pp. 45, 51, 60.

54. This, slow impoverishment is confirmed by documents left by missionary priests. In the eighteenth century, Hacquet made marginal notes dealing with individual missions which are true sociological observations of an intuitive nature. For example:

At Nieul sur Mer: 'The people, little devoted to the Gospel, are influenced by the nearby town' (page 51). At Niort: 'The soldiers of the garrison, scandalous libertines' (p. 51). At Acholet: 'The country people are good and docile while those of the village, which suffers from closeness to the town, are neither very devoted nor very flexible' (p. 61). At Champagné-les-Marais: 'This mission, by the will of Providence, has been only mediocre. . . . It is a village on the plain and this explains everything' (p. 67). At Brissac: 'The people that needed mission and to be taught, were of great spirit of adaptation. They were generous, but feel the closeness to the town' (p. 69). At Saint-Herblain: 'The closeness to Nantes makes the people little devoted, rather indifferent with very irregular attendance to Mass' (p. 80). See Pierre Fr. Hacquet, *Mémoires des missions des Mont-fortains dans l'ouest (1740–74). Cahiers de la revue du Bais-Poitou et la provinces de l'oueste Fontenay-le-Comte*, 1964. An historical survey for the region of Nantes confirms this decline and indicates an illegitimate birth-rate of 4.1 per cent at the beginning of the eighteenth century and of 10.1 per cent at its end. Cf. J. Depauw, 'Amour illégitime et société à Nantes au XVIII° siècle', *Annales*, XXVII, 45, (1972), pp. 1155–82.

55. G. Le Bras, *op. cit.*, vol. I, pp. 240–1.
56. *Ibid.*, passages cited in the preceding notes.
57. See G. Le Bras, 'Déchristianisation, mot fallacieux', *Sociologia Religiosa*, VIII, 11–12, (1964), pp. 5–12; P. Brezzi, 'Medioevo cristiano e sociologia religiosa', *Studium*, LXIV, 1, (1968), pp. 281–98.
58. See J. Schairer, *Das religiöse Volksleben am Ausgang des Mittelalters nach Augsburger Quellen*, Leipzig: Teubner, 1914; G. Reucklin-Teuscher, *Religiöses Volksleben des ausgehenden Mittelalters in den Reichsstädten und Heilbronn*, Berlin: Ebering, 1933; and L. A. Veit, *Volksfrommen, Brauchtum und Kirche in deutschen Mittelalter*, Freiburg: Herder, 1936.
59. M. Mollat, *La vie et la pratique religieuses au XIV° siècle et dans la première partie du XVe, principalement en France*, Paris: CDDU, 1963; J. Toussaert, *Le sentiment religieux en Flandre à la fin du Moyen Age*, Paris: Plon, 1963; M. Mollat, *op. cit.*, p. 1.
60. M. Mollat, *op. cit.*, p. 27.
61. *Ibid.*, p. 50.
62. *Ibid.*, p. 51.
63. *Ibid.*, p. 55.
64. *Ibid.*, p. 63.
65. J. Toussaert, *op. cit.*, p. 596.
66. *Ibid.*, p. 601.
67. *Ibid.*, p. 602.
68. M. Mollat, *op. cit.*, p. 64.
69. Cf. V. Chomel, *Bibl. École Chartres*, CXV, (1957), and Mollat, *op. cit.*
70. One almost ascetic index of the sacred which remained significant until the seventeenth century was abstinence from marital intercourse during Lent. This abstention, probably the expression of an ascetic tradition which was fairly widespread during the Middle Ages, was widely observed at the end of the medieval period, and then seems to have slowly declined. See Roger Mols, *Introduction à la Démographie*

historique des villes d'Europe du XIVᵉ au XVIIIᵉ siècle, vol. II, Louvain: Gembloux e Duculot, 1955, p. 299.

71. M. Mollat, *op. cit.*, p. 72.
72. *Ibid.*, p. 80.
73. *Ibid.*, p. 76.
74. It is true that there were extreme cases of moral decay of the clergy and decline of religious practice. But even these did not necessarily lead to a loss of the sense of the sacred, but rather to its appearance in manifestations which, to our eyes, seem totally aberrant. The situation in Sardinia is typical in this respect. In this region, social conditions were extremely depressed and religion was at a very low ebb. According to Ludovico de Cottes, out of 1,500 adults in one Sardinian diocese, less than 100 could recite the creed, and four or five hundred had not gone to confession or communion for at least twenty-five or thirty years. (These figures were reported in 1546.) See Giancarlo Sorgia, 'Due lettere i edite sulle condizioni del clero e dei fedeli in Sardegna nella prima metá del XVI secolo', *Atti del convegno di studi religiosi sardi*, Padua: Cedam, 1963, pp. 97–106.

    Christianity, in short, was not truly felt, and religiosity was largely expressed as pre-Christian sacred values which came to the surface whenever official religiosity weakened its hold. Furthermore, even in our own time, there are still in these regions clear signs of elements surviving from pagan times.

75. See C. von Höfler, *Die Ära der Bastarden am Schlusse des Mittelalters*, Bömische Gesellschaft der Wissenschaften, Prague, 1891.
76. Cf. D. Ottolenghi, 'Studi demografici sulla popolazione di Siena, dal secolo XIV al secolo XIX', *Bollettino senese di storia patria*, X, (1903), pp. 297–358.
77. Cf. G. Aleati, *La popolazione di Pavia durante il dominio spagnolo*, Milan: Giuffrè, 1957.
78. Cf. Athos Bellettini, *La Popolazione di Bologna dal secolo XV all'Unificazione italiana*, Bologna: Zanichelli, 1961.
79. R. Mols, *op. cit.*, p. 302.
80. *Ibid.*, p. 301.
81. Of particular interest are the data furnished by Dalabade, the sexton of a parish in the region of Toulouse. These data show that the number of illegitimates increased continuously.

1650–1667	1 illegitimate in every	94	births
1668–1675	,,	59	,,
1676–1699	,,	36	,,
1700–1719	,,	17.6	,,
1720–1731	,,	10.6	,,
1732–1743	,,	8.4	,,

In 1751, the percentage was already 1 in 7.2, and in 1788, 1 in 4. See Galabert, 'Les registrés paroissaux en France' in J. Cuvelier and L. Stainier, *Actes du Congrès International des Archivistes et Bibliothécaires de Bruxelles en 1910*, Brussels, 1912, pp. 118–30.

82. At St. Nicola-Waas one can distinguish three periods: 1631–50, when there were no illegitimate births; 1651–60, when there were 95 (i.e., about one per year), 16 of which took place, as Mols tells us, in 1668 when there was an invasion by a foreign army; and 1761–95, when there were 349 illegitimate births (i.e. about 10 per year). In particular about 6 for the first 5 years, and 17 for the last. See B. G. Willemsen, 'Étude sur le développement d'une commune du plat pays de Flandre au XVIIe et XVIIIe siècles (St. Nicolas-Waas)', *Annales de l'Acad. Royal d'Archéol. de Belgique*, 1904, n. 56, pp. 189–222.

83. The situation in Liège at the end of the eighteenth century was similar. See E. Helin, 'La population à Liège à la fin de l'Ancien Regime', *Bull. Stat.*, XXXVIII, (1952), pp. 481–4. See also 'La population de l'ancienne paroisse Saint Rémy à Liège', *La Vieux Liège*, 1953, nn. 101–2.

84. See Jacques Heuripin, *La population canadienne au début du XVIIIe siècle*, Paris: Presses Universitaires de France, 1954, p. 55.

85. L. Lallemand, *Histoire des enfants abandonnés et délaissés*, Paris, 1885, p. 470.

86. See R. Mols, *op. cit.*, p. 304.

87. N. S. Calisch, *Liefdadigheid te Amsterdam*, Charity in the city of Amsterdam. Summary of what has been done to improve material conditions, moral and religious, above all with the incentive (stimulus) of charity and need. Amsterdam, 1851, p. 88. The analysis is continued by S. Gargas, 'Uneheliche Kinder in den Niederlanden', *Arch. Soz. Hyg. Dem.*, III, (1928), p. 561.

88. These are Castiglioni's figures, but we take them here from Mols, *op. cit.*, p. 304.

89. P. Bandettini, *L'evoluzione demografica della Toscana, dal 1810 al 1889*, Turin, 1960.

90. R. Benini, 'La demografia italiana nell'ultimo cinquantennio', in *Cinquant'anni di vita italiana*, Rome, 1911.

91. E. Raseri, 'I fanciulli illegittimi ed esposti in Italia', *Annali di Statistica*, II, (19), 1881, p. 1.

92. See P. Bandettini, *op. cit.*

93. See S. S. Acquaviva, 'Un primo contributo alla sociologia storico-religiosa del padovano', *Sociologia religiosa*, 5–6, (1960).

94. See K. Julius Beloch, *Bevölkerungsgeschichte Italiene*, Berlin and Leipzig: W. de Gruyter & Co., I, 1937, p. 73.

95. *Ibid.*, p. 74.

96. See Beloch, *op. cit.*, p. 80.

97. See Giuseppe Parenti, 'La popolazione della Toscana sotto la reggenze lorenese', *Rivista del libro*, Florence, 1937, p. 133.

98. Pérouas reports interesting information on La Rochelle. By the middle of the seventeenth century, the clergy there had been reduced to about a quarter of their number in the mid sixteenth century. In spite of this, there was still one priest for about every four hundred inhabitants. See, Louis Pérouas, *Le diocèse de La Rochelle de 1648 à 1724, Sociologie et Pastorale*, Paris: Sevpen, 1964, p. 201.

99. See F. Casolini, *Il protomonastero di S. Chiara in Assisi, Storia e cronaca 1253-1950*, Milan: Garanti, 1950, pp. xxiv, 369, cf. p. 126.

100. A slow decline began in Tuscany even before the second half of the eighteenth century (See, G. Parenti, *op. cit.*)

The clergy in Tuscany from 1745 to 1765

	% clergy in the Population
1745	3.25
1751	3.12
1758	—
1761	3.05
1765	2.97

101. See A. Bellettini, *La popolazione di Bologna*, etc. *op. cit.*, pp. 58-9.

102. The crisis of religiosity as indicated by the usual indices is to be found in the most disparate countries, and the crisis appears at about the same time in the more developed countries. In Norway, for example, the number of priests fell by approximately 50 per cent between about 1750 and 1825 (from one priest for every 1,300 inhabitants to one for every 2,978). Before the Black Death (1349) and the Reformation there had been one priest for every 150 inhabitants. Cf. T. Flint, 'The secularisation of Norwegian society', *Comparative Studies in Society and History*, VI, 3, (1964), pp. 325-44.

103. The enormous decline in the religious vitality of France by the middle of the nineteenth century is confirmed, for example, by many data in Marcilhacy's study on the diocese of Orléans. Cf. C. Marcilhacy, *Le diocèse d'Orléans au milieu du XIXᵉ siècle*, Paris: Sirey, 1964.

104. Another index of the diminution of religious concern, although a minor one and one not always easily ascertainable, is represented by the decline in religious festivals, especially after the beginning of the eighteenth century. In the republic of Venice, for example, there was a reduction in religious feast days in 1787. In this connection cf. *Archivio di Stato di Venezia, Consultori in Jure*, filza 283, Consulta Franceschi, 12 January 1783; B. Cecchetti, *La repubblica di Venezia e la corte di Roma nei rapporti della religione*. This is taken up again by Marino Berengo, *La società veneta alla fine del 1700*, Florence: Sansoni, 1956.

105. Cf. K. H. Beloch, *op. cit.*, p. 46.

106. Cf. S. Burgalassi, *op. cit.*, p. 152.

107. For France, see, for example, Pierre Goubert, *Beauvais et le Beauvasis de 1600 à 1700*, Paris: Sevpen, 1960.
108. See M. Berengo, *op. cit.*, p. 243.
109. *Ibid.*, p. 245.
110. *Ibid.*, p. 250.
111. See Quirino Principe, 'Diocesi di Padova (1744-53)', *Sociologia religiosa*, III, 3-4, (1959), pp. 151-66.
112. As one example, F. L. Charpin reports of Marseilles that of those up to thirteen years of age, the percentage unbaptized was 2.12 per cent in 1806; then, after the crisis of the revolution, 1.17 per cent in 1821; 2.02 per cent in 1841; 1.04 per cent in 1861; 2.20 per cent in 1881; 1.30 per cent in 1901; 2.79 per cent in 1921; 2.82 per cent in 1941; 5.38 per cent in 1958. Those practising were 51 per cent in 1825, 47 per cent in 1841, 16 per cent in 1901, and about 15 per cent in 1953. Cf. F. L. Charpin, *Pratique religieuse et formation d'une grande ville*, Paris: Éditions du Centurion, 1964, pp. 93, 164.
113. On the religiously negative effect of the process of urbanization and technicization, see the interesting study of Amsterdam and other important Dutch cities by E. H. van Cleef, H. M. De Lange, P. Smits, 'De Kerk en het Vraagstuk van de Verstedelijking' (The church and the problem of urbanization), *Sociologisch Bulletin*, XI, 4, (1957), pp. 123-51.
114. The ancient city was a centre of consumption, while modern cities have increasingly acquired the character of centres of production and services: hence there is a considerable difference in the psychological context. Cf. M. Scheler, *Crisi dei valori*, Milan: Bompiani, 1937, p. 190. The thesis was originally proposed by W. Sombart.
115. That Paris already had 200,000 inhabitants in 1328 is contested by Mols who maintains that the population could not have been over 70-90,000, reaching 200,000 only around 1600. Cf. R. Mols, *Introduction à la Démographie historique des villes d'Europe du XIVe au XVIIIe siécle*, *op. cit.*
116. London, together with Paris, developed before the other great urban centres, although its greatest expansion occurred in connection with the first industrial revolution. In 1568 London had a little over 10,000 inhabitants. At the end of the seventeenth century their number had already risen to 500,000; the population had multiplied 50 times in less than 200 years. Then, in spite of some slowing in growth, it had reached 595,000 inhabitants by 1801; 1,949,277 in 1841 (an increase of 1,350,000 in 40 years); 3,830,000 in 1881 (almost 2 million in another 40 years); 4,536,063 in 1901; 8,200,000 in 1931 (Greater London).
117. G. Le Bras, *Études, op. cit.*, I, p. 249.
118. Cf. F. Boulard and J. Remy 'Pratique religieuse urbaine et régions culturelles', *Economie et Humanisme*, Paris, 1968.
119. We leave aside the general question of laicization, which in itself has

been an important aspect of desacralization. It has occurred in juridical and political structures, in schools, in mass culture, and the mass media, and this process has promoted more general desacralization.

120. See, among other things, T. Parsons and R. F. Bales, *Family, Socialization, and Interaction Process*, London: Routledge, 1956; B. Häring, *Sociologia della famiglia*, Rome: Edizioni Paoline, 2nd Edn., 1962; A. Ardigò, *Sociologia della famiglia*, Brescia: La Scuola, 1966.

121. On this point, see V. Filippone, 'Il problema del risentimento in Max Scheler', *Sociologia*, 1959, 1, pp. 5–44, esp. pp. 43–4.

122. ·See G. Le Bras, *Études, op. cit.*, I, pp. 222–3; 321–2; J. Chelini, *La Ville et l'Église, op. cit.*, pp. 100–12. On the historical dimension of this issue, see G. de Lagarde, *Naissance de l'esprit laïque au déclin du Moyen Age*, Paris: Presses Universitaires de France, 1948.

123. J. Chelini, *op. cit.*, p. 101.

124. *Ibid.*, p. 102.

125. See F. Houtart, '*Introduction à l'étude sociologique des loisirs*', *Évangéliser*, XIV, 79, (1959–60), pp. 7–33; J. Chelini, *op. cit.*, p. 105.

126. As recently as a century ago, there emerged in Italy, Lazzaretti, a man full of messianic spirit, who in our own times would scarcely be able to bring into being a large movement over vast areas of Italy, especially in the north: see Jean Séguy, 'David Lazzaretti et la sect apocalyptique des Giurisdavidici', *Archives de sociologie des religions*, III, 5, (1958), pp. 71–8; E. J. Hobsbawm, *Primitive Rebels*, Manchester: University Press, 1959, pp. 57–73. Apart from messianic phenomena, the change in mass psychology is indicated by other evidence: take, for example, the religious spirit, unthinkable today, that permeated the partisan warfare conducted throughout the ex-Kingdom of the Two Sicilies after Garibaldi's expedition. This struggle was carried on, by many if not by all, for religious reasons, and is marked by episodes of popular heroism. See A. Bianco di Saint-Jorioz, *Il brigantaggio alla frontiere pontificia dal 1860 al 1863*, Milan: G. Daelli, 1864: (the brigands of course are those who do not share the author's views and who fought for the Bourbons and the Pontiff).

127. S. S. Acquaviva, *Automazione e nuova classe*, Bologna: Il Mulino, 2nd. ed., 1964, p. 140. On the general problem of religiosity in the urban centres and in social classes see, among others, E. Pin, *Pratique religieuse et classes sociales dans une paroisse urbaine, Saint Pothin de Lyon*, Paris: Spes, 1956; J. Folliet, 'Les effets de la grande ville sur la vie religieuse', *Cronique sociale de France*, 61,(1953), pp. 539–66; G. Mury, 'Le catholicisme urbain et les classes sociales en France', *Cahiers internationaux de sociologie*, 79, (1956) pp. 31–44; Mury, 'Le prolétariat des villes et le sentiment religieux', *Cahiers, op. cit.*, 1956, n. 81, pp. 51–66; E. T. Sullenger, 'The Church in an Urban Society', *Sociology and Social Research*, 41, (1957), pp. 361–6; Paolo Tufari, 'Religiosità e cultura in una communità urbana', *Aggiornamenti sociali*, IX, 6, (1958), pp. 321–36.

128. G. Friedmann, *Ou' va le travail humain?* Paris: Gallimard, 1950, p. 21.

129. See J. M. Yinger, *op. cit.*, p. 139.

130. See on this the excellent little book by P. Barocelli, *Guida allo studio della paletnologia*, Rome: Edizioni Italjane, 1948, pp. 94, 119, 203, 222, for observations on the functional relationships of environment, technology, and culture (and thus of religiosity). See also, B. Malinowski, *Magic, Science and Religion*, Boston: Beacon Press, 1948; M. W. Agar, *Catholicism and the Progress of Science*, New York: Macmillan, 1940; R. Spiazzi, 'Scienza, Fede, Sapienza', *Sacra Doctrina*, IV, 14, (1959), pp. 124-55; and A. W. Besnard, 'La civilisation technicienne s'ouvrira-t-elle à l'Évangile?' *Lumen Vitae*, XIII, 4, (1958), pp. 632-54, and in the same journal, B. Häring, 'Mentalité technique et accès à l'univers liturgique', *ibid.*, pp. 655-64.

131. A. Desqueyrat, *La crisi religiosa del nostra tempo*, Rocca San Casciano: Cappelli, 1958, p. 51.

132. Simondon considers that religious thought tends towards synthesis, towards a cosmic vision of reality that finds its natural unity in the sacred and the divine. Technology moves more and more towards the particular, and we might add, it moulds the human mind. To the extent to which the human mind becomes more receptive to particular data, it becomes less sensitive to those synthetic visions that fascinated the generations that have gone before us. See G. Simondon, *Du mode d'existence des objets techniques*, Paris: Aubier, 1958.

133. B. Landheer, *Mind and Society: Epistomological Essays on Sociology*, The Hague: Nijhoff, 1952.

134. Distinguishing among ego, objects and others may seem artificial, but this can be justified if ultimately we do not depend too strictly on the interpretation.

135. M. Marotta, 'Il concetto di ruolo in sociologia', *Sociologia*, II, 3, (1957), pp. 269-309. In speaking of an attitude, we somewhat anticipate the discussion of individual psychology which we introduce later. We use this term only in order to emphasize the connection between attitude (psychological) and social role.

136. S. S. Acquaviva, *Automazione e nuova classe*, *op. cit.*, chap. III, paras. 1-2.

137. *Ibid.*

138. *Ibid.*

139. *Ibid.* chap. III, pp. 138-42.

140. G. Friedmann, *op. cit.*

141. With respect to the influence of natural rhythms on the human psyche, see Marcel Mauss's paper in the *Journal de Psychologie*, 1938, pp. 271-93, reprinted in *Sociologie et Anthropologie*, Paris: Presses Universitaires de France, 1950.

142. G. Friedmann, *op. cit.*, p. 29.

143. On this theme cf. also: N. Munzel, 'Técnica y Comunidad', *Estudios*

sociológicos internacionales, I, edited by the Inst. Balmes de Sociología, Consejo Superior de Investigaciones Scientificas, Madrid, 1956, pp. 417–60; F. Dessauer, *Philosophie der Technik*, Bonn, 1927; G. Siemens, 'Zur Philosophie der Technik', *Hochland*, XXIV, 2, (1926–7), p. 532 ff; J. Ortega y Gasset, *Betrachtungen über die Technik*, Stuttgart, 1949; A. Gehlen, 'Die Technik in der Sichtweise der philosophischen Anthropologie', *Merkur*, VII, (1935), p. 626 ff.

144. G. Friedmann, *op. cit.*, p. 32.
145. On the problem of the connection between the physical and psychic aspects of the human person and his socio-environmental position cf. M. Marotta, *Società e uomo in Sardegna: Ricerca di sociologia positiva*, Ann. Ec. Soc. della Sardegna, Cagliari, 1958.
146. Among the works dealing with the influence of technology and machinism on the crisis of contemporary civilization as a religious crisis, see D. Rops, *Il mondo senz'anima*, Brescia: Morcelliana, 3rd edition, 1947; D. Rops, *Al di là delle tenebre*, Milan: Garzanti, 1948.
147. G. Friedmann, *op. cit.*, p. 34.
148. B. Russell, *Religion and Science*, London: Oxford University Press, 1932.
149. Cf. S. S. Acquaviva, *op. cit.*, pp. 13–14.
150. Among the élites who have best assimilated the scientific criteria, religiosity seems to have declined, and this is precisely because of the prevalence of scientific and technical criteria over those which are religious and, so to speak, natural. The progress of unbelief should not be attributed to articulate arguments leading to negative conclusions concerning religion and its principal truths. Physics, sociology, biology, psychology and other such disciplines do not provide sufficient material and background for a competent and valid judgement on religious matters, but new mental attitudes arise among such specialists which are clearly inimical to religious belief. James H. Leuba has published two interesting tables where he seeks to measure religiosity and its decline among students in scientific disciplines.

Percentage of believers in God among four types of scientist

Discipline	1914	1933	1914	1933
	Major scientists		Minor scientists	
Physicists	50	43	34	17
Biologists	39	31	17	12
Sociologists	29	30	19	13
Psychologists	32	13	13	12

Percentage of believers in an afterlife among four types of scientist

Physicists	57	41	40	20
Biologists	45	32	25	15
Sociologists	52	31	27	10
Psychologists	27	12	9	2

From J. H. Leuba, *The Reformation of the Churches*, Boston: Beacon Press, 1955, p. 47, cited in Hoult, *The Sociology of Religion*, New York: Dryden Press, p. 359. The situation and the data may have changed considerably in the last thirty years, of course: the scientists in the study were educated at a time when science and irreligiosity were often connected. The distinction between major and minor scholars is somewhat arbitrary.

151. See S. S. Acquaviva, *op. cit.*, pp. 13–14.

152. *Ibid.*, p. 48.

153. *Ibid.*, p. 48.

154. *Ibid.*, pp. 139–40.

155. *Ibid.*, On the connections of symbols, human knowledge, and the formation of human personality, see G. Braga, 'Appunti di sociologia segnica', *Quaderni di sociologia*, 26, (1957), pp. 185–203; and *ibid.*, 27, (1958), pp. 23–43; *Idem, Communicazioni e società*, Milan: Angeli, 1961.

156. Cf. F. Barbano, 'Cultura e personalità nel pensiero sociologico americano', in *Il pensiero americano contemporaneo*, Milan: Edizioni di Comunità, 1958, p. 16.

157. F. Leonardi, *op. cit.*, p. 138.

158. *Ibid.*, p. 140.

159. Camillo Pellizzi observes that

> psychic time is never an Italian garden, neat and harmonious in its layout and design; instead it is a complex and dynamic reality full of ambiguity and multiple meanings. It will be the task of psychology to describe, from time to time, these complex situations. In the matter of definitions and in the programming of scientific work, it is very important to distinguish the 'cultural' from the 'non-cultural' aspects of value-oriented behaviour.

C. Pellizzi, 'Motivazione e comunicazione secondo nuovi concetti definitori', *Realazioni Umane*, III, 1–2, (1958), pp. 5–19.

160. *Ibid.*, p. 6.

161. *Ibid.*, p. 8.

162. *Ibid.*, p. 9.

163. *Ibid.*, p. 11.

164. Faggiotto uses the term *mithos* (sacrality) to refer to religious knowledge, *ethos* to refer to the ethical phase of knowledge, and *logos* to refer to the more markedly philosophical cognitive phase: A. Fagiotto, *Filosfia e religione, presupposti alla filosofia della religione*, Padua: University of Padua, 1951–2. See also, A. Fagiotto, *La religione nell'esperienza umana*.

165. In constructing the three categories of mythical (hierophic), ethical, and logical, Faggiotto demonstrates the interrelationship between them, A. Faggiotto, *Filosofia e religione, op. cit.*, p. 36.

166. See S. S. Acquaviva, *L'oggetto della sociologia religiosa, op. cit.*

167. This argument is valid even though it does not — indeed cannot — grasp

the essence of the experience of the sacred. We need not, however, take up a definitive stance on this matter. If the experience of the sacred is a 'spiritual' fact, it must be qualitatively different from other phenomena, which, however much they may influence and condition it, do not determine it completely. If, on the other hand, the experience of the sacred is a purely 'psychic' fact, then it fits easily into the categories of psychological experience, and its decay is even more easily explained.

168. The manifold social experiences that have modified and shaped the personality have not changed only in reference to the sacred, moving from the sacred to the non-sacred, but they have changed also in the type of sacredness for which they are relevant. As society has undergone transformation, so the significance of the spiritual life, and of the sense of the sacred, has changed. Thus arose groups of individuals who were actively, and no longer merely passively, oriented towards the sacred. Although they emerged without eliminating the sense of the sacred, their experience of a new type of society could not but leave some effects. The new type of society demanded a form of religiosity that differed considerably from that of those who, not having been affected by the corrosive action of the profane, maintained the faith that was theirs by birth and tradition. When, for example, man turned to the sacred after an experience of apostasy (if one may so call the decline of a purely interior experience), and whether he maintains his formal adhesion to a religion or not, it is said that he discovers in his relations with the sacred and their phenomenal structures, a freedom which was formerly unknown to him and which is still unknown to those who have not lived through this same experience. This topic is amply developed by N. Berdiaev, *Spirito e libertà*, Milan: Edizioni di Comunità, 2nd edition, 1947.

169. Human psychology with respect to the sacred has undergone slow, imperceptible transformations, and has fundamentally affected all other transformations. This influence of the religious component on human history must still be studied, and from this standpoint one might say that the history of the last 200 years should be rewritten. Phenomena such as the French revolution and the Marxist revolution may be grasped as something more profound than the products of political-philosophical ideologies, as being partially determined by the decay of the religious spirit — a process which unleashes in the human psychology previously contained and restrained forces.

170. If one reflects attentively on the logico-interpretive scheme developed in the previous pages, it becomes clear (contrary to what Demarchi, for example, maintains) that it is not easy to speak of secularization without the loss of the sense of the sacred. (Cf. F. Demarchi, 'Profilo sociologico della dinamica religiosa', *Humanitas*, XVI, 10, (1961), 788-809.)

CHAPTER 4

1. This was a plausible thesis in the fifties, but today things have changed. The bourgeoisie of 1960 is not the bourgeoisie of 1850 or 1750: it draws on a very different social stratum. One may then ask whether it is the old bourgeoisie that has 'again become' in part Christian, or whether there is a new bourgeoisie — recruited from social strata that never became desacralized. To some, those at managerial level appear to have a high rate of practice, but many factors affect practice, and particular influences may be felt within a restricted area of space of time. If the new technical mentality adversely affects practice, other factors may have an opposite effect — such as the more or less humanistic school training of managers, their political orientations, the bourgeois background from which some of them have come and in which they live, and which is itself very little affected by technology and science. Some students even consider that religiosity and religion are not much affected by technical and managerial milieux as such, and that technical training has little influence on religious attitudes: see C. T. Sandford and S. Griffin, 'Religious Belief and Church Attendance of Students at a College of Science and Technology', *The Church Quarterly Reveiw*, 3, (1965). (Only 17 per cent of these students declared themselves to be agnostics or atheists.) See also the issue of *Evengeliser*, XIII, 78, (1959), pp. 534-48, the articles by J. Laloux, 'La pratique religieuse des milieux indépendants'; and Y. Mergeay, 'Déficiences chrétiennes des milieux indépendants'.
2. E. Pin, *Pratique religieuse et classes sociales dans une paroisse urbaine, Saint-Pothin à Lyon*, Paris: Spes, 1956.
3. *Ibid.*, p. 190.
4. *Ibid.*, p. 196.
5. *Ibid.*, p. 213.
6. G. Kelly, *Catholics and the Practice of the Faith. A Census Study of the Diocese of St. Augustine*, The Catholic University of America Press, 1946; L. Réthy, *La pratique dominicale dans les zones urbaines de Saône et Loire*, Autun 1958; J. Chelini, 'Pratique religieuse et niveaux de culture', *Signes du Temps*, 2, 1959, pp. 11-15.
7. A. Pawelczynska, 'Les attitudes des étudiants Varsoviens envers la religion', *op. cit.*, p. 116.
8. J. Maître, 'Un sondage polonais sur les attitudes religieuses de la jeunesse', *Archives de sociologie des religions*, 12, 1961, pp. 133-43, see p. 136.
9. J. Fuseram 'Religion et opinions chez les étudiants de l'Université de Sarajevo', *Archives de sociologie des religions*, 12, 1961, pp. 145-55, see p. 154.
10. N. Greinacher, 'L'evolution de la pratique religieuse en Allemagne après la guerre', *Social Compass*, X, 4-5, (1963), pp. 345-56, see p. 350.

11. F. A. Isambert, 'Christianisme et stratification sociale', *Social Compass*, IX, 5-6, (1962), pp. 495-513.

12. In addition to Isambert's article, see G. E. Lenski, 'Some Social Correlates of Religious Interest', *American Sociological Review*, 18, (1953), pp. 533-44.

13. E. Pin, 'Hypotheses relatives a la desaffaction religieuse dans les classes inferieures', *Social Compass*, IX, 5-6, (1962), pp. 515-37.

14. E. Pin, *op. cit.*, reports on A. Cottret, *Considérations sur l'état actuel de la religion catholique en France*, Paris, 1815, p. 15-16, (also cited by F. Isambert in *Christianisme et classe ouvrière*, Paris: Casterman, 1961).

15. Pin, *op. cit.*, p. 522.

16. Our observations on the relationship between cultural level, education, and religious practice are confirmed by Fr. Toldo's study of Bologna. His survey shows that only 14.14 per cent of those who had completed primary school were practising compared with 41.17 per cent of those who had completed lower secondary school, 60.09 per cent of those who had completed higher secondary school, and 55.45 per cent of those with a university degree. The diminished participation rate in the last of the categories may be due to the fact that the 'leadership' responsibilities typically found among university graduates make practice objectively less feasible. From the occupational point of view the highest rate of practice was found among professional people, 28 per cent, while manual workers in general (self-employed and employees) show a rate of 15 per cent, and wage workers (male and female) of 7 per cent. For men alone, the rate was 4 per cent.

    The hypothesis concerning the relationship between cultural and educational level is also confirmed by the overall trend of religiosity in Italy. Burgalassi indicates that the situation is worse in the culturally less developed regions.

17. We have developed this topic in S. S. Acquaviva, *Automazione e nuova classe, op. cit.*

18. See D. H. Heath, 'Secularization and Maturity in Religious Beliefs', *Journal of Religion and Health*, 8, (1969), pp. 335-58.

19. The following table was reprinted from *Pro Mundi Vita* in *Etudes*, 1969, pp. 114-15.

Question: Croyez-vous en Dieu?

Répondent: Non	1958	1968
ensemble	13	17
garçons	18	23
filles	7	11
Catholiques non pratiquants	11	31
instruction primaire	11	13
primaire supérieure	14	15
technique ou comerc.	15	12
secondaire	11	18
supérieure	20	37

The comment is added: 'Les jeunes de 15–29 ans qui se disent athées sont en progrès particulièrement parmi ceux qui prolongent leurs études. J.-F. Six du secrétariat français pour les non croyants commente: "Comment ne pas souhaiter que l'ensemble de l'Église prenne conscience de cette situation et en tire les conséquences? Les Chrétiens sont, pour la plupart, ou bien indifférents à cette montée de l'athéisme, ou bien traumatisés" '.

Cfr. Anon, 'La jeunesse occidentale et l'avenir de l'Église', *Pro Mundi Vita*, 33, (1970), p. 19.

20. This phenomenon is considerable, but we must emphasize that the social advance affecting all industrialized countries tends to raise the educational level particularly of individuals who, because of their family background, their social context, etc., are rather disposed to deny God, or at least the more or less traditional God to which the surveys refer. In this case, atheism and agnosticism might be related to historical factors having to do with the history of culture, of classes, and of social mobility rather than with a correlation between religion and higher education. Thus the phenomenon would be analogous to that to be found among the eighteenth- and nineteenth-century bourgeoise, and therefore reversible.

21. In a certain sense one might maintain, with Mircea Eliade, that 'the symbol translates a human situation into cosmological terms and vice versa. More precisely it reveals the solidarity which exists between the structures of human existence and cosmic structures'. In a word, the symbol is, at least potentially, a vehicle of our spiritual knowledge of cosmic reality. See M. Eliade, *La symbolisme des ténèbres dans les religions archaïques*, 'Polarite de symbole, Bruges: Desclée de Brouwer, 1960, pp. 15–28.

22. See A. Faggiotto, *Storia della religioni e cristianesimo, op. cit.*, p. 7.

23. *Ibid.*, p. 12.

24. *Ibid.*, p. 13.

25. *Ibid.*, p. 17

26. See C. Pellizzi, *Elementi di sistematica sociologica*, Facoltà di scienze politiche, Florence: C. Alfieri, 1958, p. 181.

27. When we refer to the symbolic value of myth, we refer to it as an instrument of communication and knowledge. Whether the myth corresponds to an actual fact or not makes no substantial difference to the argument. Whether Buddha's experience of Nirvana was an actual fact or not, the narration of the life of Buddha becomes a vehicle for the more or less immediate and precise communication and description of principles, experiences, feelings, ideas, of a sacred character. In practice it becomes a symbol of a series of communicable entities.

28. This symbolic connection between individual and object, among various individualss, among the various aspects of the spiritual experience, etc., is grounded on a kind of basic symbiosis between

subject and object. Indeed, this symbiosis is one of the fundamental characteristics of the experience of the sacred, where on the one side whoever lives the experience always tends to become identified, to a greater or lesser extent, with the object of the experience, and sometimes, in the case of mystical union, attains a real or presumed total union with the sacred.

Undoubtedly, as Berdiaev observes:

Spiritual experience, upon which realist symbolism rests, lies altogether beyond the antithesis between subject and object and the substantialist conception of them. Spiritual life is no more subjective than it is objective. The symbolization of it, that is, its embodiment in forms belonging to the natural world, may be understood as an objectification, but that is precisely why it is not objective in the rationalist sense of the word. The symbolic mode of thought includes both subject and object within itself, and that at an infinitely deeper level of consciousness. If objectification is nothing more than a process of symbolization, then for that very reason all objective rationalism and all naïve conceptions of an object-substance cease to possess justification. What are called objective realities are in fact only realities of a secondary order, for they are merely symbolic and possess no reality in their own right. But subjective realities, such as the reality of the effective life and that of the subject and its subjective world, are likewise merely secondary and symbolic in character. (Cf. N. Berdiaev, *Freedom and the Spirit*, The Centenary Press, 1935, pp. 55–6.)

Although we cannot fully accept this crudely existentialist view, we must agree in recognizing the symbolic symbiosis between subject and object that we have just postulated.

29. See C. Pellizzi, *op. cit.*, p. 193. More recently Pellizzi has remarked: 'I do not believe that it would be semantically legitimate, and it would be even less useful, to offer a definition of 'ritual' and 'myth' that would pertain exclusively to the religious fact, even though a religious, or sacred, aspect belongs to the essence of ritual, and though it is difficult to conceive of myth as totally autonomous with respect to sacredness.' Cf. C. Pellizzi, 'Caproni, parrucche e altro', *op. cit.*, pp. 99–112 which stresses this thesis with particular vigour.

30. In expanding and deepening this subject, Camillo Pellizzi asks whether ritual should be understood as a *prius* or as a *posterius* with respect to myth. He concludes by observing that 'the mind tends to invert the order of its moves, and when it has worked out the logical figure of one of its own patterns of behaviour which has already become established as a ritual institution, then it claims that that ritual is only the translation into act of pre-existing logical concepts.

In the same way, one must hold that the genesis of religious ritual, imbued as it is with ancient "meanings" is prior to that of myth and legend, whether sacred or profane. The latter arrive later to frame it,

to co-ordinate it, to insert it into the "discourse" of a human group.'
(*Elementi di sistematica sociologica, op. cit.*, p. 195.)

31. An analysis of the characteristics of meaning and of the connections
between religious ritual and myth and social life in general is given in
J. Cazeneuve, 'Le principe de répétition dans le rite', *Cahiers internationaux de sociologie*, XXIII, 3-4, (1957), pp. 42-62.

32. No one can reasonably affirm that knowledge is only intellectual. We
may maintain with Berdiaev that 'it is a mistake to believe that
emotion is purely subjective, while thought is objective. It is a mistake
to believe that the knowing subject comes into contact with being only
through the intellect and remains in his subjective universe only with
emotion.' N. Berdiaev, *L'io e il mondo*, Milan: Bompiani, 1942, p.
26.

33. This verifies Pellizzi's remark: 'All this means that there is no communication of background significances unless whoever receives the
so-called communication has already been "initiated" to that specific
significance. However, once the latter has been incorporated into the
mind of the addressee of a communication, his mind and his emotions
re-focus on that meaning whenever anyone produces the sign'. (*Op.
cit.*, p. 202.)

34. *Op. cit.*, p. 205.

35. Among the various attempts to 'separate' religious and mystical or
sacred knowledge from ordinary knowledge, that of Lévy-Bruhl is
particularly interesting. Initially, this author denied the logical
character of the knowledge of primitive peoples, exactly because of its
'sacred or mystical' character. One consequence of this assumption,
following from Lévy-Bruhl's argument, was the denial of any logical
character to all sacred knowledge. It involved what Lévy-Bruhl
himself defined as the 'prelogical' character of primitive knowledge.
He later revised these views but did not discard them, since he could
still assert that the primitive simply did not think by means of concepts
and . . . possessed other mental habits. (See *The Notebooks*, Oxford:
Blackwell, 1975.) According to Lévy-Bruhl, for the primitives there is
an imperceptible passage from 'belief' to experience, without any
substantial distinction between the two worlds. But is the situation any
different in our own cognitive world? How much of our knowledge is
the expression of sheer belief? Naturally the beliefs of the primitives
are different from ours, but simply realizing this certainly does not
authorize us to devalue their cognitive processes. Probably, within a
thousand years our own beliefs, sacred and profane, will seem as
obviously illogical or prelogical as those of the primitives.
      Thus we cannot agree with Lévy-Bruhl when he observes that:
'impermeability to experience is another aspect of the prelogical
character of the primitive mentality, in that since this mentality feels
no need to submit traditional beliefs to criticism or to wonder if they
are acceptable, it preserves the same attitude toward experiences,

which it fails to distinguish from beliefs.' (*Ibid.*) Traditional beliefs are not subjected to criticism only because they are thought to be certainly true, that is because they are confirmed by other people's experiences, by revelation, etc. This is no different from what we do when, for example, we accept a 'historicist' interpretation of human history as a scientific one on the basis of meagre data. The majority of men behave in this way, but we do not, on this account, charge them with being illogical or prelogical. In fact, Lévy-Bruhl himself no longer believed in this distinction, remarking in *The Notebooks* that 'it is impossible to admit that there is a mentality which is typical of primitives and of them alone, and it is even more impossible to admit a distinction between societies in which the primitive mentality is dominant and other societies. This would be a discouraging picture. It is no less difficult to distinguish the logical from the prelogical in a man's head. In short, it is time I myself drew the conclusions that follow from *Mythologie Primitive* and especially from *L'experience mystique et les symboles chez les primitifs*: these require a change in the presentation of what I had to say.'

Thus, if there is a difference, it consists only in the attribution of sacred character to acts and facts that for us are not sacred, or are sacred on a different level.

36.   We have not, of course, with the considerations developed so far, even remotely exhausted the question. We have only conceptualized it as far as necessary to produce a working tool.

37.   E. De Martino, 'Mito, scienze, religiosità e civiltà moderna', *Nuovi Argomenti*, 37, (1959), p. 9.

38.   *Ibid.*, p. 13 ff.

39.   *Ibid.*, p. 217.

40.   See chapter three above.

41.   See chapter three above.

42.   See E. Durkheim, *The Division of Labor in Society*, New York: Macmillan, 1933.

43.   See E. De Martino, *op. cit.*, p. 10.

44.   The interpretations of the psychoanalytic schools are not, of course, accepted simply because they sometimes lead to the solution of some psychic problems.

45.   See H. Liechtenstein, 'Zur Phänomenologie des Wiederholungs-zwanges und des Todestriebes', *Imago*, XXI, 4 (1935), pp. 466–88; Th. Preuss, *Der religiöse Gehalt der Mythen*, Tübingen, 1933; B. Malinowski, *Myth in Primitive Psychology*, London, 1926.

46.   See M. Eliade, *Le Mythe de l'eternal retour*, Paris: Gallimard, 1949, especially the introduction and conclusions; *Images et Symboles, op. cit.*, p. 87.

47.   This sense of history is still absent in the Old Testament. The authors of the Old Testament are intensely oriented toward this projection in the primordial instant and, at the same time, into a 'timeless' ideal

future. 'All of biblical literature is constantly contrasting the un-
ceasing and ephemeral vicissitudes of human history with the immutable sovereignty of Yahweh. Yahweh is he who goes beyond all the
limits of space and time which characterize the creature. . . .
    The "Book of the Consolation of Israel" summarizes these . . .
considerations in the formula "Yahweh is the first and the
last"; where eternity is expressed unambiguously, although in
eminently concrete language. (Is. 41,4; 44,6; 48,12)'. Cf. G. Biffi,
'Eternità e tempo nel nostro destino', *La scuola cattolica*, LXXXVII,
3, (1959), pp. 196–212.

48.   'Christianity, instead, does indeed possess the sense of history, and yet
       in the Christian present the projection toward the future and eternity
       is already evident: the second future is already present and, although
       it is now enveloped in the vicissitudes of the world, it is already a living
       and working reality in the very heart of history.' G. Biffi, *op. cit.*

49.   E. De Martino, *op. cit.*, p. 33.
50.   *Ibid.*, p. 42.
51.   *Ibid.*, p. 43.
52.   Cf. Eliade, *Tecniche dello yoga, op. cit.*, p. 29.
53.   Cf. Eliade, *Le mythe de l'éternel retour*, Gallimard, Paris, 1949, p.
       228.
54.   *Ibid.*, p. 234. In the vision of history of many Eastern and Western
       religions the past appears as a prefiguration of the future, while
       nothing in the sacred vision of history is, as a value, irreversible.
       Everything may be referred to the primordial archetype which gives
       significance to the present and the future as well as to the past.
55.   Kelsen has also dealt with the problem of the logicality of the
       primitives' concept of cause in general. According to him, primitives
       ignore the concept of cause, since they consider natural events to be
       the work of persons. Kelsen attempts to demonstrate the primitive's
       inability to construct the concept of cause, a concept which is replaced
       by a close connection between nature and society. This theory can be
       easily refuted.
56.   This is the theory. In practice it seems that the correlation between
       religious practice (within a religious organization) and other forms of
       personal religiosity is very strong. In the context of a survey on Paris,
       Pin asks: 'is it not thinkable that outside of the categories of habitual
       practitioners there exists a fairly intense personal religious life which,
       instead of manifesting itself in the official religious practices of the
       church, expresses itself through a private cult of God? This possibility
       affects only a minority of the non-practising: 10 per cent of them say
       that they pray to God every day or more than once a week; a minority
       of the occasional practitioners maintains the same thing: 25 per cent.'
       Cf. E. Pin, *Religiosité et appartenance à l'Eglise dans le XX*ᵉ
       arrondissement de Paris, Rome: Ciris, 1966, p. 23.
57.   Modern is the man who has learned to rely on his own power; for

him the magical use of the 'sacred' has lost all meaning, and the aspect of need in his own existence does not cause him to turn to a supernatural source of life, but is understood as an opportunity for the exercise of his own creativity. Since he knows rationally the world in which he lives, this world has lost much of its mystery. Thus the 'sacred' is not to be found in this world, and what is emphasized is rather the transcendence of God. The 'sacred' is found instead in the intimate tendency of man to realize himself in responsible action in the world.

Cf. Theodore Steeman, 'Studio sull'ateismo', in *Dio è morto?*, Milan: Mondadori, 1968, p. 225.

58. Cf. H. Cox, *op. cit*. On the whole, Cox's thesis is rather close to that of Schillebeeckx concerning the biblical and Christian origin of secularization. Cf. E. Schillebeeckx, 'Het nieuwe mens — en Godsbeeld in conflict met het religieuze leven', *Tijdschrift voor Theologie*, 1967, p. 7.

59. T. Luckmann, *op. cit.*, p. 35.

60. *Ibid.*, p. 33.

61. *Ibid.*, p. 46.

62. See V. Sturm, 'Schwund der Religiosität', *Frankfurter Allgemeine Zeitung*, 7 October 1966, and D. Savramis, 'Das Vorurteil von der Entchristlichung der Gegenwarts-Gesellschaft', *Kölnerzeitschrift für Soziologie und Sozial-Psychologie*, XIX, (1967), 2.

63. M. Eliade, *Images and Symbols, op. cit.*, p. 120.

64. *Ibid.*, p. 160.

65. *Loc. cit.*

66. *Ibid.*, p. 18.

67. *Ibid.*, p. 19.

68. *Ibid.*, p. 33.

69. H. Marcuse, *One Dimensional Man*, Boston: Beacon Press, p. 5.

70. G. Zunini, *Homo Religiosus*, Milan: Il Saggiatore, 1966, p. 84.

71. Marcuse, *op. cit.*, p. 7.

72. *Ibid.*, p. 10.

73. *Ibid.*, p. 11.

74. *Ibid.*, p. 151.

75. J. Fourastié, *La civilisation de 1975*, Paris: Presses Universitaires de France, 1962, p. 37.

76. Cf. S. A. Stouffer, *The American Soldier*, Princeton: Princeton University Press, 1949.

77. A. Vergote, *Psychologie religieuse*, Brussels: Dessart, 1966, pp. 77, 112, 114.

78. Bergson develops an interesting argument concerning this problem, when he observes that, with the expansion of technology,

mechanics would reach their highest pitch of development. But there are certain risks which must be taken: an activity of a superior kind, which to be operative requires one of a lower order, must call forth this activity, or at least permit it to function, if necessary even at the cost of having to defend itself against it; experience shows that if, in the case of two contrary but complementary tendencies, we find one to have grown until it tries to monopolize all the room, the other will profit by this, provided it has been able to survive; its turn will come again, and it will then benefit by everything which has been done without its aid, which has even been energetically developed in specific opposition to it. However that may be, this means could only be utilized much later; in the meantime an entirely different method had to be followed. This consisted, not in contemplating a general and immediate spreading of the mystic impetus, which was obviously impossible, but in imparting it, already weakened though it was, to a tiny handful of privileged souls which together would form a spiritual society; societies of this kind might multiply; each one, through such of its members as might be exceptionally gifted, would give birth to one or several others; thus the impetus would be preserved and continued, until such time as a profound change in the material conditions imposed on humanity by nature should permit, in spiritual matters, of a radical transformation.

(H. Bergson, *The Two Sources of Morality and Religion, op. cit.*, pp. 201–2.)

Bergson's considerations lie within the context of a philosophical conception and have a teleological orientation that is useless at the empirical level, but which contains what may be taken as a valid intuition: that there is no reason to believe that what technology has done to damage the sacred in space and time must eventually lead to a total disintegration of the sacred itself. Social groups, however small, which survive the wave of desacralization may carry the sense of the sacred forward. They may sow seeds of a new expansion. The same function was performed by some lay or semi-lay groups in the centuries when society was submerged under the wave of sacrality.

79. This hypothesis appears plausible if one considers that for Jung the archetypes rest in the depths of the primordial psychic field and are part of the 'psychic structure: thus they make up the collective unconscious, common to all, "the universal foundation of every individual psyche", and *the carrier of potential meanings.*' Furthermore, the archetype exercises a very strong attraction on the conscious. In Jung's theory these potential possibilities of the archetype and of the symbol may be analysed and understood, even in relation to religious phenomenology, by reading the interesting work of J. Jacobi, 'Archétype et symbole dans la psychologie de Jung', *Polarité du Symbole*, Bruges: Desclée de Brouwer, 1960, pp. 167–206.

80. See J. Jacobi, *Complex, Archetype, Symbol, in the Psychology of C. G. Jung*, New York: Pantheon Books, 1959, pp. 42–52. The reader who is particularly interested in the dynamic that leads the archetype from the state of quiescence to that of active phenomenon should consult Jacobi's limpid scheme, *ibid.*, p. 119 ff.

Bibliography*

Abell, A. I., *The Urban Impact on American Protestantism, 1865–1900*, Harvard University Press, Cambridge, 1943.

Abrecht P., *The Churches and Rapid Social Change*, Doubleday, Garden City, 1961.

Acquaviva S. S., 'Research on Religious Practice as a Preliminary to Research on Religious Politics', *Political Research: Organisation and Design*, I (1958), n. 3.

— — 'L'oggetto della sociologia religiosa', *Notiziario di Sociologia*, I (1958), n. 4.

— — 'The Psychology of Dechristianisation in the Dynamics of the Industrial Society', *Social Compass*, 1960, n. 7.

— — 'Sociologie religieuse et sociologie des religions en Italie', *Archives de sociologie des religions*, 1961, n. 12.

— — 'Probleme der Religionssoziologie in Italien', *Probleme der Religionssoziologie*, Westdeutscher Verlag, Cologne, 1962.

— — 'Religions et développement socio-economique', *Social Compass*, X(1963), n. 3.

— — 'Sociologia religiosa', in *Antologia di scienze sociali*, vol II, Il Mulino, Bologna, 1963.

— — and G. Eisermann, 'Massmedien und Soziales Wandel', *Kölnerzeitschrift für Soziologie und Sozial Psychologie*, XX (1968), n. 4.

— — *Automazione e Nuova Classe*, Il Mulino, Bologna, 1969.

— — 'La sociologia delle religioni', in *Questioni di Sociologia*, La Scuola, Brescia, 1966.

— — 'Sociologia dell'ateismo', in *Enciclopedia dell'ateismo*, SEI, Turin, 1969.

— — *Una Scommessa sul futuro*, ISEDI, 1971.

— — and A. Guizzardi, *Religione e Irreligione nell'Età Postindustriale*, AVE, Rome, 1971.

*This bibliography does not include all of the titles referred to in the notes, and vice versa. There are a number of reasons for this, some of which are indicated in the text, and which are generally stated on page xi.

— — and A. Guizzardi (eds.), *La secolarizzazione*, Il Mulino, Bologna, 1973.

— — and Geisermann, *Der Einfluss des Fernsehens auf die Schule in der Gesellschaft von Heute und Morgen*, Enke Verlag, Stuttgart, 1973.

Adam, A., *Du mysticisme a la révolte, Les Jansénistes du XVII siècle*, Fayard, Paris, 1968.

Adam P., *La vie paroissiale en France au XIV siècle*, Préf. et avertissement de G. Le Bras, Sirey, Paris, 1964.

Adams J. L., 'Rudolf Solim Theology of Law and the Spirit', in *Religion and Culture*, Harper and Brothers, New York, 1959.

— — *Paul Tillich's Philosophy of Culture, Science and Religion*, Harper and Row, New York, 1965.

Adams J. L., *Exiles, Trapped Exiles, in the Welfare State*, University of Chicago, 1966.

Alberoni F., 'Integrazione dell'immigrato e integrazione sociale', *Studi di Sociologia*, II (1964), n. 4.

Aldrich C. R., *Mente Primitiva e civiltà moderna*, Einaudi, Turin, 1949.

Allport G. W., *The Individual and His Religion*, Macmillan Co., New York, 1950.

— — and Gillespie M., and Young J., 'The Religion of the Post-War College Student', *Journal of Psychology*, 1948.

Anon., *Lotta antireligiosa in Russia*, Edizione R. C. Bergamo, n.d.

— — *La pratique religieuse en Wallonie*, Centre des recherches socio-religieuses, Brussels, 1956.

— — *Album de sociologie religieuse*, Secrétariat social, Annecy, 1958.

— — 'Il problema del rinserimento in Max Scheler', *Sociologia*, 1959, n. 1.

— — 'La réaction religieuse des Russes soviétiques à l'Espositione de Bruxelles', *Irénikon*, XXXII (1959), n. 1.

— — *Settimana dioc. di Aggiornamento Past.*, Treviso, 24–29 September 1962, C.D.P., Treviso, 1962.

Anon. of Orleans, *Perfections de Dieu*, Ms. 1801, Orléans, mid-eighteenth century, edited by René-Jean Hesbert, Ed. de Fontenelle, 1949.

Antoine R., 'L'Hindouisme contemporain, *Rythmes du monde*, V (1957), nn. 3–4.

Argyle M., *Religious Behavior*, Free Press, Glencoe, Ill. 1959.

Aries P., 'Attitudes devant la vie et devant la mort, du XVIIe au XIXe siècle', *Population*, IV (1949).

Asch S. E., *Psicologia sociale*, SEI, Turin 1958.

Ashton T. S., *The Industrial Revolution 1760–1830*, London, 1948.

Aubry J., 'Renaissance catholique en Écosse', *Études*, 1957, n. 1.

Azzali I., *L'indagine sociologica di una parrochia*, Pizzorni, Cremona 1954.

Bagnoli A., 'Insegnamento di una statistica e rilievo statistico sulla frequenza alla messa', *Bollettino diocesano di Volterra*, XXXII (1952).

Balducci E., *L'esperienza religiosa*, Borla, Turin 1962.

Banton M. *Anthropological Approaches to the Study of Religion*, Tavistock, London 1966.

Barbano F., 'Problemi e prospettive di sociologia della religione', *Il politico*, XVIII (1953); 'Cultura e personalità nel pensiero sociologico americano', in *Il pensiero americano contemporaneo*, Edizioni di Comunità, Milan 1958.

Bardis P. D., 'The Family in a Changing Civilization', *Sociologia religiosa*, XI (1968), n. 17–18.

Barocelli P., *Guida allo studio della paletnologia*, Edizioni Italiane, Rome 1948.

Barzelloti G., *Monte Amiata e il suo profeta (David Lazzaretti)*, Treves, Milan 1910.

Battaglia R., 'Religiosità popolare italiana', *Lares*, III (1932), n. 2. 'La vecchia col fuso e la filatura del lino nelle tradizioni popolari', *Çe Fastu?*, XXV (1949), nn. 5–6.

Bayés R., *Los ingenieros, la sociedad y la religion*, Fontanella, Barcelona 1965.

Becker H., 'Current Sacred-secular Theory and its Development', in *Modern Sociological Theory in Continuity and Change*, The Dryden Press, New York 1957.

Bedeschi L., *Geografia del laicismo*, Ed. UCIIM, Rome 1957.

Beirnaert L., *Éxperience chrétienne et psychologie*, EPI, Paris 1964.

Bell D., 'Religion in the Sixties', *Social Research*, XXXVIII (1971), n. 3.

Bellah R. N., 'Religious Aspects of Modernization in Turkey and Japan', *American Journal of Sociology*, LXIV (1958), n. 1. (ed.), *Religion and Progress in Modern Asia*, Free Press, New York 1965. 'Meaning and Modernization', *Sociologia religiosa*, XI (1968), n. 17–18. 'Transcendence in Contemporary Piety', *The World Yearbook of Religion*, 1970, vol. II.

Bellah R. N., *Beyond Belief. Essays on Religion in a Post-traditional World*, Harper & Row, Evanston, 1970.

Belloc H., *La crisi della civiltà*, Morcelliana, Brescia 1948.

Berdiaev N., *L'io e il mondo*, Bompiani, Milan 1942.

Berengo M., *La società veneta alla fine del '700*, Sansoni, Florence 1956.

Berger P. L., 'Sectarianism and Religious Sociation', *American Journal of Sociology*, LXIV (1958), n. 1.

— — 'Christliche Gemeinschaft und moderne Gesellschaft', *Lutherische Rundschau*, 1960, n. 1.

— — *The Noise of Solemn Assemblies*, Doubleday, Garden City, New York 1961.

— — *The Precarious Vision*, Doubleday, Garden City, New York 1961. *Kirche obne Auftrag*, Stuttgart 1962.

— — 'Charism and Religious Innovation: The Social Location of Israelite Prophecy', *American Sociological Review*, XXVIII (1963), n. 6.

— — 'A Sociological View of the Secularisation of Theology', *Journal for the Scientific Study of Religion*, VI (1967), n. 1.

— — *The Social Reality of Religion*, Faber and Faber, London 1969.

— — *A Rumor of Angels. Modern Society and the Rediscovery of the Supernatural*, Doubleday, Garden City 1969.

Berger P. L. and Kellner H., 'Marriage and the Construction of Reality', *Diogène*, 1964, n. 44.

Berger P. L., *The Sacred Canopy*, Doubleday, New York, 1967.

Berger P. L. and Luckmann T., *The Social Construction of Reality*, Doubleday, New York, 1966.

Berger P. L. and Luckmann Th., 'Aspects sociologiques du pluralisme', *Archives de sociologie des religions*, XII (1967), n. 23.

Bergson H., *The Two Sources of Morality and Religion*, (trans. Audra, Brereton), Macmillan, London, 1935.

Berkowitz M. I. and Johnson J. E., *Social Scientific Studies of Religion. A bibliography*, University of Pittsburgh Press, Pittsburgh 1967.

Bevilacqua G., 'Cristianesimo di massa', *Humanitas*, IX (1954).

Bianchi U., 'Sardus Pater', *Atti del convegno di studi religiosi sard*, Cedam, Padua 1963.

Bianco di Saint-Jorioz A., *Il brigantaggio alla frontiera pontificia del 1860 al 1863*, G. Daelli e C. Ed., Milan 1864.

Biffi G., 'Eternità e tempo nel nostro destino', *La scuola cattolica*, LXXXVII (1959), n. 3.

Birnbaum N., 'La sociologie de la religion en Grande-Bretagne',

Archives de sociologie des religions, 1956, n. 2.

Bismarck von K., 'Kirche und Gemeinde in soziologischer Sicht', *Zeitschrift für evangelische Ethik*, 1957, n. 1.

Bittner C. J., 'Mead's Social Concept of the Self', *Sociology and Social Research*, XVI (1931), n. 1.

Blacker C., 'Le Soka Gakkai japonais. L'activisme politique d'une secte buddhiste', *Archives de sociologie des religions*, IX (1964), n. 17.

Blackmann H. J., *Religion in a modern Society*, Constable, London 1966.

Bochenski J. M., *Logik der Religion*, Bachem, Cologne 1968.

Block E. W., 'Symbols in Conflict: Official versus Folk Religion', *Journal for the Scientific Study of Religion*, V (1966), n. 2.

Bodzenta E., 'Entwicklung und Stand der speziellen kirchlichen Sozialforschung in Österreich', *Der Seelsorger*, XXVI (1957), nn. 10–11.

— — *Sozialstruktur und religiöse Praxis in einer industriellen Mittelstadt*, Icares, Abteilung Österreich, Bericht n. 29, Vienna 1957.

— — 'Forschungen in Österreich, Ergebnisse und Methoden', *Social Compass*, VI (1959), nn. 4–5.

— — *Die Katholiken in Österreich*, Herder Verlag, Vienna 1962.

Boër N., *Introduçao à Sociologia Religiosa*, Herder, San Paolo 1955.

Boisen A. T., *Religion in Crisis and Custom*, Harper Bros. Co., New York 1955.

Boldrini M., 'Biotipi e classi sociali', *Atti della XX Riunione della Soc. It. per il progresso delle scienze*, Milan 1932.

Bonhöffer D., *Auf den Wege zur Freibeit*, Haus und Schule, Berlin 1946.

— — *Sanctorum Communio*, Kaiser, Munich 1960.

— — *Ethics*, Macmillan, New York 1959.

— — *Letters and Papers from Prison*, Macmillan, New York 1963.

— — *Résistance et Soumission*, Labor et Fides, Paris 1965.

Boschini A., 'La situazione religioso-morale dei lavoratori italiani', *Orientamenti sociali*, IX (1953), n. 21.

Bossard J. H. S. and Harold C. L., 'Mixed Marriages Involving Lutherans. A Research Report', *Marriage and Family Living*, XVII (1956), n. 4.

Boulard F., *Nelle parrochie di campagna*, Morcelliana, Brescia 1948.

— — *Essor ou déclin du clergé français*, Éditions du Cerf, Paris 1950.

Bovy L., 'Une enquête de sociologie religieuse dans le Marais breton', *Revue d'Historie de l'Eglise de France*, 1965, n. 148.

Braga G., *Il comunismo fra gli italiani*, Edizioni di Comunità, Milan 1956.

— — 'Tipologia delle sottostrutture delle parocchie siciliane', *Sociologia religiosa*, I (1957), n. 1.

— — *Comunicazione e società*, Angeli Ed., Milan 1961.

Brezzi P., *Analisi ed interpretazione del 'De Civitate Dei' di S. Agostino*, Ed. Agostiniane, Tolentino 1960.

Brockmöller K., *Industriekultur und Religion*, Knecht, Frankfurt am Main 1964.

Brothers J., *Readings in the Sociology of Religion*, Pergamon Press, Oxford 1964.

— — 'Doutes et persévérances chez les jeunes catholiques d'une même année scolaire', *Lumen Vitae*, III (1964).

— — 'Sociology and Religion', in *Uses of Sociology*, Sheed and Ward, London 1968.

Brown L. B., 'The Structure of Religious Belief', *Journal for the Scientific Study of Religion*, V (1966), n. 2.

Brunetta G., 'Statistica religiosa in Italia', *Sociologia religiosa*, I (1957), n. 1.

— — *Contributo statistico allo studio delle diocesi e delle parrochie italiane*, 'Sociologia religiosa', II (1958), n. 2.

Buber M., *L'eclissi di Dio*, Edizioni di Comkità, Milan 1961.

Budd S., *Varieties of Unbelief: a Sociological Account of the Humanist Movement in Britain*, Heinemann, London, 1973.

Budd S., *Sociologists and Religion*, Collier MacMillan, London, 1973.

Buonaiuti E., *La vita dello spirito*, De Carlo, Rome 1948.

Burgalassi S., 'Il problema delle vocazioni religiose e del clero secolare in una diocesi toscana', *Orientamenti sociali*, X (1954), n. 14.

— — *Bilancio e prospettive della sociologia religiosa italiana* (bibliographical essay), Società Anonima Poligrafica Italiana, Rome 1957.

— — 'La vocazione in rapporto all'ambiente socio-religioso', *Sociologia religiosa*, I (1957), n. 1.

— — 'A proposito di una tipica parrochia siciliana', *Studi sociali*, 1965, n. 1 'Sociologia della religione in Italia dalle origini al 1967', Edizioni Pastorali, Rome 1967.

— — *Preti in crisi?*, Esperienze, Fossano 1970.

Buro de informacion y propaganda de agrupacion catolica

universitaria, *Enquesta Nacional sobre el sentimiento religioso del Pueblo de Cuba*, Havana 1954.

Bussi N., 'Sociologia della comunità parrocchiale', *Orientamenti pastorali*, I (1950).

Butterfield H., 'Reflexions on Religion and Modern Individualism', *Journal of the History of Ideas*, XXII (1961), n. 1.

Caillois R., *L'homme et le sacré*, Gallimard, Paris 1950.

— — *Le mythe et l'homme*, Gallimard, Paris 1958.

— — Après six ans d'un combat douteux', *Diogène*, VII (1959), n. 26.

Callahan D. (ed.), *The Secular City Debate*, Macmillan, New York 1966.

Campbell C., 'Humanism in Britain. The formation of a secular value-oriented movement', *A sociological yearbook of religion in Britain*, 1969, vol. 2.

Campbell C., *Toward a Sociology of Irreligion*, Macmillan, New York, 1971.

Campbell J., 'The Secularization of the Sacred', *The World Yearbook of Religion*, 1969, vol. I.

Camps A., 'Crisis of Islam in West Pakistan', *Social Compass*, IX (1962), n. 3.

Canaletti Gaudenti A., *Elementi di statistica ecclesiastica*, Giuffrè, Milan 1964.

Cancedda F., 'L'apostasia delle masse', *Testimonianze*, 1959, n. 18.

Caracciolo A., *La religione come struttura e come modo autonomo della coscienza*, Marzorati, Milan 1965.

Carli C., 'Risultati di una indagine religioso-morale (Gallarate)', *Realtà sociale d'oggi*, 1951, n. 5.

Carlton F. T., 'Technological Advance, Government and Religion', *Sociology and Social Research*, XLI (1956), n. 2.

Carrier H., 'Rôle des groupes de référence dans l'intégration des attitudes religieuses', *V Conf. int. di sociologia religiosa*, Bologna 1959.

— — 'Le rôle des groupes de référence dans l'intégration des attitudes religieuses', *Social Compass*, 1960, n. 2.

— — *Psycho-sociologie de l'appartenance religieuse*, Presses de l'Université Grégorienne, Rome 1960.

Carrier H. and Pin E., *Sociologie du christianisme, Bibliographie internationale*, Presses de l'Université Grégorienne, Rome 1964.

— — *Essais de sociologie religieuse*, Spes, Paris 1967.

Cassin E., *San Nicandro*, Plon, Paris 1957.

Cassirer E., *Filosofia delle forme simboliche*, La Nuova Italia, Florence 1961, vol. I.

Cazeneuve J., 'Le principe de répétition dans le rite', *Cahiers internationaux de sociologie*, XXIII (1957), nn. 3–4.

— — *Les rites et la condition humaine d'après des documents ethnographiques*, Presses Universitaires de France, Paris 1958.

Censi M. A., 'Una indagine campione in una parrocchia urbana. Studio sulla parrocchia Maria Santissima Immacolata nel quartiere romano Tiburtino', *Orientamenti Sociali*, IX (1953), nn. 11–23.

Chambre H., *Il marxismo nell'Unione sovietica*, Il Mulino, Bologna 1958.

Charpin M., 'Réflexion sur la pratique religieuse dans les milieux populaires de Marseille au XIXe siècle, *Les Conférences de l'Institut historique de Provence*, 1965, n. 2.

Chatelain H., 'Les conditions d'une sociologie des religions en Suisse. Remarques préliminaires sur une sociologie du protestantisme', *Archives de sociologie des religions*, III (1958), n. 5.

Chelhod J., *Introduction à la sociologie de l'Islam. De l'animisme à l'universalisme*, Maisonneuve, Paris 1958.

— — 'Pour une sociologie de l'Islam', *Revue d'Histoire et Philosophie religieuse*, 1960, n. 4.

Chelini J., *Genèse et évolution d'une paroisse suburbaine marseillaise, Le Bon Pasteur*, Imprimerie Saint-Léon, Marseilles 1953.

— — *La ville et l'Église*, Éditions du Cerf, Paris 1958.

— — 'Sociologie religieuse: science sacrée ou discipline profane?', *Signes du Temps*, 1960, n. 10.

— — 'Sociétés contemporaines et désacralisation', *Signes du Temps*, 1961, n. 11.

Chin Lee F., *G. H. Mead, Philosopher of the Social Individual*, New York 1945.

Ciscato A., *Gli ebrei in Padova (1300–1800)*, Soc. Coop. Tip., Padua 1901.

Clark D. B., *Survey of Anglicans and Methodists in Four Towns*, Epworth Press, London 1965.

Clark W. H., 'How do Social Scientists Define Religion?', *Journal of Social Psychology*, 1958, n. 1.

— — *The Psychology of Religion. An Introduction to Religious Experience and Behaviour*, Macmillan, New York 1958.

Cocchiara G., *Storia del Folklore in Europa*, Einaudi, Turin 1952.

Cochn W., 'On the problem of religion in non-western cultures. Religion culture and social change', *International Yearbook for the Sociology of Religion*, Westdeutscher Verlag, Cologne 1969, vol. 5.

Collard E. A., 'La première carte de la pratique religieuse en Belgique', *Lumen Vitae*, VII (1952), n. 4.

— — *Carte de la pratique dominicale en Belgique par commune*, Éditions du Dimanche, Mons 1952.

Converse P. E., 'Belief Systems in Mass Publics', in Apter D. E. (ed), *Ideology and Discontent*, Free Press, Glencoe, 1964.

Corrain C., 'Le tradizioni del periodo natalizio e i giorni dei presagi nel Polesine', *Lares*, XXIII (1957), nn. 1–2.

Corsano A., 'Filosofia, scienza e tecnica nella crisi del pensiero rinascimentale', *Rivista di filosofia*, XL (1949), n. 1.

Cox H., *The Secular City*, SCM Press, London 1966.

— — 'Feasibility and Fantasy, Sources of Social Transcendence', *The World Yearbook of Religion*, 1970, vol. 2.

Cragg K., 'Religious Developments in Islam in 20th Century', *Cahiers d'Histoire Mondiale*, III (1959), n. 1.

Crespi F., 'Crisi del sacro, irreligione, ateismo', *Rivista di sociologia*, 1965, n. 1.

— — 'Ateismo e situazione sociale, *Sacra Doctrina*, 1966, n. 44.

— — 'For a Sociological Classification of Types of Atheism', *Actes de la Xe Conférence Internationale de Sociologie Religieuse*, Rome 1969.

Crespy G., *Essays sur la situation actuelle de la foi*, Les éd. du cerf, Paris, 1970.

Crubellier M., *Sens de l'histoire et religion, Auguste Comte, Northrop, Sorokin, Arnold Toynbee*, Bruges 1957.

Cuny P., 'Diaspora chrétienne en Afrique du Nord', *V Conf. int. di sociologia religiosa*, Bologna 1959.

Daille R., *Pratique domincale dans l'agglomération de Roanne*, Institut de sociologie, Lyon 1957.

Daniel Y., *Aspects de la pratique religieuse à Paris*, Éditions Ouvrières, Paris 1953.

Dardel E., 'L'Histoire et notre temps', *Diogène*, 1958, n. 21.

Dawson C., *Progress and Religion*, Sheed and Ward, London, 1945.

De Azevedo T., *O Catolicismo no Brasil*, Ministerio de Educaçao e Cultura, Rio de Janeiro 1955.

Debarge L., Deconchy J. P., Leger D., Pages R., *Psychologie sociale et religion*, C.N.R.S., Paris, 1972.

Deconchy J. P., *L'orthodoxie religieuse. Essay de logique psychosociale*, Éditions Ouvrières, Paris, 1971.

De Greef E., *Psychiatrie et Religion*, Fayard, Paris 1958.

De Lagarde G., *Naissance de l'esprit laïque au déclin du Moyen Age*, Presses Universitaires de France, Paris 1948; ed. B. Nauwalaerts, Louvain-Paris 1956-58, 2 vols.

De La Rica Basagotti J. M., *La parroquia de Nuestra Señora de la Mercedes de las Arenas*, Università di Deusto, Bilbao 1957.

Delbrel M., 'Ivry, ville marxiste et présence de l'Eglise', *Parole et Mission*, 1958, n. 10.

Dellepoort J. J., Greinacher N. and Menges W., *Die Deutsche Priesterfrage. Eine soziologische Untersuchung über Klerus und Priesternachwuchs in Deutschland*, Mainz 1961.

Dellepoort J. J. and Grond L., 'Stand und Bedarf an Priestern in Österreich', *Social Compass*, IV (1957), nn. 3-4.

Del Noce A., *Il problema dell'ateismo*, Il Mulino, 2nd ed., Bologna 1965.

Delobelle A., 'Les valeurs comme expression du sacré', *Social Compass*, XV (1968), n. 6.

Delooz P., *Conditions sociologiques de la sainteté canonisée*, Faculté de Droit, Liège 1960, 2 vols.

De Marchi F., 'La religione nell'industria piemontese', *Prospettive di efficienza*, VII (1967), n. 9-10.

De Marchi F., Grumelli A., Bonicelli G., Acquaviva S. S., 'La situazione della sociologia religiosa in Italia', *Rassegna italiana di sociologia*, VII (1966), n. 1.

De Martino E., 'Mito, scienza, religiosità e civiltà moderna', *Nuovi Argomenti*, 1959, n. 37.

— — *Sud e magia*, Feltrinelli, Milan 1959.

— — 'Caproni, parrucche e altro (risposta a Camillo Pellizzi)', *Rassegna italiana di sociologia*, II (1961), n. 3.

Demerath J., 'Program and Prolegomena for a Sociology of Irreligion', *Actes de la Xe Conférence Internationale de Sociologie Religieuse*, Rome 1969.

De Noirmont P., 'L'Espagne ouvrière, est-elle catholique?', *La revue nouvelle*, VII (1957).

De Rosa G., *Fede cristiana, tecnica e secolarizzazione*, Civiltà Cattolica, Rome, 1970.

Desabie J., *La pratique dominicale dans les zones urbaines de Saône-et-Loire*, Direction des Oeuvres, Autun 1958.

— — *Le recensement de la pratique religieuse dans la Seine, 14 mars 1954*, INSEE, Paris 1958.

— — 'Sociologie religieuse dans la Seine. Recensement du 14 mars 1954', *Revue de l'Action Populaire*, 1958, n. 4.

De Sandre P., 'Religiosità e cultura di massa in Italia', *Il Mulino*, XIV (1965), n. 12.

Desqueyrat A., *La crise religieuse des temps nouveaux*, Éditions Spes, Paris.

Desroche H., 'Domaine et méthodes de la sociologie religieuse dans l'oeuvre de G. Le Bras', *Revue d'Histoire et Philosophie des Religions*, XXXIV (1954), n. 2; also in *Journal of Religion*, XXXV (1955), n. 1.

— — *Socialismes et sociologie religieuse*, Cujas, Paris 1965.

— — 'Sociologie et irreligion. A propos de Dietrich Bonhöffer', *Archives de sociologie des religions*, X (1965), n. 19.

— — *Sociologies Religieuses*, Presses Universitaires de France, Paris 1968.

Dessauer F., *Philosophie der Technik*, Bonn 1927.

De Volder N., 'La sociologie religieuse en Belgique', *Actes du IVe Congrès international de sociologie*, Éditions Ouvrières, Paris 1955.

Dittes J. E., 'Secular Religion Dilemma of Churches and Researches, The H. Paul Douglas Lectures of 1968', *Review of Religious Research*, X (1969), n. 2.

Donini A., *Sociologia y Religion*, Ed. Sudamericana, Buenos Aires 1961. 'Práctica y actitudes religiosas, Estudio sociológico de "Santa Maria alle Fornaci" en el "quartiere" Aurelio de Roma, *Sociologia religiosa*, V (1961), n. 7; VI (1962), n. 8.

Dreyfus F. G., 'Le Protestantisme Alsacien', *Archives de sociologie des religions*, II (1957), n. 3.

— — 'Vocation et limites d'une sociologie du protestantisme en France', *V. Conf. int. di sociologia religiosa*, Bologna 1959.

Dufrenne M., *La personnalité de base. Un concept sociologique*, Presses Universitaires de France, Paris 1953.

— — *La notion d' 'A Priori'*, Presses Universitaires de France, Paris 1959.

Droulers P., Martina G., Tufari P., *La vita religiosa a Roma intorno al 1870*, Gregoriana, Rome, 1971.

Dumas A., 'Dietrich Bonhoeffer et L'Interpretation du Christianisme comme non-religion', *Archives de sociologie des religions*, 1965, n. 19.

Dumermuth F., 'Religion in Sociological Prospective', *Contemporary Religions in Japan*, 9, 1968.

Dumont F., 'La sociologie religieuse au Canada français', *Actes du*

IVe Congrès international de sociologie, Éditions Ouvrières, Paris 1955.

Dumont J., 'Sondage sur la mentalité religieuse d'ouvriers industriels en Wallonie', *Vocation de la sociologie religieuse, Ve Conference internationale de sociologie religieuse*, Casterman, Paris 1958.

Duocastella R., *Mataró 1955*, Consejo Superior de Inv. Científicas, Barcelona 1961.

Durkheim E., 'Le problème religieux de la dualité de la nature humaine', *Bulletin de la Société Française de Philosophie*, XIII (1912-13).

Duroselle J. B., 'Un projet de "mission ouvrière" à Paris au milieu du XIXe siècle', *Archives de sociologie des religions*, III (1958), n. 6.

Eisermann G., 'Pareto V., als Nationalökonom und Soziologe', *Recht und Staat* (Heft 236-37), Mohr, Tubingen 1961.

Eister A. W., *The Cult as a Social Group: Some Hypotheses*, copy of a Ph.D. thesis in 'Summaries of Doctoral Dissertations, University of Wisconsin', vol. IX, later published by Duke University Press, 1950.

— — 'Religious Institutions in Complex Societies: Difficulties in the Theoretic Specification of Functions', *American Sociological Review*, XXII (1957), n. 4.

Eliade M., *Le mythe de l'éternel retour*, Gallimard, Paris, 1949.

— — *Images et Symboles*, Gallimard, Paris, 1952.

— — *Tecniche dello yoga*, Einaudi, Turin, 1952.

— — *Le chamanisme et les techniques archaiques de l'extase*, Payot, Paris, 1951.

— — *Traité d'histoire des religions*, Payot, Paris.

— — *Comparative Patterns of Religion*, New York, 1958.

— — *The Sacred and the Profane*, Harcourt Brace, New York, 1958-59.

— — *Aspects du mythe*, Gallimard, Paris, 1963.

— — 'Survivance et camouflage des mythes', *Diogène*, 1963, n. 41.

— — *The Quest. History and Meaning in Religion*, Univ. of Chicago Press, Chicago, 1969.

Elwell-Sutton L. P., 'Nationalism and Neutralism in Iran', *Mej*, 1958, n. 12.

Erkes E., *La situazione religiosa nella Cina odierna*, from 'Numen' in 'Il Ponte', supplement to the April 1956 issue entitled *La Cina d'oggi*.

Estus H. W. and Doeringtond M. A., 'The meaning and end of religiosity', *American Journal of Sociology*, 1970, vol. 75, n. 5.

Ettinger R. C. W., *Ibernazione nuova era*, Rizzoli, Milan 1967.

Faggiotto A., *Storia delle religioni e cristianesimo*, Tip. Penada, Padua, 1937. *Filosofia e religione, presupposti alla filosofia della religione*, Unversità di Padua, Advanced course in History of Religion, Academic Year 1951–52, Liviana Ed., Padua 1951–52.

— — 'Remoti indizi della Magna Mater nell'Estremo Oriente', *Atti e memorie dell'Accademia Patavina di Scienze, Lettere ed Arti*, LXVI (1953–54).

— — *Pour une méthodologie des études historico-religieuses*, Padua 1955.

— — 'L'attualità del problema storico-religioso', *Atti e memorie dell'Accademia Patavina di Scienze, Lettere ed Arti*, LXVIII (1955–56).

Falardeau J. C., 'Recherches de la sociologie religieuse au Canada', *Lumen Vitae*, VI (1951), nn. 1–2.

Falcão M. F., 'Sondangem â assistência a Misa dominical no patriarcado de Lisboa', *Novellae Olivarum*, 1956, n. 25.

Falconi C., 'Primo tentativo di una statistica dell'organizzazione cattolica in Italia', *Nuovi Argomenti*, III (1955), n. 12.

— — *La Chiesa e le organizzazioni cattoliche in Italia (1945–55)*, Einaudi, Turin 1956.

— — *Gli spretati*, Parenti Editore, Florence 1958.

— — *La Chiesa e le organizzazione cattoliche in Europe*, Edizioni di Comunità, Milan 1960.

— — *La religiosità in Italia*, Editori Riuniti, Rome 1963.

Fay B., *La massoneria e la rivoluzione intellettuale del secolo XVIII*, Einaudi, 2nd ed., Turin 1945.

Febvre L., 'Sensibilité et Histoire', *Annales d'Histoire Sociale*, 1941, n. 1.

Fenn R. K., 'The secularization of values', *Journal for the Scientikc Study of Religion*, 1969, vol. 8, n. 1.

Fenn R. K., 'The Process of Secularisation: a Post-Parsonian View', *Journal of the Scientific Study of Religion*, IX (1970), n. 2.

Fermi E. (Falconi C.), 'La parrocchia, piccola comunità', *Comunità*, VIII (1954), n. 27.

— — 'La Chiesa in Inghilterra' *Comunità*, XII (1958), n. 62.

Ferrarotti F., *Sociologia e realtà sociale*, Opere Nuove, Rome 1958.

— — *Macchina e uomo nella società industriale*, ERI, Turin 1963.

Ferte J., *La vie religieuse dans les campagnes parisiennes (1662-1695)*, Librairie philosophique J. Vrin, Paris 1962.

Feuer L. and Perrine M. W., 'Religion in a Northern Vermont Town', *Journal for the Scientific Study of Religion*, V (1966), n. 3.

Fiamengo A., 'Croyances religieuses et changements technologiques en Yugoslavie', *Archives de sociologie des religions*, VIII (1963), n. 15.

Fichter J. H., 'Urban Mobility and Religious Observance', *The American Catholic Sociological Review*, XI (1950), n. 3.

— — 'Sociological measurements of religiosity', *Review of Religious Research*, 1969, vol. 10, n. 3.

Fletcher R., 'Religion in Modern Society', *Plain View*, XI (1957), n. 4.

Folliet J., 'Les effets de la grande ville sur la vie religieuse', *Chronique sociale de France*, 1953, n. 61.

Fourastié J., *La civilisation de 1975*, Presses Universitaires de France, Paris 1962.

Freytag J., 'Zur Entwicklung der Religionssoziologie in Deutschland', *Lutherische Rundschau*, IX (1959), n. 3.

Friedmann G., *Prolemi umani del macchinismo industriale*, Einaudi, Turin 1949.

— — *Humanisme du Travail et Humanité*, Colin, Paris 1950.

— — *Der Mensch in der Mechanisierten Produktion*, Cologne 1952.

— — *Dove va il lavoro umano?*, Edizioni di Comunità, Milan 1955.

— — *Industrial Society; The Emergence of the Human Problems of Automation*, Free Press, Glencoe, Ill. 1955.

Friess H. L. and Schneider H. W., *Religion in Various Cultures*, New York 1938.

Fromm E., *Psicanalisi e religione*, Edizioni di Comunità, 2nd ed., Milan 1971.

Fürstenberg F., 'Soziologische Strukturprobleme der Kirchengemeinde', *Zeitschrift für Evangelische Ethik*, VII (1963), n. 4.

Gabelli A., *L'istruzione in Italia*, Zanichelli, Bologna 1891, 2 vols.

Galli D., *Sociologismo e religione*, 'Filosofia e sociologia', Il Mulino, Bologna 1954.

Galli N. and Sarti S., 'Le vocazioni nei Seminari della Diocesi di

Modena a partire dal primo dopoguerra', *Orientamenti pedagogici*, XIII (1966), nn. 1-2.

Garcia A. M., 'Perspectivas actuales del catolicismo español', *Cuadernos Hispanoamericanos*, 1955.

Geck A., 'Die Sozialtheologie im Dienste der Rewaltigung der Sozialordnung', in *Gesellschaft, Staat, Wirtschaft*, Tyrolia Verlag, Innsbruck 1961.

— — *Zur Theologie des Industriebetriebes*, Duncker & Humbolt, Berlin 1967.

— — *Aufbuch zur sozialen Pastoral*, Liegerns Verlag, Essen 1969.

Geetz C., 'Religion as a Cultural System', *The World Yearbook of Religion*, 1969, vol. 1 ('Commentary' by Talcott Parsons).

Gehlen A., 'Die Technik in der Sichtweise der philosophischen Anthropologie', *Merkur*, VII (1935).

— — *Die Seele im technischen Zeitalter*, Rowohlt, Hamburg 1957.

— — *Der Mensch, seine Natur und seine Stellung in der Welt*, Frankfurt am Main 1962.

Gilkey L., *Religion and the Scientific Future*, Harper & Row, New York 1970.

Girardi G., 'Pour une définition de l'athéisme', *Salesianum*, XXV (1963), n. 1.

Glock C. Y., 'On the Study of Religious Commitment', *Research Supplement, Religious Education*, LVII (1951), n. 4.

— — 'Sociology of Religion', in *Sociology Today, Problems and Prospects*, edited by R. K. Merton, L. Broom, L. S. Cottrell Jr., New York 1959.

Glock C. Y., Ringer B. B., Babbie E. R., *To Comfort and to Challenge, A Dilemma of the Contemporary Church*, University of California Press, Berkeley and Los Angeles 1967.

Glock C. Y. and Stark R., *American Piety: The Nature of Religious Commitment*, University of California Press, Berkeley and Los Angeles 1967.

Glock C. Y. and Stark R., *Religion and Society in Tension*, Rand McNally, Chicago 1965.

Goddijn H. P., 'The Sociology of Religious Orders and Congregations', *Social Compass*, VII (1960), nn. 5-6.

Goddijn W., 'Die Katholische Pfarrsoziologie in Westeurope', in *Soziologie der Kirchengemeinde*, edited by D. Goldschmidt, F. Greiner, H. Schelsky, Enke Verlag, Stuttgart 1960.

Goddijn W. and H. P., *Godsdienstsociologie*, Het Spectrum, Utrecht Antwerp 1960.

Godin A., 'À propos des variables affectant le rôle integrateur de la religion', *V Conf. int. di sociologia religiosa*, Bologna 1959.

Goldammer K., *Die Formenwelt des Religiösen*, Stuttgart 1960.

Goldschmidt D., Greiner F. and Schelsky H., *Soziologie der Kirchengemeinde*, Enke Verlag, Stuttgart 1960.

Gonzáles C. M., *El precepto de la Misa en la diócesis de Bilbao*, Bilbao 1952.

Goode E., 'Social Class and Church Participation', *American Journal of Sociology*, 1966, n. 7.

— — 'Some sociological implications of religious secularization', *Social Compass*, XVI (1969), n. 2.

— — Another look at social class and church', *American Journal of Sociology*, 1970, n. 5.

Gorer G., *Death, Grief and Mourning*, Cresset Press, London 1965.

Gouyon P., *La pratique religieuse d'une ville girondine, Libourne*, Libourne 1957.

Grasso P. G., *Elementi di sociologia religiosa*, PAS, Turin 1955.

— — 'Ricerca sociologica e sociologia religiosa', *Enciclopedia Social*, Edizioni Paoline, Alba 1958.

— — 'La struttura della personalità morale sociale di giovani italiani quale risulta dal-l'analisi fattoriale dei risultati di una prova di giudizio morale', *Orientamenti pedagogici*, IX (1962), n. 3.

Greinacher N., *Soziologie der Pfarrei, Wege zur Untersuchung*, Colmar and Freiburg 1955.

— — 'Entwicklung und heutiger Stand der Religionssoziologie', *Anima*, XII (1957), n. 1.

— — 'Evolution de la pratique religieuse en Allemagne après la guerre', *Social Compass*, X (1963), n. 4–5.

— — *Die Kirche in der Städtischen Gesellschaft*, Matthias Grünewald, Mainz 1966.

Grond L., 'Der Katholizismus in Europa. Einige statistische und soziologische Betrachtungen im Zusammenhang mit der europäischen Integration', *Herder-Korrespondenz*, July 1960; see also 'Bilan du Monde', part II, Paris 1960.

Groner F., *Kirchliches Handbuch, Amtliches statistisches Jahrbuch der katholischen Kirche Deutschlands*, vol. XXIII, Cologne 1944–51.

— — *Kirchliche Statistik Deutschlands, für das Jahr 1957*, Amtliche Zentralstelle für kirchliche Statistik des katholischen Deutschlands, Cologne 1958.

Grumelli A. and Bolino G., 'For a Tipology of Atheism', *Actes de la X Conférence Internationale de Sociologie Religieuse*, Rome 1969.

Guiart J., 'Des multiples niveaux de signification du mythe', *Archives de sociologie des religions*, XIII (1968), n. 26.

Gurvitch G., 'Sociologie de la connaissance et psychologie collective', *L'Année Sociologique*, 1940–48, n. 1.

Hacquet P. Fr., 'Mémoires des missions des Montfortains dans l'ouest (1740–1779), Contribution à la sociologie religieuse historique', *Cahiers de la revue du Bas-Poitou et des provinces de l'Ouest*, Fontenay-le-Comte, 1964.

Hahn P., 'Le symbole dans la psychologie sociale de G. H. Mead', *Cahiers internationaux de sociologie*, VI (1949).

Hamelin L. E. and Hamelin C., *Quelques matèriaux de sociologie religieuse canadienne*, Les Éditions du Lévrier, Montreal 1956.

Hamer J., 'Ecclésiologie et sociologie', *Social Compass*, 1960, n. 4.

Harenberg W. (ed.), *Was glauben die Deutschen*, Kaiser-Grünewald, Munich, 1969.

Häring B., *Macht und Ohnmacht der Religion, Religionssoziologie als Anruf*, Otto Müller Ed., Salsburg 1957. *Sociologia della famiglia*, Edizioni Paoline, 2nd ed., Rome 1962.

Harding V., 'The Religion of Black Power', *The World Yearbook of Religion*, 1969, vol. 1.

Heiderscheid A., *Aspects de sociologie religieuse du Diocèse de Luxembourg*, Ed. de l'Imprimerie Saint-Paul, Luxemburg 1961.

Heim K., 'Christian Faith and the Growing Power of Secularism', in *Religion and Culture, Essays in Honor of Paul Tillich*, edited by Leibrecht W., Harper & Bros., New York 1959.

Henriques N., *Religious Toleration in England, 1787–1833*, Routledge, London 1961.

Highet J., *The Churches in Scotland Today. A Survey of their Principles, Strength, Work and Statements*, Glasgow 1950.

Hilare Y. M., *La pratique religieuse de 1815 à 1878*, 'L'information historique', 1963, n. 2.

Hoeffner J., 'Industrielle Revolution and religiöse Krise. Arbeitsgemeinschaft für Forschung des Landes Nordrhein-Westfalen', Heft 97, Westdeutscher Verlag, Cologne 1961.

Hoffman H., *Gott im Underground*, Furche, Hamburg 1972.

Hoge R., 'Religious Commitments of College Students over Five Decades', *Jahrbuch für Religionssoziologie*, (7), 1971, pp. 184–211.

Honigsheim P., 'Sociology of Religion: Complementary Analyses of Religious Institutions', in *Modern Sociological Theory in*

Continuity and Change, The Dryden Press, New York 1957.

Hoult T. F., *The Sociology of Religion*, The Dryden Press, New York 1958.

Hourdin G., *La Nouvelle Vague croit-Elle en Dieu?*, Éditions du Cerf, Paris 1961.

Houtart F., 'Les paroisses de Bruxelles', *Bulletin de l'Institut de recherches économiques et sociales*, November 1955.

— — *Aspects sociologiques du catholicisme américain*, Éditions Ouvrières, Paris 1958.

— — 'The variables affecting the integrating role of religion', *V Conf. int. di sociologia religiosa*, Bologna 1959.

— — *L'Église latino-américaine à l'heure du concile*, Feres, Freiburg 1963. *Sociologia e Pastorale*, Ave, Rome 1966.

Houtart F. and Pin E., *L'Église à l'heure de l'Amérique latine*, Casterman, Tournai 1965.

Houtart P., 'Sociologiczne Aspekty Znakowczasu', *Chrzescijaninw Swiecie*, 1969, n. 1.

Hsu F. L., *Religion, Science and Human Crises: a Study of China in Transition and its Implication for the West*, Routledge and Kegan Paul, London 1952.

Huet-Pleuroux P., *La vie chrétienne dans le Doubs et la Haute Saône de 1860 à 1900*, Université de Paris, Paris 1966.

Huizinga J., *La crisi della civiltà*, Einaudi, Turin 1937.

Hunt C. L., 'The Sociology of Religion', in *Contemporary Sociology*, edited by J. Roucek, New York 1958.

Husserl E., *Esperienza e giudizio*, Silva, Milan 1960.

Huxley J., *The Destiny of Man*, London 1959.

Ikado F., 'Trend and Problems of New Religions: Religion in Urban Society', *Journal of Asian and African Studies*, III (1968), nn. 1–2.

Iribarren J., *Introdución a la sociología religiosa*, Madrid 1955.

Isambert F. A., *Christianisme et classe ouvrière*, Casterman, Tournai 1961.

— — 'L'analyse des attitudes religieuses', *Archives de sociologie des religions*, 1961, n. 11.

— — 'Christianisme et stratification sociale', *Social Compass*, IX (1962), n. 4–5.

Jacobi J., *Complex, Archetype, Symbols, in the Psychology of C. G. Jung*, Pantheon Books, New York 1959.

Jackson J. and Jobling R., 'Towards an analysis of contemporary cults', *A sociological yearbook of religion in Britain*, 1968, vol. 1.

Jahoda G., 'The Genesis of non Belief', *New Outlook*, I, London 1952.

James P., 'De la paysannerie chrétienne au paganisme urbain', *Masses ouvrières*, 1963, n. 192.

James W., *Le varie forme della coscienza religiosa*, F.lli Bocca Ed., Milan 1945.

Jammes J. M. and Mendras H., 'La sociologie religieuse aux États-Unis', *Lumen Vitae*, VI (1951), nn. 1-2.

Jeannin J., *Visages religieux de l'Anjou en 1961*, Ed. CNRS, Angers 1963.

Jung C. G., *Psicologia e religione*, Edizioni di Comunità, 3rd ed., Milan 1966.

Kadlecova E., 'Vyzkum religiozity Severomoravského Kraje (Metoda a technika)', *Sociologicky Casopis*, 1965, n. 1.

Kanters R., *Essai sur l'avenir de la religion*, Julliard, Paris 1945.

Kanwar M. A., 'Tradition vs. Modern Trends in Pakistan: a Muslim Society in Transition', *Social Compass*, XVIII (1971), n. 2.

Kardiner A., *The Individual and his Society, The Psychodynamics of Primitive Social Organisation*, Columbia University Press, New York 1939.

Kardiner A. et. al., *The Psychological Frontiers of Society*, Columbia University Press, New York 1945.

Kehrer G., *Religionssoziologie*, De Gruyter, Berlin 1968.

— — 'Religion and sozialer Wander', *Int. Jahrbuch für Religionssoziologie*, (7), 1972, pp. 31-59.

Kibedi G., 'Une enquête en Amérique latine. Influence du milieu sur la vie religieuse et morale de la classe ouvrière de Bogota', *Lumen Vitae*, VI (1951), nn. 1-2.

Kitagawa J., *Sociology of Religion*, London 1947.

Klapp O. E., 'Ritual and Cult, A Sociological Interpretation', *Annals of American Sociology*, VIII (1956).

Kloetzli W., *The City Church: Death or Renewal*, Philadelphia 1961.

Kloppenburg B., 'Der brasilianische Spiritismus als religiöse Gefahr', *Social Compass*, V (1957-58), nn. 5-6.

Klügl J., 'Premier colloque international de sociologie religieuse dans les pays socialistes', *Archives de sociologie des religions*, XI (1966), n. 21.

Koester R., *Die Kirchentreuen, Erfahrungen und Ergebnisse einer soziologischen Untersuchung in einer grosstädtischen evangelischen Kirchengemeinde*, Enke Verlag, Stuttgart 1959.

Kogon E., 'Kirche und Heimat, Bemerkungen zu den Thesen eines Warschauer Philosophen', *Frankfurterhefte*, XVI (1961), n. 12.

Kolakowski L., 'Kleine Thesen de Sacro et Profano', *Frankfurterhefte*, XVI (1961), n. 11.

Koutnik S., 'Ateismo in Cecoslovacchia', *Studi Cattolici*, Jan.-Feb. 1961.

Krausz E., 'Religion and Secularisation. A Matter of Definitions', *Social Compass*, XVIII (1971), n. 2.

Kruijt J. P., 'Verklaringen van de geographische verbreiding der Kerkelijke gezindten in ons land', *Sociologisch Bulletin*, II (1948), n. 2.

— — 'La vie religieuse protestante aux Pays-Bas', *Revue de psychologie des peuples*, V (1950), n. 1.

— — 'Het Kerkelijk-godsdienstig leven in de Verenigde Staten', *Sociologisch Bulletin*, VIII (1954), n. 4.

Labbens J., *Les 99 autre, . . . ou l'Église aussi recense*, Vitte, Lyon 1954.

— — *La pratique dominicale dans l'agglomération lyonnaise*; *I*. L'équipement religieux, 1955; *II*. Paroisses et chapelles, 1956; *III*. L'instruction, la ville et les pratiquants (in collaboration with R. Daille), 1957.

— — 'Déchristianisation-sécularisation?', *Chronique sociale de France*, 1964, n. 12.

Lacroix J., *Le sens de l'athéisme moderne*, Casterman, Tournai 1964.

Laloux J., 'Analyse sociologique du changement social et religieux', *V Conf. int. di sociologia religiosa*, Bologna 1959.

Landis B. Y., 'Trends in Church Membership in the United States', *The Annals of the American Academy of Political and Social Science*, November 1960.

Laslett P., *The World We Have Lost*, Methuen, London 1965.

Laurent P., 'Tecnica e religione', *Aggiornamenti sociali*, X (1959), n. 7.

Lazerwitz B., 'Some Factors Associated with Variations in Church Attendance', *Social Forces*, XXXIX (1961), n. 4.

Le Bras G., 'Secteurs et aspects nouveaux de la sociologie religieuse', *Cahiers internationaux de sociologie*, 1946, n. 1.

— — 'Mesure de la vitalité sociale du catholicisme en France', *Cahiers internationaux de sociologie*, VIII (1950).

— — 'Structure et vie d'une société religieuse', *Revue d'Histoire et Philosophie religieuse*, XXXI (1951), n. 4.

– – 'Lo stato attuale della sociologia religiosa', *Realtà sociale d'oggi*, VII (1952).

– – *Études de sociologie religieuse*, Presses Universitaires de France, Paris, vol. I, 1955; vol. II, 1956.

– – 'Sociologie religieuse et science des religions', *Archives de sociologie des religions*, I (1956), n. 1.

– – 'L'explication en sociologie religieuse' *Cahiers internationaux de sociologie*, XXI (1956), n. 2.

– – 'La sociologie religieuse parmi les sciences humaines', in *Sociologie et religion*, Fayard, Paris 1958.

Lee R. and Marty M. E. (eds.), *Religion and Social Conflict*, Oxford University Press, New York 1964.

Lefebvre des Noëttes, *L'attelage, le cheval de selle à travers les âges*, Paris 1931.

– – 'Le gouvernail: contribution à l'histoire de l'esclavage', *Mémoires de la société des Antiquaires de France*, 1932, vol. LXXVIII.

Leif J., *La sociologie de Tönnies*, Presses Universitaires de France, Paris 1946.

Lengauer M., 'Soziale Veränderungen und Pfarrstruktur in Linz', *Der Seelsorger*, XXVI (1957), nn. 10–11.

Lengauer M. and Bodzenta E., 'Ergebnisse einer exakten Kirchenbesuchszahlung', *Der Seelsorger*, XXVI (1957), nn. 10–11.

Lenski G., *The Religious Factor*, Doubleday, Garden City 1961.

Leonardi F., *Introduzione allo studio del comportamento sociale*, Giuffrè, Milan 1957.

Leoni A., 'Elementi di spiegazione sociologica e geografica sulla pratica religiosa della diocesi di Mantova', *Realtà sociale d'oggi*, 1951, n. 9.

– – 'La situazione religiosa in Italia', *Realtà sociale d'oggi*, VIII (1953), nn. 11–12.

– – *Aggiornamento e processo di adeguamento degli Istituti religiosi femminili alle esigenze della società*, under the auspices of the Sacra Congregazione dei Religiosi, Rome 1958.

Lesourd J. A., 'La déchristianisation en Angleterre vers le milieu du XIX siècle', *Cahiers d'Histoire*, IX (1964), n. 3.

Lestocquoy M., *La vie religieuse en France du VII au XX siècle*, Albin Michel, Paris 1964.

Lévy-Bruhl L.., *Les Carnets*, Presses Universitaires de France, Paris, 1949.

Lewin K., *A Dynamic Theory of Personality*, McGraw-Hill, New York-London-Toronto 1935.

Linton R., *The Study of Man*, Appleton Century Co., New York 1936.

– – *The Cultural Background of Personality*, Kegan Paul, London 1947.

Lizcano M., 'État et possibilités de la sociologie des religions en Espagne', *Archives de sociologie des religions*, II (1957), n. 3.

Locke J. H., Sabagh G. and Thomes M. M., 'Interfaith Marriages', *Social Problems*, IV (1957), n. 4.

Loew J. and Cottier G. M. M. *Dynamisme de la foi et incroyance*, Éditions du Cerf, Paris 1963.

Long E. L., *The Religious Beliefs of American Scientists*, Philadelphia: Westminster Press, 1964.

Lubbe H., *La secolarizzazione*, Il Mulino, Bologna 1970.

Luckmann T., *Das Problem der Religion in der modernen Gesellschaft*, Rombach, Freiburg 1963.

– – 'On Religion in Modern Society', *Journal for the Scientific Study of Religion*, 1963, n. 2.

Lutz K. M., 'Zur gegenwärtigen Situation der Seelsorgischen Praxis', *Zeitschrift für Evangelische Ethik*, VII (1963), n. 3.

Macintyre A. *Secularisation and Moral Change*, Oxford University Press, London, 1967.

Macintyre A. and Ricoeur P., *The religious significance of atheism*, Columbia University Press, New York 1969.

Maertens T., 'La situation de l'Église en Haute-Volta', *La Revue Nouvelle*, XXIX (1959), n. 6.

– – 'L'Église dans le monde: où va le Sénégal?', *La Revue Nouvelle*, XXIX (1959), n. 6.

Magistretti F., 'Psicologia e scienze sociali' *Rivista internazionale di scienze sociali*, LXI (1953).

Magli I.. *Gli uomini della penitenza*, Cappelli, Rocca S. Casciano 1966.

Mailloux N. and Ancona L., 'La dinamica del conflitto religioso', *Archivio di psicologia neurologia e psichiatria*, XVIII (1957).

Maître J., 'Les dénombrements des catholiques pratiquants en France', *Archives de sociologie des religions*, II (1957), n. 3.

– – 'Quelques problèmes méthodologiques en sociologie du Catholicisme français, *Social Compass*, VI (1958), n. 6 and *Sociologia religiosa*, V (1960), nn. 5–6.

– – 'Le rôle la religion dans le changement social', *V Conf. int. di sociologia religiosa*, Bologna 1959.

– – 'Religion populaire et populations religieuses', *Cahiers internationaux de sociologie*, VI (1959), n. 2.

— — 'Religion et changement social', *Social Compass*, 1960, n. 2.

— — 'Utilizzazione dell'analisi gerarchica in sociologia del cattolicesimo', *Rassegna italiana di sociologia*, 1960, n. 2.

— — 'Structure et mesure en sociologie du catholicisme', *Archives de sociologie des religions*, 1961, n. 11.

— — 'Les sondages sur les attitudes religieuses des français', *Revue française de sociologie*, II (1961), n. 1.

Malinowski B., *Magic, Science and Religion*, The Beacon Press, Boston 1948.

Malley F., 'Quelques sondages sur la pratique religieuse à Barcelone', *L'Actualité religieuse dans le monde*, 1954, n. 22.

— — 'La pratique religieuse dans les grandes villes françaises', *L'Actualité religieuse dans le monde*, 1955, n. 52.

Mankeliunas M. V., *Psicología de la religiosidad*, Religion y cultura, Madrid 1961.

Mannheim K., *Ideology and Utopia, an Introduction to the Sociology of Knowledge*, London 1936.

— — *Essay on Sociology and Social Psychology*, Routledge and Kegan Paul, London 1953.

Manzini G. M., 'Autori e temi della recente etnologia religiosa in Italia', *Sociologia religiosa*, III (1959), nn. 3–4.

Marcilhacy C., 'L'anticléricalisme dans l'Orléanais pendant la première moitié du XIXᵉ siècle', *Archives de sociologie des religions*, III (1959), n. 6.

Marcuse H., *One Dimensional Man*, Beacon Press, Boston, 1964.

Maritain J., *Cristianesimo e democrazia*, Edizioni di Comunità, Milan 1953.

— — *Le paysan de la Garonne*, Desclée de Brouwer, Paris, 1966.

— — *Le philosophie dans la cité*, Alsatia, Paris, 1960.

Marle' R., 'Secularisation', *Lumen Vitae*, XXIII (1968), n. 3, pp. 401–14.

Marotta M., 'Il concetto di ruolo in sociologia', *Sociologia*, II (1957), n. 3.

Martin D. A., 'The Denomination', *British Journal of Sociology*, XIII (1962), n. 1.

— — 'Toward Eliminating the Concept of Secularisation', in J. Gould (ed.), *Penguin Survey of the Social Sciences*, Penguin, Harmondsworth 1965.

— — 'Some Utopian Aspects of the Concept of Secularisation', *Internationales Jahrbuch für Religionssoziologie*, 1966, n. 2.

— — *A Sociology of English Religion*, Heinemann, London, 1968.

— — *The religious and the secular. Studies in secularization,*

Routledge and Kegan Paul, London 1969.

Marty M. E., 'Sects and Cults', *The Annals Am.*, 1960, n. 332.

Masi G., *Organizzazione ecclesiastica e ceti rurali in Puglia nella seconda metà del '500*, Adriatica, Bari 1957.

Matthes J., *Die Emigration der Kirche aus der Gesellschaft*, Furche, Hamburg 1964.

Mauss M., presented to the 17 May 1937 meeting of the Psychology Society and published in *Journal de Psychologie*, 1938; Reprinted in *Sociologie et Antropologie*, Presses Universitaires de France, Paris, 1950.

McAvoy T., 'The le Bras Approach to the History of the Diocese of Fort Wayne', *The Indiana Magazine of History*, III (1956), n. 4.

Mead G. H., 'Social Consciousness and the Consciousness of Meaning', *Psychological Bulletin*, VII (1910).

— — 'A Behavioristic Account of the Self and Social Control', *International Journal of Ethics*, 1925.

— — *Mind, Self and Society*, University of Chicago Press, Chicago 1934.

— — *The Philosophy of the Act*, University of Chicago Press, Chicago 1938.

Mehl R., *Traité de sociologie du protestantisme*, Delachaux et Niestlé, Paris 1965. *Traité de sociologie due protestantisme*, Delachaux et Niestlé, Neuchâtel 1966.

Meneghini G., *La peste del 1576 a Padova*, Stediv, Padua 1956, from 'Padova' (1955).

Menges W., 'Entwicklung und Stand der religionssoziologischen Forschung in Deutschland', *Social Compass*, VI (1959), nn. 4–5.

Mensching G., *Sociologie religieuse. Le rôle de la religion dans les relations communautaires des humains*, Payot, Paris 1951.

— — 'Zur Geschichte und Aufgabe der Religionssoziologie', *Archivio di Filosofia*, 1955, n. 2.

— — *Die Religion, Erscheinungsformen, Strukturtypen und Lebensgesetze*, Curt E. Schwab-Verlag, Stuttgart 1959.

Merlau-Ponty M., *Le Visible et l'Invisible*, Paris 1964.

Merton R. K., 'La sociologie de la connaissance', in *La Sociologie au XXe siècle*, Paris 1947, eds. Gurvitch and Moore, 2 vols.

Milanesi G., 'Insegnamento della religione e dubbio religioso nella tarda adolescenza', *Orientamenti pedagogici*, XII (1965), n. 4.

— — 'Il pensiero magico nella tarda adolescenza', *Orientamenti pedagogici*, XIV (1967), n. 3.

Minon P., *Le peuple liégeois, structures sociales et attitudes religieuses*, Secrétariat interparoissial, Liège 1955.

Mitford J., *The American Way of Death*, The Cresset Press, London 1965.

Moberg D. O., 'Religion and Society in the Netherlands and in America', *Social Compass*, IX (1962), n. 1-2.

Moberg D. O., 'The Encounter of Scientific and Religious Values Pertinent to Man's Spirtual Nature,' *Sociological Analysis*, XXVIII (1967), n. 1.

Mollat M., *La vie et la pratique religieuses au XIVe siècle et dans la première partie du XVe, principalement en France*, Centre de documentation universitaire, Paris 1963.

— — *La vie religieuse au XIVe et XVe siècle (jusqu'en 1449)*, Centre de documentation universitaire, Paris 1964, 2 vols.

Mol H., *Western Religion*, Mouton, The Hague, 1972.

Mols R., *Introduction à la Démographie historique des villes d'Europe du XIVe au XVIIIe siècle*, Gembloux and Duculot, Louvain 1954-6, 3 vols.

Mombusho S., *Shukyo Nenkan (The Year Book of Religion)*, Ministry of Education, Tokyo 1949-1967.

Monier, Cardascia, Imbert, *Histoire des institutions et des faits sociaux des origines à l'aube du Moyen Age*, Paris 1956.

Morandi F., 'Automazione e cultura', *Analisi e prospettive*, III (1957), n. 2.

— — 'Civiltà e movimento operaio', *Analisi e prospettive*, III (1957), nn. 8-9-10.

— — *Neocapitalismo e movimento operaio*, Studium, Rome 1958.

Morel G., 'Déchristianisation?', *Etudes*, 1964, n. 5.

Moreux C., *Fin d'une religion*, Presses Univ. de Montréal, Montreal, 1969.

Moroka K., 'Les religions contemporaines du Japon: Coexistence et conflict', *Revue française de sociologie*, n. 8, 1967.

Morra G., *La riscoperta del sacro*, Pàtron, Bologna 1964.

Morris C., *Lineamenti di una teoria dei segni*, Paravia, Turin 1954.

Muchembled R., 'Sorcellerie, cultura populaire et christianisme au XVIe siècle', *Annales*, XXVIII (1973).

Munzel N., 'Técnica y Comunidad', in *Estudios sociológicos internacionales*, vol. I, edited by the Inst. Balmes de Sociologia, Consejo Superior de Investigaciones Scientíficas, Madrid 1956.

Murakami S., 'Les religions nouvelles au Japan', *Social Compass*, XVII (1970), n. 1.

Mury G., 'Le catholicisme urbain et les classes sociales en France',

Cahiers internationaux de sociologie, 1956, n. 79.

— — 'Le prolétariat des villes et le sentiment religieux', *Cahiers internationaux de sociologie*, 1956, n. 81.

Nesti A., 'Comunità di base e chiesa istituzionale in Italia', *Idoc*, I (1970), n. 8.

Newman Association Demographic Survey, 'Youth and Religion. A Scientific Inquiry into the Religious Attitudes, Belief and Practice of Urban Youth', *New Life*, IV (1958), nn. 1–2.

Niceforo A., 'Y a-t-il des faits constants dans la structure et dans la vie des sociétés humaines, et quels sont ils?', *Scientia*, 1957, n. 2.

Nirchio G., 'La sociologia religiosa in Francia', *Idea*, XV (1959), n. 8.

Noirhomme G., de Craemer W., de Wilde d'Estmael M., *L'Église au Congo en 1963, Rapport d'une enquête socio-religieuse*, Centre de Recherches sociologiques, Leopoldville 1963.

Nottingham E. K., *Religion and Society*, Doubleday and Co., New York 1954.

Oates W. E., *The Religious Dimensions of Personality*, Association Press, New York 1957.

Obsborne W. A., 'L'Église et les changements culturels', *Idoc International*, 1 June 1969, n. 3.

Ochavkov J., 'Problèmes méthodologiques d'une enquête sur la religiosité en Bulgarie', *Archives de sociologie des religions*, XI (1966), n. 21.

O'Dea T. F., 'Crisis en la cristianidad', *Mensaje*, VIII (1959), n. 77. 'Five Dilemmas in the Institutionalization of Religion', *Social Compass*, VI (1960), n. 1.

O'Dea Th., *The Catholic Crisis*, Beacon Press, Boston, 1968.

Ogburn W. F., 'How Technology Changes Society', *The Annals of the Am. Ac. of Pol. and Soc. Sciences*, 1947.

Olt R., *An Approach to the Psychology of Religion*, Christopher Pub. House, Boston 1956.

Ortega y Gasset J., *Betrachtungen über die Technik*, Stuttgart 1949.

Otto R., *The Idea of the Holy*, Oxford Univ. Press, London 1923.

Pagani C., 'Una inchiesta religioso-morale tra le maestranze di un centro industriale (Saronno)', *Realtà d'oggi*, 1951, n. 6.

Pareto V., *I sistemi socialisti*, Utet, Turin 1951.

— — *Trattato di sociologia generale*, Edizioni di Comunità, Milan 1964, 2 vols.

Parker, E. C., Barry D. W., Smithe D. W., *The Television-Radio Audience and Religion*, Harper, New York 1955.

Parsons A., *Belief, Magic and Anomie. Essays in Psychosocial Anthropology*, The Free Press, New York 1969.

— — *Phenomenology of Religion. Eight Modern Descriptions of the Essence of Religion*, edited by J. D. Bettis, SCM Press, London 1969.

Parsons T., 'The Place of Ultimate Values in Sociological Theory', *International Journal of Ethics*, 1935, n. 45.

— — 'The Theoretical Development of the Sociology of Religion', *Journal of the History of Ideas*, 1944, n. 5.

— — 'Religious Perspectives in College Teaching, Sociology and Social Psychology', in *Religious Perspectives in College Teaching*. The Ronald Press, New York 1952.

— — 'Réflexion sur les organisations religieuses aux États-Unis', *Archives de sociologie des religions*, II (1957), n. 3.

— — 'Death in American Society. A Brief Working Paper', *American Behavioral Scientist*, VI (1963), n. 9.

— — *Structure and Process in Modern Societies*, Free Press, New York 1960.

Parsons T. and Bales R. F., *Family, Socialization and Interaction Process*, Routledge and Kegan Paul, London 1956.

Pederson D., Owen B., *Jesus People*, Compass Press, Pasadena, 1971.

Pellizzi C., *Simbolo e società*, Società Italiana di Sociologia, Rome 1950.

— — 'La struttura elementare del comportamento consapevole', in *Scritti di sociologia e politica in onore di Luigi Sturzo*, Rome 1954.

— — 'Motivazione e comunicazione secondo nuovi concetti definitori', *Relazioni Umane*, III (1958), nn. 1–2.

— — 'Caproni, parrucche e altro (Commenti e quesiti a E. De Martino)', *Rassegna italiana di sociologia*, II (1961), n. 1.

Peltier H., 'Souvenirs et réflexions sur le christianisme en URSS', *Études*, December 1958.

Pemberton P. L., 'An Examination of Some Criticism of Talcott Parsons's Sociology of Religion', *The Journal of Religion*, XXXVI (1956), n. 4.

Pennati E., 'Determinismi e regolarità nella dinamica delle strutture globali', *Atti del XVIII congresso internazionale di sociologia*, Nuremberg 1958.

Pennesi D., *Resoconto di un'inchiesta religiosa*, Grafica Emiliana, Bologna 1966.

Pereira de Queiroz M., *La guerre sainte au Brésil: le mouvement messianique du 'Contestado'*, Univ. di S. Paolo, 1957.

— — 'L'influence du milieu social interne sur les mouvements messianiques brésiliens', *Archives de sociologie des religions*, III (1958), n. 5.

Pérouas L., *Le diocèse de la Rochelle de 1648 à 1724, Sociologie et Pastorale*, Sevpen, Paris 1964.

Petit J., 'Structure sociale et vie religieuse d'une paroisse parisienne', *Archives de sociologie des religions*, I (1956), n. 1.

Pfautz H. W., 'The Sociology of Secularization: Religious Groups', *American Journal of Sociology*, LXI (1955), n. 2.

Pfliegler M., *Die Religiöse Situation*, Verlag Anton Pustet, Graz-Salsburg-Vienna 1948.

Pickering W. S. F., 'Religious movements of Church members in two working-class towns in England', *Archives de sociologie des religions*, 1951, n. 11.

— — 'Quelques résultats d'interviews religieuses', *Vocation de la sociologie religieuse, Ve Conférence internationale de sociologie religieuse*, Casterman, Paris 1958.

Pin E., *Introduction à l'étude sociologique des paroisses catholiques. Critères de classification et typologies*, Paris 1956.

— — *Pratique religieuse et classes sociales dans une paroisse urbaine, Saint-Pothin à Lyon*, Spes, Paris 1956.

— — 'Désaffection religieuse dans les classes inférieures', *Social Compass*, VI (1962), nn. 4–5.

— — *Religiosité et appartenence à l'Église dans le XXe arrondissement de Paris*, Ciris, Rome 1968.

— — 'Tensions internes et crise de communication dans l'Église', *Idoc International*, 1 Dec. 1969, n. 13.

Plattel M. G., 'Het geseculariseerd mens-en wereldbeedl in verband met het godsdienstig verschijnsel', *Sociale Wetenschappen*, X (1967), n. 4.

Pleijel H., *Die Erforschung des religiösen Volkslebens in Schweden*, Lund 1953.

Pleuroux H. P., *La vie chrétienne dans le Doubs et la Haute-Saône*, Ed. Université de Paris, Paris 1966.

Poblete R., *Crisis sacerdotal*, Ed. del Pacifico, Santiago, Chile 1965.

Poggi G., *Catholic Action in Italy—The Sociology of a Sponsored Organization*, Stanford University Press, Stanford.

Potel J., Huot-Pleuroux P., Maître J., *Le clergé français*, Ed. du Centurion, Paris 1967.

Potestà L., 'Istituzioni religiose e struttura sociale', *Rassegna italiana di sociologia*, 1960, n. 2.

Pothacamury T., 'Position présent de l'Église en Inde', *Rythmes du monde*, V (1957), nn. 3–4.

Poulat E., 'La découverte de la ville par le catholicisme français contemporain', *Annales*, 1960.

— — 'Les nouveaux espaces urbains du catholicisme français', *Cahiers internationaux de sociologie*, 1960, n. 1.

Pratt J. B., *The Religious Consciousness, a Psychological Study*, Macmillan, New York 1959 (1st ed. 1920).

Principe Q., 'Diocesi di Padova. Pratica religiosa (1744–53)', *Sociologia religiosa*, III (1959), nn. 3–4.

Quaritch W. (a cura), *Prehistory and Religion in South-East Asia*, London 1957.

Querido A., 'Eléments pour une sociologie du conformisme catholique au Portugal', *Archives de sociologie des religions*, IV (1959), n. 7.

Quoist M., *La ville et l'homme*, Éditions Ouvrières, Paris 1952.

Rabut O., *L'espèrience religieuse fondamentale*, Casterman, Tournai 1969.

Radhakamal Mukerjee, *The Symbolic Life of Man*, Hindikitabs, Bombay 1959.

Radhakrishnan S., *Religion and Society*, New York 1947.

— — 'Indian Religious Thought and Modern Civilization', *Indo-Asian Culture*, VII (1958), n. 1.

Rapp H. R., *Mensch, Gott und Zahl*, Furche, Hamburg, 1967.

Rapporto n. 11, *La pratique religieuse en Wallonie*, CDRSR, Brussels. For the 38th waloon social week.

Rapport n. 12, *Le Canton et le Doyenné de Beauraing*, CDRSR, Brussels.

Rapporto n. 13, *Enquête sur la mentalité et le comportement religieux d'ouvriers de la grosse industrie à Liège et à Charleroi*, CDRSR, Brussels.

Rapporto n. 17, *Étude socio-religieuse de Braine-le-Comte*, CDRSR, Brussels.

Rapporto n. 19, *Étude socio-religieuse de la paroisse du Béguinage à Bruxelles*, CDRSR, Brussels.

Rapporto n. 30, *Structure sociale et vie religieuse d'une paroisse de grande ville: la paroisse de la Sainte-Trinité à Bruxelles*, CDRSR, Brussels.

Rapporto n. 32. *La paroisse Ste-Famille à Schaerbeek*, CDRSR, Brussels.

Rapporto n. 33, *Godsdienstige praktijk in Zaventem*, CDRSR, Brussels.

Rapporto n. 36, *Complément à l'étude socio-religieuse du Doyenné de Beauraing*, CDRSR, Brussels.

Rapporto n. 45, *Étude socio-religieuse du Doyenné de Frasnes-les-Buissenal*, CDRSR, Brussels.

Rapporto n. 48, *Étude sociologique du Doyenné de Marche-en-Famenne*, I. 'Le donné humain', 1958; II 'Étude socio-religieuse', 1959, CDRSR, Brussels.

Rapporto n. 49, *La pratique religieuse à Tournai*, CDRSR, Brussels 1959.

Rapport n. 52, *Socio-religieuze studie van het Bisdom Brugge*, Centrum voor Socio-Religieuze Onderzoek, en Diocesane Kommissie, Brugge 1959.

Remy J., 'Conséquences socio-culturelles de la concentration urbaine', *Social Compass*, VII (1960), n. 4.

Rhoades D. H. 'What Social Science has done to Religion', *Numen*, IX (1962), n. 9.

Riccitelli B., *Ascoli Piceno, frequenze alla S. Messa festiva*, Ed. Centro Catechistico diocesano, Ascoli Piceno 1962.

Richard E. and Hughes K., *Religion in China*, Hutchinson's University Library, London 1950.

Rimoldi A., 'Les études de sociologie religieuse en Italie', *Atti della VI conferenza internazionale di sociologia religiosa di La Tourette*, Economie et Humanisme e Éditions Ouvrières, Paris 1955.

Robertson R., *A sociological Yearbook of Religion in Britain*, vol. 2 edited by D. Martin, SCM Press, London 1969. *The Sociological Interpretation of Religion*, Blackwell, Oxford 1970.

Rondot P., 'L'Islam et les Musulmans d'aujourd'hui'. II: *De Dakar à Djakarta, L'Islam en devenir*, Ed. de l'Oriente, Paris 1960.

Rosier I. (ed.), *Essays on the Pastoral Problems of the Catholic in the World Today*, Institut Carmélitain, s.l., 1961.

Rostagnat M. L., 'Les visites pastorales de Mgr. Camille de Neufville dans le diocèse de Lyon au XVIIᵉ siècle, *Cahiers d'Histoire*, 1960, n. 3.

Rotureau G., *Coscienza religiosa e mentalità tecnica*, LDC, Turin 1966.

Ruppin A., *Gli ebrei d'oggi dall'aspetto sociale*, F.lli Bocca Ed., Turin 1922.

Saatman J. W., 'Protestantisme américain', *Nouvelle revue théologique*, May 1956.

Salisbury W. S., 'Faith, Ritual, Charismatic Leadership and Religious Behaviour', *Social Forces*, XXXIV (1956), n. 3.

Salvemini T., 'Il clero secolare, i religiosi e le religiose in Italia secondo il censimento del 1936', *Statistica*, X (1949), n. 2.

Sambin P., *L'ordinamento parrocchiale di Padova nel medioevo*, Cedam, Padua 1941.

Savramis D., 'Das Vorurteil von der Entchristlichung der Gegen-warts-Gesellschaft', *Kölnerzeitschrift für Soziologie und Sozial-Psychologie*, XIX (1967), n. 2.

Schelsky H., 'Religionssoziologie und Theologie', *Zeitschrift für evangelische Ethik*, 1959, n. 4.

Schillebeeckx E., *Theological Reflexions on Religion; Sociological Interpretations of Modern 'Irreligion'*, 1963. *Personale Begegrung mit Gott*, Mainz 1964.

Schneider L. and Dornbusch S. M., *Popular Religion. American Inspirational Literature*, University of Chicago Press, Chicago 1958.

Schreuder O., 'Sociologie religieuse et recherche socio-ecclésiastique au cours de la période 1962–1964, *Social Compass*, XIII (1966), n. 3.

Schroeder W. and Obenhaus V., *Religion in American Culture*, The Free Press, Gencoe 1964.

Schuyler J. B., 'Religious Behaviour in a Northern Parish. A Study of Motivating Values', *American Catholic Sociological Review*, XIX (1958), n. 2.

Sciascia L., *Feste religiose in Sicilia*, Leonardo, Bari 1965.

Simmel G., 'Beitrag zur Soziologie der Religion', *The American Journal of Sociology*, XI (1905). 'Die Religion' ('Die Gesellschaft', vol. II), Frankfurt am Main 1912.

Smith H., 'Secularization and the Sacred. The Contemporary Sense', *The World Yearbook of Religion*, 1969, vol. 1.

Spiazzi R., *Prospettive religiose del nostro tempo*, Idea, Rome 1964.

Spinks G. S., *Psychology and Religion*, Methuen, London 1963.

Spinks G. S., Allen E. L. and Parkes J., *Religion in Britain since 1900*, London 1952.

Stammler E., *Protestanten ohne Kirche*, Kreuz-Verlag, Stuttgart 1960.

Starbuch E., *The Psychology of Religion*, London 1901.

Steeman Th. M., 'L'Église d'aujourd'hui. Une exploration de la Hollande Catholique en 1966', *Social Compass*, XIV (1967), n. 3.

Sticklel G., 'L'attitudine religiosa dei giovani. Risultati di una ricerca sperimentale', *Rivista di pedagogia e scienze religiose*, 1963, n. 4.

Storck H., *Die Zeit drängt. Die evangelische Kirche stellt sich den Fragen der Industriegesellschaft*, Berlin 1957.

Stouffer S. A., *American Soldier: Combat and its Aftermath*, Princeton University Press, Princeton 1949.

Struve N., *Les Chrétiens en URSS*, Seuil, Paris 1963.

Sturm V., 'Schwund der Religiosität', *Frankfurter Allgemeine Zeitung*, 1966, n. 233.

Suk W., 'Die soziale Wirklichkeit als Gegebenheit der Seelsorge in der Pfarre St. Johannes von Nepomuk', *Der Seelsorger*, XXVI (1957), nn. 10–11.

Sullenger E. T., 'The Church in an Urban Society', *Sociology and Social Research*, XL (1957), n. 41.

Swanson G. E., 'Modern secularity. Its meaning, sources and interpretation', *The World Yearbook of Religion*, 1969, vol. I.

Tacchi Venturi P., *Stato della religione in Italia alla metà del secolo XVI*, Rome-Milan 1908.

Tezkereh-i-Evlia, *Tadhkiratu l'avliya* (Memories of the friends of God), French trans. by de Courteille, Paris 1880.

Thompson R. H. T., *The Church's Understanding of Itself. A Study of Four Birmingham Parishes*, S.C.M. Press, London 1957.

Thouless R. H., *An Introduction to the Psychology of Religion*, Cambridge University Press, Cambridge 1961.

Tillich P., *Religionphilosophie der Kultur; Zwei Entwurfe von Gustav Radbruch und Paul Tillich*, Reuther und Reichard, Berlin 1919.

— —'Die Kategorie des "Heiligen" bei Rudolf Otto', *Theologische Blätter*, II (1923), n. 11–12.

Toffanin G., *Storia dell'umanesimo*, Perella ed., Napoli-Città di Castello 1933.

— —*Il secolo senza Roma*, Zanichelli, Bologna 1943.

— —*L'uomo antico nel pensiero del Rinascimento*, Zanichelli, Bologna 1957.

Toldo A., *Il senso dell'appartenenza psico-sociologica alla chiesa tra i fedeli di una grande città e diocesi d'Italia (Bologna)*, Edizioni Isab, Bologna 1962.

Toniolo G., *Opera Omnia*, edited by the Comitato Opera Omnia di G. Toniolo, Vatican City 1940.

Tönnies F., *Comunità e società*, Edizioni di Comunità, Milan 1963.

Toussaert J., *Le sentiment religieux en Flandre à la fin du Moyen Age*, Plon, Paris 1963.

Trénard L., 'Aux origines de la déchristianisation: le diocèse de Cambrai de 1830 à 1848', *Revue du Nord*, 1965, n. 3.

Trevelyan G. M., *English Social History (A Survey of Six Centuries, Chaucer to Queen Victoria)*, Longmans Green & Co. Ltd., London 1944.

Triviere L., 'L'Église catholique en Chine continentale', *Saturne*, 1957, nn. 5-7-8-9-10-11.

Tufari P., 'Religiosità e cultura in una comunità urbana', *Aggiornamenti sociali*, IX (1958), n. 6.

— — 'Sixty Years of Psychology of Religion', *Social Compass*, 1960, n. 4.

— — 'L'analisi funzionale in sociologia religiosa', *Sociologia religiosa*, IV (1960), n. 5.

Turner D. S., 'Belief, Ritual and Experience: the Case of Methodism', *Social Compass*, XVIII (1971), n. 2.

Uggè A., 'La scristianizzazione del proletariato', *Atti del Congresso di Charleroi*, Morcelliana, Brescia 1950.

Untersteiner M., *Fisiologia del mito*, Bocca, Milan 1946.

Various authors, *Le basi fisiche del pensiero*, Einaudi, Turin 1953.

Various authors, *Ricerche sulla zona di Torino-Lucento*, research group in religious sociology, Istituto di Scienze politiche University of Turin, 1956.

Various authors, *L'anima religiosa del mondo d'oggi*, A.C.I., Rome 1957.

Various authors, *Coutances, sociologie et pastorale*, Coutances 1958.

Various authors, *Die Europäische Priesterfrage*, Int. Kath. Institut für kirchliche Sozialforschung, Vienna 1959.

Various authors, *Polarité du symbole*, Desclée de Brouwer, Bruges 1960.

Various authors, 'Probleme der Religions Soziologie', Herausg. D. Goldschmidt und J. Matthes, Sonderheft 6, della *Kölner Zeitschrift für Soziologie und Sozialpsychologie*, Cologne 1962.

Various authors, *Proceedings of the Hazen International Conference of the Sociology of Religion, Sociology and Religion*, Washington 1962.

Various authors, 'Soziale Verantwortung in der säkularisierten Gesellschaft', *Zeitschrift für evangelische Ethik*, VII (1963), n. 2.

Various authors, *Atti del I Symposion di Sociologia religiosa*, Morcelliana, Brescia 1963.

Various authors, 'The Meaning and End of Religion: A Symposium', *The Harvard Theological Review*, LVIII (1965), n. 4.

Various authors, *Perché non credo?*, Cittadella, Assisi 1966.

Various authors, *Culturologia del sacro e del profano*, Feltrinelli, Milan 1966.

Various authors, *Dio è morto?*, Mondadori, Milan 1967.

Various authors, *Sacerdoce, clergé et changement social*, CRSR, Louvain 1967.

Various authors, *Religione e pregiudizio*, Cappelli, Rocca S. Casciano 1968.

Various authors, *Processo alla religione*, Mondadori, Milan 1968.

Van Buren P. M., *The Secular Meaning of the Gospel*, Macmillan, New York 1963.

Van der Leeuw G., *L'uomo primitivo e la religione*, Boringhieri, Turin 1961.

Van Hooydonk P., 'De religieuse practijk van de katholieke bevolking in de stad Groningen en in het bijzonder in de Oosterparkbuurt', *Social Compass*, V (1957), n. 3.

Vansina J., 'Religions et sociétés en Afrique Centrale', *Cahiers des Religions Africaines*, 1968, n.2.

Varga I., 'La sécularisation de la jeunesse hongroise', *Archives de sociologie des religions*, XII (1967), n. 23.

Vasquez J. M., *Así viven y mueren* . . .,OPE, Pamplona 1958.

Vecchi A., 'Appunti sul gesto rituale', *Sociologia religiosa*, VIII (1964), nn. 11–12.

— — 'Riti del fuoco e dell'acqua nel folklore del basso Veneto', *Ateneo Veneto*, II (1964), n. 2.

— — *Il culto delle immagini nelle stampe popolari*, Olschki, Florence 1968.

Veit O., *La tragedia dell'età della tecnica*, Bompiani, Milan 1937.

Vekemans R., 'La sociographie du catholicisme aux Pays-Bas', *Archives de sociologie des religions*, II (1957), n. 3.

Vergote A., *Psychologie religieuse*, Dessart, Brussels 1966.

Vinot-Prefontaine J., 'Sanctions prises dans l'ancien diocèse de Beauvais au XVIIe siècle contre les réfractaires au devoir pascal', *Revue d'histoire de l'Église de France*, XLV (1959), n. 142 (pub. 1961).

Violante C., *La società milanese nell'età precomunale*, Laterza, Bari 1953.

Vogt E., 'Religious Sociology and the Standardization of its Methods', *Euntes Docete*, VIII (1955), n. 2.

— —'La definizione della sociologia religiosa', *Sociologia religiosa*, I (1957), n. 1. 'Problemi di sociologia religiosa', Rome 1958–59, 2 vols.

Vrcan S., 'Some Theoretical Implications of the Religiosity as a Mass Phenomenon in a Contemporary Socialist Society', *Int Jahrbuch für Religionssoziologie* (7), 1972, pp. 150–67.

Wach J., *Sociologie de la religion*, Payot, Paris 1955.

Ward C. K., 'Church Attendance in Great Britain', *Sociologia religiosa*, III (1959), nn. 3–4.

— —*Priests and People*, Liverpool University Press Social Research Series, Liverpool 1961.

— —'Sociology and Christian Life', in *Uses of Sociology*, Sheed and Ward, London 1966.

Watelet D. G., 'L'artisan à l'âge de la machine', *Annales des classes moyennes de Belgique*, 1958, n. 2.

Watzke J., 'Paganization and dechristianization or the crisis in institutional symbols. A Problem in sociological interpretation', *Social Compass*, XVI (1969), n. 1.

Webb C. C. J., *Group Theories of Religion and the Individual*, London 1961.

Webb S. and B., *Il comunismo sovietico: una nuova civiltà*, Einaudi, Turin 1950.

Weber M., *Gesammelte Aufsätze zur Religionssoziologie*, J. B. Mohr, Tübingen 1947.

Weijer A., van de, *De Religieuse practijk in een Brabantse industriestad*, Assen 1955.

Weil S., *La condizione operaia*, Edizioni di Comunità, 2nd ed., Milan 1965.

Wetter G. A., *Il materialismo dialettico sovietico*, Einaudi, Turin 1941.

Whitehead, A. N., *Science and the Modern World*, Cambridge University Press, London 1926.

Wickham E. R., *Church and People in an Industrial City*, Lutherworth Press, London 1957.

Willems E., *Followers of the New Faith, Culture Change and the Rise of Protestantism in Brazil and Chile*, Vanderbilt University Press, Nashville 1967.

Wilson B. R., 'An Analysis of Sect Development', *American Sociological Review*, XXIV (1959), n. 1.

— — *Sects and Society*, Heinemann, London 1961.

— — 'The Paul Report Examined', *Theology*, LXVIII (1965), n. 536.

— — *Religion in Secular Society*, Watts & Co., London, 1966; and Penguin Books, London 1969.

— — (ed.) *Rationality*, Blackwell, Oxford 1970.

— — *Religious Sects*, Weidenfeld and Nicolson, London 1971.

Winninger P., *'Eléments de géographie religieuse de l'agglomération strasbourgeoise'. Le Catholicisme*, 'Bulletin de l'association géographique d'Alsace', 1956, n. 3.

Winter E. K., 'Probleme der Religionssoziologie', *Zeitschrift für die ges. Staatswissenschaft*, 1931.

Winter G., *Religious identity. A study of religious organisation*, Macmillan, New York 1968.

Wölberg H. A., *Religion ohne Entscheidung*, Vandenhoeck und Ruprecht, Göttingen 1965.

Wösser J., (ed.) *Religion in Umbruch*, Enke, Stuttgart, 1972.

Yinger J. M., 'Present Status of the Sociology of Religion', *Journal of Religion*, XXXI (1951).

— — *Religion, Society and the Individual*, Macmillan Co., New York 1957.

— — 'Influence of Anthropology on Sociological Theories of Religion', *American Anthropologist*, LX (1958).

— — 'Areas for Research in the Sociology of Religion', *Sociology and Social Research*, XLII (1958), n. 6.

— — 'Religion and Social Change', *Review of Religious Research*, IV (1963), nn. 2–3.

— — *The world yearbook of religion. The religious situation*, edited by D. R. Cutler, Evans, London, vol. I, 1969; vol. II, 1970.

— — *The scientific study of religion*, Macmillan, New York 1970.

— — 'Toward a Theory of Religion and Social Change', *Int. Jahrbuch für Religionssoziologie* (7), 1971, pp. 7–8.

Zadra D., *La dinamica della affiliazione religiosa in una società pluralista*, Degree thesis, Milan 1967.

— — *Sociologia della religione*, Hoepli, Milan 1969.

Zolla E., 'Sociologia religiosa', *Tempo presen?, III (1958)*.

Zulehuer P. M., *Religion ohne Kirche? Das religiöse Verhalten von Industriearbeiten*, Herder, Vienna 1969.

Zunini G., *Homo Religiosus*, Il Saggiatore, Milan 1966.

Index